YOU HEAR ME, BARACK?

PC-FREE CONSERVATIVE SATIRE

STEVE GRAMMATICO

WITH FOREWORD BY MICHAEL WALSH

'13

You Hear Me, Barack?
Copyright © 2013 by Steve Grammatico. All rights reserved.
First Print Edition: July 2013

ISBN-10: 1-4903-7378-0
ISBN-13: 978-1-4903-7378-2

Contact: stevegrammatico@yahoo.com

Cover and Formatting: Streetlight Graphics

You Hear Me, Barack? is a collection of satire by Steve Grammatico and is not intended maliciously. Steve Grammatico has invented all names and situations in the selections, except in cases where public figures are being satirized. Any other use of real names is accidental and coincidental, or used as a fictional depiction or personality parody (permitted under Hustler Magazine v. Falwell, 485 US 46, 108 S.Ct 876, 99 L.Ed.2d 41 (1988)).

TABLE OF CONTENTS

DEDICATION

For Josh Goldberg--too soon, too soon; and Kathleen, my daughter, my muse

TESTIMONIALS

Sharp, smart, original and fall down funny, Steve Grammatico belongs in the political pundit hall of fame with Iowahawk, Mark Steyn and P.J. O'Rourke.

~Lucianne Goldberg

Steve Grammatico. . . . runs the risk of a secret subpoena snatching his phone records and email trove, and of, eventually, bunking with Julian Assange. We in the fake-but-true news industry stand by our brother.

~Scott Ott, editor of ScrappleFace.com, author of *Laughing at Obama: Volume I, Hope That Changes*, and *Our Fickle Constitution*; and host at *pjtv.com*

So sit back, relax and enjoy this parade of poltroons, hoist high with their own petards. You're in the hands of a master.

~Michael Walsh, from the Foreword to *You Hear Me, Barack?*

FOREWORD BY MICHAEL WALSH

When the late Andrew Breitbart asked me in the fall of 2009 to start a new website called Big Journalism, the first thing I looked for in potential contributors was a sharp wit and a way with words. Luckily for me, one of the first people who signed on was Steve Grammatico, who quickly carved out a place for himself as our house satirist par excellence—the scourge of leftist cant, pious liberal nonsense and pie-in-the-sky progressivism.

Steve began his rise to punchlines and punditry in a typically 21st-century way, as the commenter "sagman" on the influential lucianne.com website, where his sparkling insouciance quickly won him a loyal following. Wrote one fan: "Writing good political satire involves more than wit and words; it requires exceptional knowledge of personalities, politics, and policies."

Satire, as the great playwright George S. Kaufman famously noted, is what closes on Saturday night. As someone who, under the nom de plume of "David Kahane," has written a fair amount of satire myself, I would amend that wisecrack to "bad satire." Good satire—biting, crackling and always on target, but never simply mean and insulting—is what plays and plays. Because, at its heart, everybody knows it's true. And even when it's not, it is anyway.

If you doubt me, consider this: "The Beggar's Opera," a work of the English musical theater which skewered contemporary politicians, manners and mores has been playing, more or less continuously, since 1728. Yes, you read that right: for nearly *three hundred years*, both in its original form by John Gay and Johann Pepusch, and in its German incarnation by Bert Brecht and Kurt Weill, "The Threepenny Opera." And you know what? It's still funny.

Hence, this book, drawn from Steve's work for Big Journalism and elsewhere. Chief among these pieces are the Obama War Room parodies, in which all the villains of the administration are given free reign to express their innermost thoughts to a largely bewildered and clueless Barry, with the fun almost invariably ending when Michelle breaks into the room to berate the hapless president, her tirades ending with the words, "You hear me, Barack?"

In short, you'll laugh, you'll cry, you'll wonder aloud, "What the hell were we thinking?" in electing Barack Hussein Obama president in 2008 and again in 2012. "My goal," Steve says, "is to get people to laugh, to see my scenarios as a warped and often not so warped reflection of reality. For me, incongruity is at the heart of satire."

So sit back, relax and enjoy this parade of poltroons, hoist high with their own petards. You're in the hands of a master.

Author and screenwriter Michael Walsh is weekly op-ed columnist for the New York Post*, a featured columnist at PJ Media, and regular contributor to National Review Online. He is the author of more than a dozen books, including* Rules for Radical Conservatives*, written under his satiric pseudonym, David Kahane.*

INTRODUCTION

The Moving Finger writes; and, having writ,
Moves on: nor all thy Piety nor Wit
Shall lure it back to cancel half a Line,
Nor all thy Tears wash out a Word of it.

~From *The Rubáiyát of Omar Khayyam*

Unchallenged wisdom, right? A poetic way of saying, you can't unring the bell.

Except . . . if Omar were alive today to witness the president routinely turning history on its head, he'd scrub those lines. Obama unrings bells like nobody's business.

In a moment of Khayyamic candor at one of his briefings, White House Press Secretary Jay Carney might utter these words:

Whatever we did is done, or maybe not.
Move on, for all your probes will come to naught
Since evidence to prove the truth is gone,
And those who might betray are scared or bought.

I write political satire untainted by political correctness. I am not trying to score points. My goal is to make readers laugh by employing ridicule and mockery (not the same thing) to expose the hypocrisy and pretensions of politicians and their media and celebrity allies.

Be forewarned (as if you weren't already): my targets are all on the left. I suspect hard-core liberals and their country cousins, denizens of the Democrats' fever swamp, won't crack a page after a look at the book's cover. And to Obama worshippers, that dwindling subset of the Party, I'll be a heretic whose head belongs on a stake.

Everyone else with even a passing interest in politics: if I can't amuse you using wit and wordplay, without being vicious or crude or vulgar, I've failed. Please read at least a portion of the Sampler to determine if *You Hear Me, Barack?* is worth your time and money. It contains seven representative and independent pieces of satire: two fly-on-the-wall Obama War Room dialogues, a mock interview, a news spoof, an "alternate universe" scenario, a presidential heart-to-heart with the nation's schoolkids, and a parody poem, "The Raving," by Robert Gibbs. Another hundred stand-alone parodies follow in sixteen chapters. Check out the Table of Contents.

Political humor generally has the shelf life of a gnat. So everything in this book must be dated, right? Wrong. *You Hear Me, Barack?* is not an extended Leno monologue about one day's forgettable events. I stay focused on politicians and their acolytes whose contempt for the rest of us is palpable; public policy issues (ObamaCare, Green Energy, gun control, immigration, etc.); and scandals (IRS, NSA, Benghazi, "Fast and Furious," on and on).

In his foreword, Michael Walsh quotes me as saying that "incongruity is at the heart of satire." What does this mean? Words and actions are incongruous if they are in stark contrast to what's expected, if they appear out of place yet ring familiar. In the world of *You Hear Me, Barack?*, Obama, Holder, Hillary and the rest are unguarded, uninhibited, and over the top. From these written caricatures arises the humor: Obama appearing on Shalom TV to announce his conversion to Judaism; Holder and Khalid Sheikh Mohammed proposing construction of a seaside resort for Gitmo detainees in Mecca, Florida; Biden suggesting the "mortarboarding" of captured jihadists; Kerry informing Israelis our support is unconditional unless they refuse to recognize a Palestinian state bent on driving them into the sea.

To be effective and entertaining, satire must present more than a humorous premise followed by 500 words of filler. My guiding principle when I wrote the pieces in this book (not always achieved, for sure): every line had to be funny or witty or serve to introduce a funny or witty line. Eye of the beholder, of course. You judge.

Steve Grammatico
July 9, 2013

SAMPLER

OBAMA WAR ROOM: DIE HARD

OBAMA: No way out, no way out. Seniors with a lick of common sense are blasting us as we implement ObamaCare. Why the hell didn't we call it "BidenCare"?

JOE BIDEN: Geezers are gonna have our guts for garters when they realize they're payin' more even as we take resources away from them.

DAN PFEIFFER: Let's use guilt to divert attention from our screwup, sir. For example, a TV spot featuring a "doctor" saying, "Is the new pacemaker you've been prescribed more important than your grandchild's flu shot?"

OBAMA: That'll help but it's not a killer fix. Somebody, come up with something big that'll turn this thing around. I want the elderly a non-factor by midterms.

KATHLEEN SEBELIUS: Sir, millions of seniors own pets they regard as family. I'll announce that attorneys reviewing the bill found language suggesting the animals may be considered "partners" and therefore eligible for coverage as dependents.

JOE BIDEN: Nice thinkin', Kathleen. But . . . who'd vet the claims? Hahahahaha....

OBAMA: Dan, call Hillary. If she hasn't fallen down and suffered a concussion recently, ask her to consider replacing Joe on the ticket in 2016.

VALERIE JARRETT: Kathleen's proposal would be costly, sir, unless we added fine print specifying lethal injection as the only option for sick animals.

JACK LEW: There's probably just enough scratch in the budget we haven't formulated yet to put felines down. Dogs, not a chance.

OBAMA: Okay. We call the supplementary program we discovered "Medicat." "Peticare" is too . . . inclusive. Other ideas to get old people back in the fold?

BIDEN: How 'bout a "Cash for Clunker Viscera" promotion, Chief? "Replace your worn-out heart or liver, earn a $5,000 rebate from Uncle Sam."

OBAMA: Good! We'll fund the program with two billion pulled from the VA's budget. Limited time offer. Jack, write the bill with Waxman, and make the application procedure impossibly complicated. Last thing we want is a run on the organ banks.

LEW: Yes, sir. I can assure you no one will qualify. Then you can brag about the two billion you saved taxpayers.

BIDEN: I dunno, Boss. Every time we do something to help this ObamaCare rat puke go down like cream of wheat, support declines. We need professional advice. Why not hire a New York ad agency to pitch our proposals?

OBAMA: Hmm. Madisonian Avenue Democracy. Jefferson would gag. Well, he's dead. Jack, find a top firm to take on selling our pets and body parts initiatives or face an IRS probe.

LEW: Doesn't matter if support increases, sir. We're still looking at fiscal Armageddon. People are living longer and accessing healthcare into their 90s.

OBAMA: Well, let's incentivize dying. Set up an ad shoot. I'll say, "Social Security and Medicare really *are* unsustainable because people are retiring early and consuming medical resources when they should be in the ground. I call on Americans to work till you die. And die younger . . . for the children."

SEBELIUS: I'll arrange working groups with Big Pharma, Big Insurance, and Big Hospital. We'll have retirees' death rates spiking by 2015.

LEW: One of Pelosi's House automatons can propose legislation halving the death tax for anyone who volunteers to pass away prematurely. The NSA has given us the goods on thirty House Republicans, sir, more than enough to get us the votes we need.

JARRETT: We'll need massive revenue infusions to make it all click, sir. I suggest you grant undocumenteds temporary citizenship. That's twenty million more people paying taxes. When they retire, we'll ship them back to their home countries before they can apply for Social Security and Medicare.

OBAMA: Works for me. Reverend?

JESSE JACKSON: What?

OBAMA: We'll need some Johnnie Cochran wordplay for ads.

JACKSON: Oh. How about, "Early croak, kin won't go broke," or, "Take a fall, kids get it all."

MICHELLE: Barack, ask Hillary to write a sequel to her book. The title for this one: *It Takes an Early Grave to Save the Village*.

JARRETT: Following up on an earlier suggestion, sir: speak from the Oval Office about the imminent bankruptcy of convalescent homes across the country. Announce their nationalization. Cast it as an urgent measure to stave off an economic and humanitarian catastrophe.

BIDEN: I gotcha! Then we run 'em like Third World clinics to boost death rates.

OBAMA: Hmm, a riff on the "Roach Motel" ads: they check in, but they don't check out. Kathleen, consult with Pelosi and Reid on the takeover legislation. Do a backroom deal to get the AMA on board. Tell 'em, tell 'em . . . we'll consider tort reform if they cooperate [snort].

SEBELIUS: HHS can help, sir. We'll offer promotions for free cremation, but you have to book early.

PFEIFFER: After midterms, we should propose a national conversation on end-of-life options. Ah, [winking] Mr. Vice President, you have an opinion on euthanasia?

BIDEN: Um, they're highly susceptible to al Qaeda recruitment, especially in Jakarta?

MICHELLE: Dan, Joe's special. Tease him again and I'll rip your heart out and eat it in front of your family, Chicago-style.

OBAMA: Stop squabbling; time's short. Valerie, hush-hush, reach out to Dr. Kevorkian. Ask him to come out of mortification to implement ObamaCare.

BIDEN: Back to the fogies, Boss. I say, tell 'em straight up: "I'm the One. I can cut Medicare and privatize Social Security with a word; sic the IRS on your kids; tax Roth accounts retroactively. Cross me and kiss your skinny old butts good bye."

CARNEY: Sir, I agree with the vice president. Take that message straight to the elderly in a televised "conversation" as they gather for lunch in senior centers and nursing homes around the country. Guarantee audience by using grants to make the fare that day five-star quality.

SEBELIUS: Live from the Oval Office, time-delayed on the West Coast. Attendance mandatory in facilities getting federal aid. Alzheimer's patients excused.

OBAMA: I'm not sure . . .

MICHELLE: You can't make an Obamalet without breaking eggs. Don't go wobbly on us. You hear me, Barack?

LIVE, FROM THE WHITE HOUSE MESS, THE CHIEF EXECUTIVE BROADCASTING SYSTEM PRESENTS *THE CEBS NIGHTLY NEWS WITH JAY CARNEY*

JAY CARNEY: Good evening. On our broadcast tonight:

*Rigging it—EPA mandates fuel nozzles reconfigured to fit only Chevy Volts.

*Miracle in Detroit—first Sharia law zone in nation records falling crime rates as word of amputations spreads.

*Breakthrough—Iran pledges to halt ICBM production at 250.

*Finally, Wisconsin professors' paramilitary units seize legislature.

Those stories and more later, but first, a conversation with Attorney General Eric Holder and Khalid Sheikh Mohammed, who comes to us on a satellite feed from his home in Guantanamo Bay, Cuba. Welcome, gentlemen.

HOLDER: Pleasure, Jay.

SHEIKH: May Allah grant you a merciful death.

CARNEY: Um, thanks. General, the court proceedings you've . . .

HOLDER: Trial's off, Jay. The Sheik hired Ramsey Clark to represent the detainees. We realized Clark would make a shambles of the proceedings for years, the legal equivalent of bringing down the towers.

CARNEY: What's Plan B, sir?

HOLDER: Drastic action on Gitmo to regain the president's credibility with Whoopi Goldberg, Jay. As we speak, SEIU mercenaries are on their way to Gitmo to replace military personnel. When they've assumed control, I'll dispatch federal marshals to pick up prisoners for transport to a U.S. facility.

CARNEY: How does that . . . ?

HOLDER: The marshals will arrive to find SEIU picket lines deployed around the camp. And who's standing shoulder-to-shoulder with them, singing "We Shall Overcome"? President Obama, who flew in secretly earlier after getting word that I'd gone rogue.

CARNEY: A Mexican stand-off?

HOLDER: No, we don't send Cartel people to Gitmo. Accompanying the president: Brian Williams, Scott Pelley, Diane Sawyer, Wolf Blitzen, Donner, Prancer . . .

CARNEY: Pardon?

HOLDER: Sorry. I was listening to Christmas songs on the way here and I . . .

CARNEY: Never mind. You were saying?

HOLDER: So, on live television, President Obama orders the jackbooted thugs home. Our base is pleased, and independents admire the Commander-in-Chief's *cojones.*

CARNEY: Almost 170 jihadists remain at Gitmo, off a high of 700 plus during the Bush years. Why is *anyone* still there?

SHEIKH: Excuse me. Am I—how do you say—a potted plant?

6

HOLDER: [rolling his eyes] Here it comes.

SHEIKH: Azerbaijan's president has offered to take two of my associates for a year before they're allowed to escape; in exchange, he reasonably requests a state dinner and a round of golf at Congressional.

HOLDER: We countered with lunch at McDonald's and a bucket of balls at East Potomac Driving Range, Jay. Impasse.

CARNEY: Rumor is, you and the Sheikh co-chair the super-secret "Gitmo Working Group," which will make such horse-trading moot. When will you report your conclusions to the president?

HOLDER: Soon, Jay. We'll present him with two options that close the facility but keep the remaining man-made disaster suspects on ice until we're legally bound to return them to the battlefield. Khalid?

SHEIKH: Option One: General Holder does an end run around Congress and offers us asylum in America.

HOLDER: We'd house them at a Best Western in Mecca, Florida while the Army Corps of Engineers completes a maximum security seaside resort nearby.

CARNEY: Mecca, Florida?

HOLDER: Khalid's idea, Bob. He wants to be a good neighbor. Says if we put it on the map, pilgrims making the Hajj will visit by mistake and spend money. Here's a brochure the Sheikh developed to sell his fellow detainees on the move.

CARNEY: [reading] ". . . coastal enclave . . . dining and entertainment hub ringed by ethnically dedicated neighborhoods—Yemeni Glen, Afghan Acres, Uighur Court, Saudi Meadows . . ." Impressive. Maximum security?

HOLDER: Absolutely. No expense spared to protect our guests from local yahoos.

SHEIKH: Your benefit: the resort's a magnet for jihadists; no need to chase them all over the planet. Our benefit: it's a haven for the burn-outs who require R & R before returning to the field. Win-win.

CARNEY: How would you get word to al-Qaeda's far-flung network, sir?

HOLDER: Ad buys on *Al Jazeera* and *MSNBC*, Jay. Our pitch: "Jihadists! You do not have to die to attain Paradise. Come, come to America."

CARNEY: What's Option Two?

SHEIKH: The Saudis finance construction of "Bayside Villas," Guantanamo's first high-end condo development. Right after we move into our units, I incorporate the Bayside Villas Homeowners Association.

HOLDER: The Board then votes to remain in their gated community on Cuba's east shore. President Obama respects their decision. End of story.

CARNEY: Neat. Are you in agreement on a choice?

HOLDER: We are, Jay. In a humanitarian gesture, the administration will cede Gitmo to Castro, helping him accommodate his exploding population of political prisoners.

CARNEY: Sheikh, will you pursue the American dream during your Florida sojourn?

SHEIKH: Absolutely. I intend to acquire property near the community and build OsamaTown™, a working al Qaeda hamlet similar to your Old Sturbridge Village in Massachusetts.

We'll feature daily hand loppings; workshops on suicide vest design and the etiquette of beheadings; and children's recitals, with standards like, "The IED in the Dead Cat Next to the Hat." Perhaps Disney would be interested in a reciprocal relationship.

CARNEY: Sounds interesting. Hey, you'll need a flack who knows the territory. There's a man named Gibbs who . . .

KERRY ON *MEET THE PRESS*

DAVID GREGORY: Our guest this morning, Secretary of State John Kerry. Welcome, sir.

KERRY: Hello, Tim. I heard you'd passed away. Glad you're back.

GREGORY: Uh, thanks. How do you see the Afghan struggle playing out?

KERRY: Well, Theresa and I agreed on a Turkestan Kunduz in the Persian style for my office at Foggy Bottom, but she insists I use it as a wall covering. I prefer a rug. We've hired a mediator.

GREGORY: Hillary had Huma. Any Muslim in the Kerry State Department?

KERRY: Yes, Tim. I picked muslin with cheery Wide Ruffles® for my conference rooms and muslin backdrops for videographic contrast in our studios.

GREGORY: The administration's sending out mixed signals about the military coup in Egypt, sir. Would you clarify?

KERRY: Certainly. We were against the coup before we were for it.

GREGORY: Suppose widespread civil strife breaks out. The Egyptian military might very well start a war with Israel to unite the population. How do we prevent this scenario?

KERRY: We have two carriers in the area now, the Eisenhower and the Truman. If things escalate, we'll seize the Suez Canal from Egypt. That'll unite the Egyptians against us and likely forestall an attack on Israel.

GREGORY: Seize Suez! Sir, that's an act of war.

KERRY: Not necessarily. We'll explain it away as a military exercise gone wrong because of miscommunication. By the time we get it all sorted out, the generals will have Egypt under control. A dozen more F-16s will encourage them to forgive and forget.

GREGORY: Let's move on. The "ticking time bomb" scenario, sir. You capture a jihadist after he's hidden a nuke in New York. Now what?

KERRY: We get him out of harm's way, unfortunately denying him his martyrdom. Of course, that's a violation of his religious rights. He'd probably retain Ramsey Clark and sue us at The International Court in The Hague. We'd lose.

GREGORY: Would you embed journalists in State Department special operations teams?

KERRY: I resent the question, Tim. I'm a happily married man.

GREGORY: Sorry. President Obama wants to be Jimmy Carter to the Palestinians and Bush 43 to the Israelis. How can he pull this off?

KERRY: Supply Hamas with surplus self-propelled howitzers. Simultaneously, give Israel Northrop's Skyguard Laser Defender™ to fry those howitzer shells in mid-flight. No harm, no foul.

GREGORY: What will the president say to Palestinian President Abbas and Israeli Prime Minister Netanyahu at next week's summit?

KERRY: He'll demand Palestinians acknowledge Israel's determination to avoid another holocaust. And he'll tell Israelis our support is unconditional unless they refuse to recognize a Palestinian state bent on driving them into the sea.

GREGORY: What's happening in Gaza now, sir?

KERRY: Where the pyramids are?

GREGORY: No, that's Giza. How about the West Bank?

KERRY: The big savings and loan in Houston?

GREGORY: Never mind. Today, the *Times* suggested a temporary solution to the Palestinian-Israeli stalemate: a buffer zone between the two sides patrolled by evangelical survivalists from Idaho. Your thoughts?

KERRY: Well, nobody messes with those people. Easy to recruit them, too: they'd be close to the holy places when Iran gets the bomb and the balloon goes up.

GREGORY: But how would it look in Damascus?

KERRY: Um, nice, I think, in silk or maybe organic cotton, woven in a stylized floral motif.

GREGORY: Right. Any last-resort plan to keep the Israelis and Palestinians from each other's throats?

KERRY: Yes, Tim. We force Israel to abandon the Palestinians' homeland and resettle its population in a semi-autonomous enclave in Utah. The president favors this option.

GREGORY: Turning to the terror threat, estimate the number of al Qaeda interlopers in the U.S. today.

KERRY: Um, the middle distance, a handful from Pakistan. Plus another fifty or so five kilometer specialists from northern Africa. Finally, about a dozen 30K people from Somalia. The CIA keeps a running total.

GREGORY: Sure. Morale's okay at State?

KERRY: I posted Morales to Nicaragua last week. He wasn't happy.

GREGORY: Is it true we've captured Mullah Omar and are holding him at a secure State Department facility? If so, why is State involved, not the CIA?

KERRY: It's true, Tim. He arrived in Washington yesterday and was immediately given his Miranda warning by Eric Holder. We were concerned the CIA might skip that step.

After a decent meal and a good night's sleep, we began interrogating him this morning, with his attorney, Ramsey Clark, present. The president authorized us to waterballoon Omar to extract information—permissible, according to the ACLU, as long as the subject is able to return fire.

GREGORY: And?

KERRY: Just received the report. They had a lot of fun, but we learned nothing. I want to assure the American people that Mullah Omar has been treated with dignity and respect.

GREGORY: Now what?

KERRY: We'll tie him to a stake in a field outside Islamabad and take him out with a drone.

GREGORY: Are we meeting with the rest of the Taliban leadership in theater, sir?

KERRY: Soon. The Department ran a competition for best "Let's talk" invitation to them. A Jamaican *attaché* won with, "Come, Mr. Tali Ban. Dally, you're bananas. Play this right, mon, we gonna go home."

GREGORY: Regarding Iran, sir: what's going on with their nuclear program?

KERRY: State's team of, uh, overt co-operatives is . . .

GREGORY: Overt co . . . you mean covert operatives?

KERRY: Whatever. They're in the region right now monitoring Iran's progress. The minute Israel is nuked, I'll be alerted even if, as likely, I'll be on my boat off Nantucket.

GREGORY: The spy swap with Russia a few years back was never fully explained, sir. Ten for them, four for us. A bad deal?

KERRY: Not at all, Tim. Check the fine print on the Memorandum of Understanding: we got three more agents to be named later and a first round pick in next year's draft.

GREGORY: Last question, sir: who's running things in China?

KERRY: Uh, it's Wen, not Hu, Tim. I've met both. Hu knows where, or Wen.

GREGORY: Secretary of State John Kerry. Thanks for your time.

THE GREAT WALL OF MEXICO

Washington (AP)—Former Democratic National Committee Chairman Howard Dean is under fire over remarks he made following a speech last week at a University of Mexico symposium on immigration.

The event was sponsored by the National Council of La Raza [The Race] and Reconquista, a loose affiliation of groups whose goal is to reclaim the southwestern United States for Mexico.

Surreptitiously taped, Dean's appearance was posted on YouTube Monday afternoon and pulled Tuesday morning, hours after President Obama ordered the FCC to put its boot on YouTube's neck until the site removed all obscene anti-Alinksy/anti-Obama videos and replaced them with fawning, misty reminiscences of the good old days of the class struggle.

A high-ranking administration source told *ABC News* the president dissociates himself from Dean's comments for the time being: "We sent him as an observer, not a participant. Former DNC chair Dean was wrong in revealing private discussions with the White House about how to make the border with Mexico more porous while appearing to secure it."

Press Secretary Jay Carney weighed in at his briefing yesterday, calling Dean's statements at the symposium a Republican dirty trick.

"Fishy," Carney said. "Who organized the event? Who invited Dean? Who gave him the floor? This smells, my friends."

[begin transcript]

UNIDENTIFIED MAN: *Señor*, we hear rumors President Obama intends to build a wall between Mexico and the U.S. to satisfy his critics on the right.

DEAN: It's more complicated than that, *amigo*. Fact is, our economy's in the toilet. Debt's going through the roof. We go under, you folks get hurt, too. Where'll your excess population go? Honduras? And you *Reconquistas*—you want to annex territory poorer than Sonora?

If you've been paying attention, you know China's been propping us up for years. Now they've threatened to stop buying our Treasuries unless we solve one of their nagging internal problems: rising Muslim unrest in Xinjiang province.

They've proposed a *quid pro quo*: they'll keep purchasing T-bills if we commit to the biggest shovel-ready project since the Panama Canal: the Great Wall of Mexico, built by 750,000 expatriated Chinese Uighur Muslims doing jobs no American would. The president has accepted the offer.

UNIDENTIFIED MAN: I see no benefit to us from your arrangement with China, *Señor*.

DEAN: Think clearly, my friend. Our border fanatics will be silenced because we are finally building the barrier they want. With the influx of Chinese laborers, service industries in the Southwest will boom, to the president's credit. With issues like enforced boundaries and jobs now favoring Democrats, your natural allies in Washington, your prospects are bright.

UNIDENTIFIED WOMAN: Empty words! There will still be the Wall to keep us out and the gangs to terrorize us.

DEAN: Look, *Señora*, the narcotics trade is a plague on both our countries, impossible to eradicate. Agreed? So, if we can't eliminate trafficking, the next best thing is to co-opt the traffickers. How? By offering them unfettered access to a huge new market, the wall builders—on condition they leave the rest of us alone. A no-brainer for them.

As for your concerns about immigrating to the U.S., we understand that Mexico needs a relief valve. The president is committed to increasing his "undocumented Americans" constituency, the bloc he's sure guarantees him a third term once he lops off the 22nd Amendment and signs an amnesty bill. Experienced narcotunnelers will work closely with Wall architects to design "easy through" passages to America.

Let me add, the Obama administration is also determined to prevent non-Hispanics entering Mexico illegally from the U.S. There will be no *Norte Americano* Cultivadors ranging south to entice campesinos to pick strawberries in California for a pittance. That era of exploitation is over.

Reconquistas, you're in my thoughts, as always. The president intends to cede California to Mexico right after he's reelected or the state goes bankrupt, whichever comes first. Remember though: there's a no-return policy.

[crowd] Viva Obama! Viva Dean!

DEAN: *Muchas gracias.* [to aide] How do you scream YEEHAWRRRG in Spanish?

15

ROBERT GIBBS' 'THE RAVING' WINS POETRY AWARD

New York (AP)—Robert Gibbs has won the Ars Poetica Society's prize for 2012's best parody poem, "The Raving," a work drawn on his two-year stint as President Obama's Press Secretary. Accepting the honor at the group's awards ceremony, Gibbs thanked the Society and asked, "What's a parody?"

The work is reprinted below.

"THE RAVING" BY ROBERT GIBBS

Lay, O Lord, a curse on press men, rude and churlish,
sad, obsessed men
Who persist to query me on matters that they know I
must ignore.
As I parry, neatly jinking, Tapper stares at me,
unblinking;
No doubt he is thinking, thinking Robert Gibbs is short
one oar.
"Jake the Malcontent," I murmur, "never one to seek
rapport."
Of them all, him I abhor.

Yes, the fire's now an ember from that long-ago
November
When every media staff member bowed and scraped
outside my door.
Confident, I held each presser (Helen! Old as earth, God
bless her),

Brushing off reporters—lessers, lessers who were such a
bore,
Including Jake the Tapper, whom the gods named my
bête noire.
From the start, we've been at war.

There! He rises, smarmy, sassy; I feel dizzy, bloated,
gassy,
Sickened, stricken with the urge to swat this gadfly to
the floor.
As I tamp down nauseation, purge my thoughts of his
castration,
Jake the Tapper, this . . . crustacean floats a challenge
like a spore.
Yes, Jake Tapper the crustacean floats a challenge like a
spore,
And it roots inside my core.

Shaken now, I face him squarely, caustic tongue in
check, just barely:
"Scribe," I bark, "or journo, hotly your aspersion I
deplore.
Blurted out while I was wrapping, in the middle of
recapping,
Just to get your mates to clapping, clapping because
you're plainly sore.
Well, be careful, sir," I warn him, "you are swimming far
from shore."
Says he louder: "Lie no more."

The rabble stand, and all are cheering; I hold my ground,
erect and sneering,
Mulling whether it is possible for order to restore.
Eventually, the room grows still; then Knoller shouts
out, sounding shrill:
"Robert Gibbs has stained his office and has much to
answer for."

Now the rest of them repeat it: "Gibbs has much to answer for."
Back comes Jake with, "Lie no more."

"Leave," I snarl, my stomach churning. "Briefing's done, we are adjourning."
No one speaks, but Jake is humming with a backup group of four.
"Come on," I say, "really, you can't hang out here to do a . . . coup chant."
But Jake just laughs to underscore they will dish me out what-for;
And so they sing a rap refrain where they dish me out what-for
From their slammin' gangsta score:

Gibbsy doan wants ya mussin' wid 'im
Doan wants ya fussin' wid 'im
Wants ya to be a playa pushin' single paya
So shut your faces ya know your places
Stay in the traces *and ya'll score some primo dope*
And he'll let ya stay inside the rope

Jake the Rapper, never droning, keeps intoning, keeps intoning
In the press room I abandoned, oh, a few months heretofore.
And that shattering refrain, I shall hear it in my brain—
Evermore!

SUFFER THE CHILDREN

REP. CHARLES RANGEL: Good morning, kids. I'm your Uncle Chollie in Washington. I help your Uncle Sam take care of you and your family.

Today, I'm here to introduce a special person. He'll explain how you, our youngest citizens, can partner with him to make America a country we can all be proud of, even if you're not a minority. Girls and boys, the President of the United States, Barack Obama.

PRESIDENT OBAMA: Thanks, Uncle Chollie. Hi kids. I enjoyed our last visit. Lots of your teachers asked if I would come back every week, preferably Friday afternoons. I've agreed because I know how much you need your sleep.

Don't worry, I'll still have plenty of time to fix the broken country George Bush left me. Like my Saturday radio speeches to grownups, these talks are all taped in advance when I'm not playing golf, so all I do is read what somebody else wrote from marvelous inventions called "teleprompters."

Anyway, in weeks to come, I'll discuss fun topics like *Hot Czars*™, the souped-up, small-scale vehicles my former Michigan auto company will build for kids who are into power trips; and we'll play *Tic Tax Dough*, a new *Monopoly*-like board game developed by a youngster who used to be in my Cabinet, Timmy Geithner. A special treat: the First Lady will sub for me one day next month and tell you a story about the Keebler Elf's plans to turn you into a gobblin' if you don't eat right.

Okay if I get serious for a few minutes? Last year, when folks were in a better mood, I spoke about the importance of a good education and setting high goals for yourselves. Today, with people still talking about me like a dog, I'll explain what adults call "politics."

Here's a question: how do you know if your mom and her partner are Democrats or Republicans?

Democrats believe a powerful government will watch over you all your life in exchange for loyalty, just about every dime you make, and your willingness to abide by the decisions of Washington bureaucrats concerning your medical needs.

Republicans are taught to be self-reliant, thrifty and privately generous, which is hurtful to the millions of people who work for our wonderful bureaucracy in order to help their fellow citizens from 9 to 4, weekdays, and not too close to the end of their shift.

Now, I don't care what Party your folks belong to. Criticism from any corner hurts my self-esteem and distresses me. You don't want someone with thousands of nuclear weapons at his fingertips feeling depressed, do you?

You're just kids, so how you can stop adults from talking trash about me? Act out. For example, elementary schoolers, put salt in the sugar bowl at home. Or run away. Junior and high school students, flip the grownups a sneaky bird. (Check out my technique on *YouTube*.) Or program a parental block on *Fox News*, NFL games, *Dancing with the Stars*, and *Playboy after Dark*.

Sure, these actions will have consequences. But anyone punished for taking my side is a victim of domestic political abuse. Don't remain silent. Tell a teacher. Tell a counselor. Teleprompter. Believe me, I'll hear about it. Then a man named Mr. Holder will be in touch with you to get a statement.

Let's talk about money briefly. If you're lucky, Mom and her partner support you and your brothers and sisters. Well, Mrs. Obama and I are like your second set of parents. We give you and your family tons of cool stuff you probably take for granted: tasteless but healthy school lunches and buses and nice roads and beautiful parks and food stamps and disability benefits and weather forecasts, so forth. I pay for these goodies. Where do *I* get the money?

Most comes from working people, maybe like your folks. Just as you get an allowance, they give me an allowance, too. Is *your* allowance enough to buy what *you* want? Neither is mine. So pretty soon, I'll ask your Mom and Dad to make some sacrifices, for example, going out to dinner once a month instead of weekly so they can increase my allowance.

I know you wish you could do more to help. Uncle Chollie and his friends Harry and Nancy are working on that. In a few weeks, they'll ask me to bypass Congress and issue a directive giving kids from first grade up the right to register and vote at school the day before elections. You're never too young to participate in the "Democratic" process. Ha ha.

Soon, people called "pollsters" will visit classrooms across America. They'll ask questions about what you and your folks think about me and what I'm doing to the country. Your teachers will give you the questions in advance, and the correct answers, too. It'll count as a major test grade.

Well, that's enough for today. For show-and-tell next week, I'll bring a copy of our dead Constitution and two guests, Dr. Kagan and Dr. Sotomayor, who'll explain how they intend to breathe new life into this decaying charter of negative liberties.

See you soon, kids.

OBAMA WAR ROOM: THROUGH A PRISM, DARKLY

VALERIE JARRETT: The president of Russia is on line one, sir.

OBAMA: Vladimir, my good friend. How are you?

So, I understand you and your entourage are staying at the Taj Lake Palace Hotel in Udaipur, India, preparing for your Himalayan adventure.

You should know. A little bird told me. It's called a NaSA. The first "a" is silent.

But the Taj, Vladimir? One of the world's best hotels. You really are Putin on the Ritz.

It was a joke, Mr. President. All right, to business then.

[listens]

Agreed. We will not fuss about Russian air bases in Venezuela and you will not object to missile defense installations in Eastern Europe which I have no intention of building.

Senate approval is unnecessary, Vladimir. This is a private understanding, not a formal treaty.

What? No, I heard no . . . sound. Yes, call me after you've skied Everest and brought back a Yeti's head. *Ciao.*

[hangs up]

Jay, get me the NSA Director. On speaker.

General Alexander, good morning. Are you monitoring my phones?

ALEXANDER: Yes, sir.

OBAMA: The Residence, too?

ALEXANDER: Yes, sir.

OBAMA: The girls' cells.

ALEXANDER: One never knows where the threat will come from, sir.

OBAMA: General, when I took over from Bush and approved the expansion of PRISM to gather intimate details on all earth's sentient beings, I wasn't including myself. Eric, do you know how I became a mark?

ERIC HOLDER: It's possible I orally okayed surveillance on you and yours, sir. I can't recall.

OBAMA: But this is wonderful! Like millions of Americans, I've been caught up in the sweep, my privacy rights violated. I'm a victim!

Jack, instruct the IRS to reveal my last return was audited and contained irregularities.

LEW: I'll inform House Oversight you'll be glad to testify about additional breaches of trust by our government, sir.

OBAMA: Jay, schedule a news conference for tomorrow morning. I'll alert the nation the president is also subject to overreach by the executive branch, and I will do everything in my power to find out what happened when I leave office and have more time.

JOE BIDEN: Jeez, Boss, I had no idea the NSA was checking everyone's underwear.

OBAMA: You weren't cleared, Joe.

BIDEN: Gives me the creeps.

OBAMA: Joe, have faith in me to do some good with our new information gathering techniques. Here, put this headset on and take a listen.

[a minute later]

BIDEN: That was Boehner, and then McConnell, right?

OBAMA: What you heard was recorded last Wednesday, Joe. The Speaker just finished number 4 at Burning Tree. He's telling the group he had a bogey. Now I'll cue up the video on the monitor.

Look there! That's a couple minutes earlier. He's searching for his ball in the woods, finds it behind a bush, glances around, then kicks the ball clear. Bogey my butt.

BIDEN: McConnell?

OBAMA: Pillow talk. You wanna see the video?

BIDEN: Not really, Boss. I don't get . . .

OBAMA: Joe, there's Top Secret; Top Secret, National Security Classification; and Top Secret, Obama Eyes Only. You wonder why the Speaker and the Majority Leader have been pretty quiet lately? I know what kind of toilet paper they use. Leverage, Joe. Information is power.

[enter First Lady]

MICHELLE: Listen up! I'm tired of sharing a plane. I want my own and I want it modeled after Air Force One. And don't give me that poor mouth speech or O'Reilly'll find a copy of your senior thesis in his mailbox. You hear me, Barack?

YOU HEAR ME, BARACK?

CHAPTER 1: HEALTH SNARE

OBAMA WAR ROOM: PUBLIC OPTION

KATHLEEN SEBELIUS: Postponing the employer mandate until 2015 is good politics, sir, but it'll be just as much a loser then as now. Better just to cut it out of the bill tomorrow using your Executive Excision power.

JOE BIDEN: Katy's right, Boss. Same's true for the individual mandrake.

OBAMA: I can't. Those two features are the heart and soul of . . . You meant "mandate," Joe. A mandrake is a plant that's said to shriek when pulled from the ground.

[silence]

Okay, okay, I see where you're coming from. But absent the two mandrakes, we don't even have ObamaCare Lite.

VALERIE JARRETT: It would be a bold move and a big part of your legacy, sir. You'd be the man responsible for protecting the American people from the consequences of a poor decision by the previous administration.

[phone rings; Jay Carney answers, listen, and hangs up]

JAY CARNEY: That was Edward Snowden, sir. Apparently, he's still plugged into the NSA network. He said to tell you he agrees with Valerie.

OBAMA: No. We stay the course. We owe it to the people we've conned into believing ObamaCare is the answer to our problems.

Kathleen, what've you come up with so far to reduce life expectancy and keep healthcare costs down?

SEBELIUS: Our databases contain the personal records of every senior—their ages, maladies, marital status, tickle spots, firearm preferences, dietary eccentricities, bowel habits, so forth. We'll assign attrition goals to their doctors. If they meet or exceed natural deaths quotas assigned to their practice, they may remain providers.

OBAMA: Good. Those who don't measure up we'll encourage to retrain as veterinarians. Anything else?

SEBELIUS: A flu shot lottery, sir. We've ordered 100 million doses for fall, 2013, 200 million short of what we'll need. A one in three chance to get the vaccine. Everyone takes their chances, including kids and seniors. Only exceptions: Executive Branch officials and key Congressional Democrats.

OBAMA: That it?

SEBELIUS: A promotion: for every elderly relative who signs a living will leaving life and death decisions to a Board-approved healthcare bureaucrat, your wait for any elective procedure is reduced six months.

OBAMA: Nice. Other ideas?

JACK LEW: Close suburban hospitals. Establish mega health complexes in the worst urban neighborhoods. Suburbanites will be afraid to come into the city for care. Less strain on resources.

OBAMA: Still, what about people living longer despite our best efforts?

SEBELIUS: Covered, sir. Section 6402, (A) (2) (b) (1) (c) automatically enrolls citizens in "Dying with Dignity" programs when they hit 60.

OBAMA: Gimme two more.

DAN PFEIFFER: Encourage smoking to become cool again. Mr. President. Give tobacco growers subsidies to make their products affordable. Cigarettes should be food-stamp eligible, too.

By the time millions of America are terminally ill from tobacco use, HHS can invoke that footnote on page 843 of the PPACA denying treatment to those who ignored warnings about the filthy habit.

JARRETT: All half measures, sir. My thought: nationalize drug companies. Pull life-saving medications off the shelves. Put cancer research on a back burner and launch a crash program to develop a whole new range of placebos.

OBAMA: Now you're talkin'! Remember, our ultimate goal is to encourage people to flee to Canada for their health needs.

OBAMA WAR ROOM: PPACA 2.0

OBAMA: Serendipity. Iran couldn't have nuked Tel Aviv at a better time. The Supreme Court revisiting and overturning ObamaCare because it violates the Origination Clause was relegated to a paragraph on A18.

JAY CARNEY: Damn the *Times*! They promised two sentences on B37. Well, the news will leak eventually, sir. We need to deflect responsibility for the fiasco from you.

OBAMA: Agreed. Jay, at your next briefing, acknowledge the Court's decision and start blasting Republicans for goading me into signing the bill before I was able to study it. *Consigliere*?

VALERIE JARRETT: I say we ignore the Supremes, sir. Tell Sebelius to continue implementing the PPACA while we appeal the ruling at the International Court of Justice in The Hague.

JOE BIDEN: Bad idea, Boss. We'd be twistin' in the wind for months while the thing played out. Accept the rebuke and throw your weight behind symbolic Congressional repeal. Cauterize the wound.

DAN PFEIFFER: But . . . that would mean abandoning the 145 million uninsured Americans and proto-citizens with preexisting conditions.

BIDEN: Dan, ya gotta know when to fold 'em. The whole shebang blew up in our faces 'cause we weren't anticipating widespread resistance.

OBAMA: Right. So, the act's history and we lie low. Voters will forget by midterms who birthed the monster.

BIDEN: Havin' nothin' to defend, we Democrats can reoccupy our usual gauzy moral high ground. We'll keep the Senate and take back the House. At that point we push through PPACA 2.0. Only this time, we anticipate the pratfalls, uh, pitfalls. Reminds me. [grabs pen, makes note on wrist]

OBAMA: What'd you write, Joe?

BIDEN: [reads from wrist] "Don't forget 'severability.'"

OBAMA: You know, I'll catch hell for reversing field from people we twisted like pretzels in the run-up to ObamaCare's passage— Landrieu, Bill Nelson, Blanche Lincoln, some of the Blue Dogs. Wish I could do something to reward their loyalty.

ERIC BOEHLERT: *Media Matters* can plant fake stories in the *National Enquirer* about them, sir. Drugs, gambling, infidelity, bathroom assignations. Then, at your direction, the DOJ investigates and discovers "evidence" Hannity ginned it all up.

OBAMA: Excellent! They'll be eternally grateful I used the power of my office to clear their names.

CARNEY: The *Enquirer* won't take unsourced material, Eric. I'll ask Jill Abramson at the *Times* to spread the rumors, even though her paper doesn't have the credibility or stature of the *Enquirer*.

VALERIE JARRETT: Who'd be the best person to fashion "ObamaCare—the Sequel" in the next Congress?

KATHLEEN SEBELIUS: Up until he announced his retirement, my first thought was Senator Baucus of Montana, ObamaCare's architect. He's less ignorant about the PPACA than anyone. But the doctors say his mind is gone now.

MICHELLE: Waxman of California is the next logical choice. He has a nose for this stuff.

OBAMA: When the time comes, we'll employ a "single bullet" stratagem to get around any hint of Congressional gridlock. Kathleen will explain.

SEBELIUS: Senator Reid passes an "Aid to Military Orphans Act" 100 to 0. Before sending it to the House, he surreptitiously attaches an amendment: Waxman's 3000 page ObamaCare 2.0 bill. Pelosi rushes a vote and sends the measure to the president.

OBAMA: Fine. First, we rebuke the Court for finding the Act constitutional to begin with, then we smother the thing in its crib. Dan, inform House and Senate leaders I'll sign the repeal as soon as it reaches my desk.

SEBELIUS: Regarding ObamaCare 2.0, sir: we'll need to do a better job of getting public support.

OBAMA: Right. Jay, alert the media: this fall I'll host the nationally televised "Teddy Kennedy Bipartisan Memorial Health Insurance Conference" at Camp David.

JARRETT: Nice, sir. Never too early to lay the groundwork for the next go-round. What's your plan?

OBAMA: Convince the country once again we're taking the initiative on reform. I want a controlled environment. At the

Republican breakfast caucus each morning, SEIU stewards will spike Paul Ryan's coffee with Xanax. Let's see how he does against me with a little buzz on.

PFEIFFER: I'll arrange to have AFL-CIO plants outside the gates wearing Palin T-shirts. They'll hold signs reading, "Hands off Insurance Companies" and "WellPoint IS America." Friendly anchors will switch to them whenever a Republican seems about to score.

OBAMA: Perfect. Oh, I'll need a reason to cut out during the afternoon sessions to get nine holes in.

Joe, when I scratch my forehead, you "answer" your cell, listen, hang up, come up to me looking worried, and whisper something in my ear. I'll nod and leave hurriedly. Sweet, no?

BIDEN: Gotcha, Boss. When I scratch my head, you'll approach me looking concerned and whisper sweet nothings in my ear. Then we leave together.

MICHELLE: From now on, I want Joe on permanent overseas funeral duty. You hear me, Barack?

CHAPTER 2: WHATEVER IT FAKES

OBAMA ANNOUNCES CONVERSION TO JUDAISM ON *SHALOM TV*

MAX RESNIK: Welcome President and Mrs. Obama. Sir, are you here because your support among Jews is cratering?

OBAMA: Correct, Max.

RESNIK: Mr. President, short of declaring Hagel is anti-Semitic and that Israel had nothing to do with 9/11, how can you regain Jews' trust?

OBAMA: Are your viewers aware Nation of Islam's Louis Farrakhan recently called me "the first Jewish President," Max? Or that yesterday I ruled out a freeze on Jewish construction on Manhattan's Upper East Side? And, and . . .

MICHELLE: Go ahead, tell him.

OBAMA: Well, you heard it here first, Max: I've changed my named to Barach [Baracchhk] Obauma and converted to Judaism.

RESNIK: You're kidding me.

MICHELLE: My idea, Max. Now we can play both the race and anti-Semite cards.

RESNIK: But . . . conversion rituals may take anywhere from six months to a year. You live in a bubble, Mr. President. When did you do this?

OBAUMA: March. I was in Chicago chairing a symposium on anti-Semitism with Reverend Farrakhan. Only it wasn't me. It was my former impersonator on *Saturday Night Live*, Fred Armisen, filling in for me.

RESNIK: Where were you?

OBAUMA: At Bed 'n Beth El, an African-American Reform synagogue in New York. Rabbi Ezekiel Okombo agreed to fast-track my conversion. To anticipate your next question, I chose "Reform" rather than "Orthodox" because I wasn't willing to give up my Saturday golf.

RESNIK: Sounds like a conversion of convenience, sir.

OBAUMA: Wrong, Max. I commemorated Passover this year by sneaking away to Arizona's Dunes Resort and playing 40 holes in the desert, straight through.

RESNIK: Shows commitment, sir. Ah, a delicate matter: how . . .

OBAUMA: Rabbi Okombo accepted without question a certified copy of my Certificate of Circumcision, Max, which I had a guy at Treasury forge for me.

RESNIK: About the Armisen substitution, sir. Who knew?

OBAUMA: Just Michelle and Vice President Biden. Worked out fine, except when Fred started fooling with the "nuclear football." Biden aborted the launch with minutes to spare. No harm, no foul.

RESNIK: Mr. President, Jews wonder if you'll help Israel in a death struggle with Hamas, Hezbollah, and Iran.

OBAUMA: Name someone who's tried harder to prevent the situation from escalating, Max. Earlier this year I said to

Netanyahu, "Let the Palestinians have their country back, and I'll use the Feds' eminent domain power to carve out an 8000 square mile enclave for you guys in West Texas in the, uh, Crawford area." He just laughed and accused me of wanting to stick it to Bush 43.

RESNIK: Sir, I asked if you would come to Israel's aid in a crisis.

OBAUMA: Of course, Max. I warned Ahmadinejad last year American warships won't brook interference when they pick up Israeli refugees drifting in the Red Sea.

MICHELLE: Baruch . . .

OBAUMA: "Baracchhk," dear.

MICHELLE: Baracchhk [cough cough] has guaranteed victims of the coming Israeli Diaspora right of return to Brooklyn, Max.

OBAUMA: All down the road. In the short term, I'll focus like a laser beam on the major threat to Jewish-Americans: Bible-thumping evangelicals. On my order, the FCC now monitors the Christian Television Network for hate speech and will exempt Jewish World Radio from the soon-to-be-imposed Fairness Doctrine.

MICHELLE: The president's religiosity is going to play a big part during his second and third terms, Max. Beginning Sundays in October, we'll televise non-denominational services live from the East Room on Presidential Productions, LLC's *White House of Worship*. Each week will feature an ordinary American Democrat telling the audience of a miraculous government intervention in her life.

OBAUMA: In related news, my proposed Cabinet-level Department of Guilt and Self-Flagellation organized this month under a temporary administrator. At 2:00 a.m. next Wednesday, I'll recess-appoint Michelle to take over. She's looking forward to her role as America's official Jewish Mother.

MICHELLE: Baracchhk believes it's long past time our government took responsibility for all the bad things that happened in the world before he became president, Max.

RESNIK: Sir, your approval rating is down across the board. You'll need more than Jewish support to abrogate the 22nd Amendment and be elected to serve a third term.

OBAUMA: My campaign bus is rolling, Max. The 22nd Amendment's just a speed bump. Once that's out of the way, we'll pursue the standard Democratic Party "building blocs" strategy to offset the Republicans' advantage among rational voters.

We're depending on minorities, of course, "white guilt" liberals, academics, intellectuals, unionists, feminists, undocumented proto-Americans, federal employees, compromised former Democratic Secretaries of State, the transgendered disabled, and other aggrieved segments of American society. We turn these folks out, and instead of an Inaugural Ball in January 2017, I'll throw the biggest bloc party in history.

RESNIK: Your most important constituency, sir, aside from African-Americans?

OBAUMA: Absentee voters, Max. They always cast ballots in numbers disproportionate to their existence. [glancing at watch] Well, we'd better run.

RESNIK: Thank you for coming on, Mr. President. And *shalom*. Perhaps you'll visit us again soon.

OBAUMA: *Inshallah*, Max. [Michelle elbows him] What? Oh. Excuse me. Got a little ahead of myself there. See, we're due at the CAIR TV studios shortly, where I will make an important announcement regarding . . .

MICHELLE: Say *"Shalom*, Max," Baracchhk.

OBAUMA: *Shalom*, Max, Baracchhk.

PRESIDENT TO GUEST ON *SWAMP LOGGERS* SPECIAL

Washington (AP)—In an interview yesterday on *MSNBC*'s *Hardball*, White House Press Secretary Jay Carney revealed that President Obama will appear in a Swamp Loggers special to be aired this fall. Cancelled several years ago, the *Discovery Channel*'s reality show followed a family-owned logging company plying its trade in all but inaccessible North Carolina wetlands.

[begin transcript]

CHRIS MATTHEWS: *Swamp Loggers*? Why?

CARNEY: Well, Chris, as ObamaCare finally starts kicking in, people are beginning to realize they were conned. Our poll numbers are heading south.

Some months ago, the president said to me, "Jay, John Kerry just told me something I'll never forget: 'Inside every demigod, every patrician, every politician, there's a common man trying to get out.'"

At that moment the president decided to reconnect with the American people. He figured he wouldn't find them at a tony compound on Martha's Vineyard or his palatial Hawaiian retreat, though he wouldn't give those places up. He said, "I want to carve out more free time and spend it with regular folks, like the women on *The View*. I want to learn how ordinary people live, see through their eyes as my policies take hold and the American dream disappears. And I want a big heartland audience watch me descend to earth."

I'm a *Discovery Channel* fan. I suggested a guest spot on *Deadliest Catch*, the network's top-rated reality series. The president considered it, but decided the only relationship he wanted with large crustaceans was tucking into their legs with a cup of melted butter nearby.

Then I remembered the *Swamp Loggers* special was in the works. I ran a proposal by the president, which he accepted. We made the necessary contacts and taped the show.

MATTHEWS: Wait a second. You mean it's in the can? The president's dodged the press pool once or twice for a few hours, but he had to be away for at least a few days for taping. How could no one know? When did he do this?

CARNEY: Last May, Chris, during the G8 summit. We asked *Saturday Night Live*'s former Obama impersonator, Fred Armisen, to fill in for the president at the meetings. He's done it before.

It all worked out fine, except when Fred got carried away and committed the U.S. to adopting the euro in January. We hadn't planned on implementing the switchover until spring, but we'll adjust. Our money's already being printed in funny colors, so nobody will notice the difference.

Anyway, President Obama was excited about his appearance. Marine One deposited him at the All-Terrain Logging, Inc. (ATL) work site on a spit of land in the middle of Possum Swamp in southeastern North Carolina. Initially, he was upset

MATTHEWS: Why?

CARNEY: It was a snafu. I took full responsibility. Seems the president thought he heard me say *Swamp Bloggers* not *Swamp Loggers* and assumed he'd sit down for a *View*-like gab with some Internet-savvy hayseeds.

MATTHEWS: Oh. His reaction when he learned the truth?

CARNEY: He was a good sport. Met with ATL Chief Bobby Goodson and they hit it off at first. Goodson invited the president to take the co-pilot seat on a haul to the mill and let him play with the controls of a grapple skidder. We took some great footage.

The president got an earful about the difficulty of logging in a foot of water. He promised Goodson that when he returned to Washington, he'd ask former House Speaker Pelosi to come down to North Carolina and drain the swamp. Later, though, things went south.

MATTHEWS: What happened?

CARNEY: They started talking politics. President Obama asked Goodson if he thought Palin was presidential timber. Goodson exclaimed, "Damn straight she is!" The president burst out laughing; said if she had won the nomination in 2012, he'd have gone through her like a Husqvarna 365 through yellow pine.

Then Goodson got in the president's face: "Laugh while you can, 'cause your Dem field, including the old growth, is facing a clear-cutting next time round."

Well, that did it. Marine One flew us out an hour later. The president was furious. Ordered OSHA to cite ATL for allowing him on site without a hardhat; the IRS to pursue Goodson and his family into bankruptcy; the NSA to send a copy of their file on Goodson to the *Times*; and the FCC to pull *Discovery Channel*'s license if it aired the special.

MATTHEWS: Suppose a court rules the show may be aired.

CARNEY: Should that happen, the NSA assures me a localized atmospheric electromagnetic anomaly will interfere with the broadcast.

MATTHEWS: Gotcha. What's up next for the Chief Executive and Reality TV?

CARNEY: New TV series premieres in January: *Bad Boys on Wall Street*. In the first episode, the president rides along with federal marshals when they bust some hedge fund freaks. Talk it up, Chris.

[end transcript]

STEVE GRAMMATICO

CARVILLE NAMED "RIGHT WING THREAT ASSESSMENT CZAR"

WASHINGTON (AP)—President Obama introduced James Carville today as Homeland Security's new "Right Wing Threat Assessment Czar." A political science professor at Tulane, Carville is inexplicably married to Republican strategist Mary Matalin.

The president praised Dr. Carville's "unparalleled understanding of the danger the right poses to his vision for America. He will work with Attorney General Holder and the IRS to ferret out and expose subversion masquerading as dissent."

Carville—or "Serpenthead," as he is known to political herpetologists—announced he will launch an investigation into the origins and funding of the "tea party" movement that has spread across the country and cost Democrats at the polls despite the efforts of the DNC to portray Tea Partiers as the American Taliban.

"Ya got these here 'tea pirates' hijackin' the national conversation, talkin' trash, holdin' up the Constitution as some kinda sacred text 'at empowers 'em. They messin' wid simple, hard workin' folks' heads, people never give the IRS nor deficits no never mind before, getting' 'em riled up 'n spoutin' anti-gummint nonsense.

"Limbaugh, Hannity, Levin, the Reynolds fella," Carville continued, "they leadin' the pack, but I'm gonna call in my own dogs to wet the fire when the hunt's done, the moon's come over the bayou, we've et the mudbugs, and the jambalaya's simmerin' in the pot." Asked to explain, Mr. Carville responded, "Say what?"

OBAMA WAR ROOM: REVERSE POLLARITY

JOE BIDEN: [handing president phone] Axelrod calling from Chicago, Boss. He sounds pissed.

OBAMA: Whassup, Axe?

No, I don't know who leaked our decision to abandon blue collar whites. Soon's we find the SOB, we'll dress him up like a corporate type and drop him in the middle of an OWS demonstration.

You're kidding. We gotta play the game just because word got out?

Okay, I understand: you want me and Joe to be regular people for a while. Suggestions?

Avoid Camp David. Fine. Too rustic for my taste, anyway.

Wait until after midterms to eminent domain Lafayette Square and build a White House pitch and putt complex? Agreed. Anything else?

What?! Aw, c'mon, man! You can't be serious. It'd demean the office of the presidency.

All right, all right. Yeah, we'll brainstorm more ideas, too. Later.

[hangs up]

BIDEN: Chief?

OBAMA: Joe, first thing tomorrow you and I begin hanging new drapery in the East Room.

JAY CARNEY: I'll alert *Good Morning America*.

VALERIE JARRETT: And I'll cancel your 9:00 o'clock tee time with Tiger, Mr. President.

OBAMA: I forgot about that. Ixnay! *SNL*'s Jay Pharaoh owes me big for resuscitating his career as my impersonator. Jay, request his presence here at dawn in work clothes and cap. And don't give the signal to start taping until Pharaoh and Joe are atop their ladders. No close ups. |

DAN PFEIFFER: I just signed you and Michelle up for the Tuesday night mixed league at the Lucky Strikes Lanes in Bethesda, sir. First-timers bring beer.

OBAMA: Oh joy. Well, anyway, Versace'll need a few weeks to design Michelle's ball bag. We'll start after we get back from our Hawaiian sojourn in . . . Val, what?

JARRETT: Um, normal folks don't go to the islands on holiday for weeks with a 500 person entourage, sir. Better stick close this year.

BIDEN: She's right, Skipper. How 'bout us two and the wives do some day trips, like Busch Gardens in Williamsburg, maybe. We don't like it, we say it's Busch's fault. Or maybe we check out *Bob's Reptile House* in Manassas. Or we take a bird walk at the National Zoo.

CARNEY: I'll announce at today's briefing that you and Mrs. Obama will spend August clearing brush at Camp David.

OBAMA: This is getting out of hand.

BIDEN: Ooh, that sparks a thought, Number One. The prop kids are coming on Wednesday to sit at your feet when you tape the new ObamaCare spot.

Afterwards, let's you and me do a Bush-Cheney sock puppet show for them in the Rose Garden. Bush and Cheney are quail hunting in Jersey, see, when Cheney accidentally discharges his weapon, winging Jon Corzine who's nearby throwing bags of money into a big hole he's dug. Meanwhile . . .

OBAMA: Wait, wait, wait. We're going about this bass ackwards. I won't get my numbers back up because the great unwashed think I'm one of them; I'll become popular again if the economy booms. Or, conversely, if it tanks and everyone panics and comes running to hold my pant leg.

PFEIFFER: Choosing the boom scenario, sir—you could bring Rick Santelli in and make him Economy Czar.

JARRETT: The president will not abandon his war on capitalism, Dan.

OBAMA: Look, unemployment just fell to 13.6%. Why? Because employers are buoyed by the fact I'm looking more like a lame duck every day. They're anticipating a Republican takeover of Congress in 2014 and my agenda in tatters

PFEIFFER: I think I get where you're going, sir. We keep doing what we've been doing to drive your numbers down further, through the 30s and even into the 20s. The lower you go, the more hoarded cash gets pumped into the marketplace. By the middle of 2014, the economy's ignited, leaving Republican candidates gasping like a landed fish.

OBAMA: Exactly. Naturally, my numbers and the Party's rebound dramatically, with businesses too committed to expansion to pull back even though we're surging. Their tough luck when we own Congress and punish them for trying to profit on the backs of their customers.

JARRETT: On another front, sir: Senator Collins has agreed to break ranks with Senate Republicans and sign on to your American Jobs Bill.

OBAMA: What did we give up for her support?

PFEIFFER: She remains a Republican, but she gets a vote in Reid's caucus.

OBAMA: Not too bad in exchange for . . .

PFEIFFER: There's more: she has first call on the White House movie theater. Also, next vacancy, you're nominating her for the Supreme Court.

OBAMA: Ouch! The pain in Maine weighs heav'ly on my brain. Still, nice having a token Republican on our side.

BIDEN: Whew! All this Machovellan stuff is making my head spin. Hey, you haven't had any down time since yesterday, Chief. Whyncha reach out to Tiger and Michael Jordan. Check if they're available to fly to Pebble Beach this weekend.

JARRETT: Collins already reserved Air Force One through Sunday, sir.

OBAMA: Oh? Has she moved into the Residence yet? What more can possibly happen to . . . ?

[enter First Lady]

MICHELLE: Hey, who booked the Blue Room Friday night for "An Old-Fashioned Maine Snowbound Hoedown"? I need it for my seminar on "Weak Men, and the Strong Women Who Push Them to Greatness." Move the Maine shindig to your basketball court. You hear me, Barack?

INSIDE THE DNC: YOU'RE NEVER TOO DEAD TO VOTE

MINUTES

Democratic National Committee
Oval Office Meeting
January 8, 2014

MEMBERS PRESENT

Debbie Whassupman Schultz, Chairman

Howard Dean, Chairman Emeritus Idiotis

Dennis Kucinich, DNC mascot

Nancy Pelosi, Speaker-in-Waiting

Harry Reid, Senate Majority Misleader

Senator Charles Schumer, Majority Misleader-in-Waiting

Brian Williams, Network Lieaison [sic]

Eric Boehlert, *Media Matters*

Chris Matthews, DNC Cable Guy

ALSO PRESENT

President Obama

Jack Lew, Secretary of Disbursements

Michael Moore, fabulist

George Soros, DNC Sugar Daddy

Stan Greenberg, pollster

Marcia L. Fudge, Congressional Black Caucus

Eric Holder, Attorney General for Minorities

Lawrence ("Shilling-for-Your-Thought, Mr. President") O'Donnell

Unidentified Hamas Observer

PROCEEDINGS

Chairman Schultz called the meeting to order at 9:00 a.m. in the Oval Office after aides fetched a booster seat for Mr. Kucinich and removed American flags from the room per request Mr. Moore and Mr. Soros.

President Obama left, pleading a golf date.

Minutes of last month's meeting were amended to remove unsettling references to recent opinion polls. Motion to Approve. Accepted.

NEW BUSINESS

1. Chairman Whassupman Schultz asked for fresh ideas to boost Party prospects for midterms.

Mr. Dean suggested expansion of the 2008 "Dead Pool" pilot program, noting dead Democrats outnumber dead Republicans by 2 to 1.

He urged the Party to nationalize its urban get-out-the-dead vote operations: "The passed are being passed over. Democrats are dying every day and taking their votes with them," he said.

Mr. Williams promised that *NBC* would begin framing incorporeality as a disability, not a disqualification.

Senator Schumer will sponsor legislation restoring the Founders' original intent of "one dead man, one vote."

Mr. Soros offered to buy "phooneral" parlors in Democratic strongholds so "ven dey go, ve know."

Mr. Dean advised the Committee to have DNC attorneys monitor morgues in those cities to advise the deceased of their rights and counter Republican shenanigans.

Motion to approve all measures related to the "Dead Vote Project." Accepted.

2. AG Holder said he will inform registrars across the country that showing up to vote in future elections constitutes proof of eligibility.

3. Ms. Pelosi expressed concern about the enthusiasm of the Republican Party's base. She advocated preemptive voter suppression.

Mr. Williams promised the networks would run stories implying there isn't a nickel's worth of difference between the parties and candidates.

Mr. Moore offered to produce and star in a series of TV spots endorsing Republicans.

Mr. Greenberg revealed the question for voters in his next poll: "Would you be more likely or less likely to vote for Republicans while they're sabotaging the president's efforts to revive the economy?"

Motion to approve voter suppression recommendations. Accepted.

3. Senate Majority Misleader Reid requested an update on the Committee's work to compromise the right's leading voices.

Mr. O'Donnell apologized for not meeting his quarterly slander quota. This month he's targeting Laura Ingraham, Glenn Reynolds, Hannity, and Mallard Fillmore.

Mr. Moore reported our friend at the skin-magazine-that-must-not-be-named-but-whose-title-rhymes-with-rustler has compiled a list of Republican targets, is checking it twice, and will get it to the Committee well before midterms.

4. Ms. Whassupman Schultz revealed SEIU and UAW Rapid Response Force units are now available to help Democratic candidates manage their campaigns. She thanked Mr. Soros for underwriting the cost.

On request, RRF squads will be dispatched to selected town hall meetings to:

a. Confiscate the opposition's signs, recording devices, and cell phones

b. Screen attendees for party affiliation

c. Assure audiences are racially and ethnically balanced

d. Vet pre-chosen questioners before the meeting begins.

e. Assault anyone who interrupts candidates with anything but approbation.

Agents will wear distinctive black T-shirts with a smiling President Obama on the front. On the back, the logo, "Yes, we can! Hurt you."

Ms. Whassupman Schultz waived charges for this service but said, "One day, I might tap a congressman on the shoulder and say, 'I need a favor.'"

5. Mr. Kucinich will appeal to Munchkins to come home to the Democrats.

Motion to adjourn. Approved.

OBAMA WAR ROOM: SHAKIN' UP IS HARD TO DO

JAY CARNEY: The *Times* and the *Post* are still with us, sir, but *MSNBC* has revolted.

OBAMA: Man! Five years ago those people thought I walked on water. Now they crucify me because I can't transmogrify private coverage into single payer. What happened, Jeremiah?

REVEREND WRIGHT: By embracing your humanity, you denied your divinity, Barack. Subsequently, believers suffered a crisis of faith. And then the Tea Party sect seized the Mount of Public Opinion, for which they were rightly targeted by your acolytes at the IRS. The agitators must be evicted and cast into the Slough of Despond.

OBAMA: To put things right. I'll set humility aside and found my own religion—The Church O' the Redeemer; Sunday services broadcast live from the Rose Garden; Homilies on public policy matters.

Is there a church-state separation issue here, Eric?

HOLDER: No, sir, since you embody both.

OBAMA: Uh, Jay who's that young man sitting in the corner?

CARNEY: His name's Ezra Klein, sir, founder of the now defunct JournoList web clique I told you about.

OBAMA: What's he doing here?

CARNEY: You wanted our outreach programs on the same page, sir. Klein's reconstituted JournoList, only this time with 400 Hispanic journalists and bloggers. They'll communicate in code to reduce the chance of exposure. Sort of like *Codetalkers en Espanol.*

DAN PFEIFFER: Klein's attending our strategy sessions to take in firsthand the spin he'll be disseminating, sir.

OBAMA: *Si, se puede!*

KLEIN: I . . .

PFEIFFER: Ezra, do not speak unless you are directly addressed; when responding to the president, keep your gaze downcast. Sir, cut him some slack. He's only 14.

OBAMA: [to Klein] Stand up, son, stand up. So, no more "*Journolistas.*" What do you people in the new listserv call yourselves?

KLEIN: The *Cabal-leros, Jefe.* We . . .

OBAMA: Sit down, son.

VALERIE JARRETT: Sir, the *MSNBC* firebreathers, their anger is troubling. They speak for the base, and the base *is* restless.

OBAMA: I know. Absent Bush's retroactive impeachment or the disbandment of the military, they'll sit on their hands in 2014. We can't afford that.

JOE BIDEN: Here's an idea, Boss: satisfy the nutroots' bloodlust by publicly purging high-profile advisors for failin' you. That'll play in the *barrios*, too, won't it Ezra?

KLEIN: I . . .

OBAMA: Quiet, son. You're here to listen.

BIDEN: I spoke with Rahm Emanuel in Chicago, Chief: he volunteered to be a scapegoat. Said he'd be willing to commit—whatamacallit—suburu at your next presser.

OBAMA: That's *seppuku*, Joe: Japanese ritualistic suicide. Well, his call. Jay, seat Jake Tapper and Fox's Ed Henry within spurting distance. I want them to feel responsible for Rahm's sacrifice.

MICHELLE: The Secret Service won't let Rahm take a ritual blade into the East Room to perform the rite, guys.

BIDEN: No problem. He can disembowel himself in the corridor, then hold things in till he gets to the podium.

OBAMA: Any other volunteers to take the heat for my failures? Um, Joe?

BIDEN: I'd resign in an instant, Boss, but your numbers would go through the floor if people thought I had what it takes to be president.

OBAMA: Good point. Jay?

CARNEY: I've replaced Bob Gibbs as a supercilious prig, sir. Fire me and hold daily press briefings yourself.

OBAMA: Done. If I can't answer a question, I'll say I'll check with myself later and get back to the reporter, ho ho. Eric?

HOLDER: I've reversed 40 years of racial progress as Attorney General, sir. I'll resign and resume representing Guantanamo detainees.

OBAMA: Okay. Ramsey Clark will take your place after he's filed his war crimes brief against me in The Hague. Jack?

LEW: I'm in over my head, sir. Bernie Madoff could turn things around on a dime.

OBAMA: Reach out to Madoff, Valerie. Offer him a pardon if he takes Treasury and keeps Social Security going another twenty years; after all nobody knows Ponzi schemes like Bernie. John?

KERRY: In the midst of world gloom, I've made people laugh again with my gaffes. So, I'm good, sir.

OBAMA: I suppose. Well, the bloodletting should mollify the MoveOn folks. Son, you want to say something?

KLEIN: [timidly] I'll instruct the *Cabal-leros* to push the machismo angle of your aides' sacrifice, El Caudillo. [cell rings] Yes? With a what? Okay, I'll tell them. [hangs up] Trouble. Whoopi Goldberg just lost it on *The View*. Hit Ann Coulter in the face with an old fruitcake instead of a cream pie.

BIDEN: And the problem with that is?

OBAMA: We could use one more high-profile sacrifice. Maybe . . .

MICHELLE: Who you lookin' at? Come after me and your *real* long form birth certificate goes right to Hannity. You hear me, Barack?

SECRETARY OF STATE DESIGNEE JOE BIDEN SAILS THROUGH CONFIRMATION HEARING

Washington (AP)—If all goes as expected, Vice President Joe Biden and Secretary of State John Kerry will officially trade places at an unprecedented swearing-in ceremony next week in the Rose Garden.

As a mark of courtesy to their former Chairman, Senate Democrats on the Foreign Relations Committee appointed Mr. Kerry Chairman *Pro Tempore* to allow him to conduct Mr. Biden's confirmation hearing.

[partial transcript]

JOHN KERRY: Good morning. In recent weeks, the president realized what a disaster I am on the international stage. He correctly reasons I would do less damage to the administration as his Number Two.

Joe Biden is uniquely qualified to take the reins at State and oversee the steaming pile of dung Mrs. Clinton and I left him. I have no doubt Joe can handle the load, at least in the short term.

America is a nation in decline, a nation hurtling toward the depths. With his misplaced sense of humor, endearing ineptitude, and characteristic superciliousness, Joe is well-equipped to lead us into irrelevance.

Before we begin the questioning, I would like to offer a few thoughts about my tenure at State and some initiatives I hope Joe will pursue:

. . . defeating the worldwide scourge of male pattern baldness and preventing loss of innocent follicles . . .

. . . extraditing Dick Cheney to The Hague to stand trial for. . .

. . . returning Texas and California to Mexico, from whom we unjustly . . .

. . . calming Americans' unreasoning dread of a Global Caliphate . . .

. . . reversing the Industrial Revolution, so that the Earth may once again . . .

Now, to save time, we'll dispense with a self-serving statement from the Ranking Member and go right to questioning. Suit you, Mr. Vice President?

BIDEN: Sure. [looks into camera and nods at Kerry] Don't let the long face and sober mien fool ya, folks. Kerry's a regular guy. The other day we were playin' bumslap in the locker room at the New York Athletic Club, and he . . .

KERRY: That was Bob Kerrey, Joe.

BIDEN: Whatever.

KERRY: Let's do a foreign policy word association exercise first.

BIDEN: Shoot.

KERRY: Palestinians.

BIDEN: Give 'em a chunk of money to ignore Israel, then sic 'em on Iran.

KERRY: Guantanamo.

BIDEN: Release the detainees. Say, "We grab you on the battlefield again, we'll shave your beard and feed you pulled pork sandwiches." To hell with *Human Rights Watch*.

KERRY: Nicarugula

BIDEN: [hesitates] Um, nice, with a light balsamic, maybe some parmesan shards?

KERRY: Bumslap, huh? Gotcha.

BIDEN: Damn.

KERRY: North Korea.

BIDEN: They're paranoid. Hand over Bill Clinton to serve as hostage to our good behavior.

KERRY: Muslim Brotherhood.

51

BIDEN: Appoint Minister Farrakhan Special Envoy to the brothas.

KERRY: On a more personal note: what was your proudest moment in the foreign arena as Vice President

BIDEN: Tell you a story was never reported.

April 2009, a few months after we took over. The standoff between the USS Bainbridge and Somali pirates holdin' the captain of an American-flagged ship in a lifeboat was in its fourth day and showed no signs of endin'.

I said to the president, "Lemme fly out there, Boss, settle this thing. I grew up with workin'-class stiffs tryin' to make an easy buck any way they could. I'll get down and dirty if I hafta."

The Big O says, "Do it, Joe."

Twelve hours later I was aboard the Bainbridge and had assumed command of the ship. I parleyed with the pirates in Somali, which I speak fluently. They musta been hopped up. Wouldn't listen. So, I decided to move on 'em.

I nixed a proposal for a SEAL dive team to surface next to the boat, climb in and overwhelm the bad guys. "No waterboarding," I told the SEALs. "Not in this administration." Instead, I stationed snipers on the ship's fantail, spottin' for one of them.

When the time was right, I gave the order and my team took 'em down. Then I dove in, grabbed our hostage, and got 'im back to the ship in twelve foot seas.

KERRY: Amazing.

BIDEN: Don't make me out like a hero, now. Just doin' my job.

KERRY: How can we prevent such a situation from happening again?

BIDEN: Piracy was allowed to grow and fester under the previous administration, John. President Bush never reached out to the pirates; he dismissed them as barbarians and thieves.

In fact, the Obama Administration has developed evidence these high seas entrepreneurs often mistakenly target American vessels because of dense fog caused by global warming.

The president authorized me to share ship identification technology with responsible members of the pirate community to reduce the chance of a repeat incident.

KERRY: Ah, time's up. Before I yield, I want to thank Mr. Biden for his advice on registering my yacht in Panama, beyond the reach of Massachusetts tax collectors who . . .

BIDEN: Don't go there, John.

CHAPTER 3: THE DAYS OF GUNS AND POSES

OBAMA WAR ROOM: ARMS AND "THE MAN"

VALERIE JARRETT: Treasury Secretary Lew's here to brief you on your blind trust, sir.

OBAMA: Great. The usual, Jack. I'll close my eyes, you tell me how my portfolio's doing.

LEW: Good news, sir. Your decision to invest heavily in publicly traded firearms manufacturers before being elected in 2008 has paid off.

OBAMA: Told ya so. Nothing causes guns to fly off the shelves like a Democrat in the White House.

LEW: Your investment in ammunition manufacturers was prescient, too, sir. Factories are running three shifts since you ordered 15 billion hollow points for your new Civilian National Security Force.

OBAMA: You can't be too thin or too rich or have too many bullets, Jack.

Has Feinstein shown any sign of tumbling to my real agenda—repeal of the 22nd Amendment limiting me to two terms, not the 2nd?

DAN PFEIFFER: Negative, sir. The plan is still operative: the public turns against Republicans for politicizing Benghazi the IRS, NSA, your vacations, so on; we blow them out in 2014; a Constitutional Convention repeals the 2nd Amendment after GOP state legislators learn what the NSA and IRS have on them.

JARRETT: The repeal is then encapsulated in a formal document published by the Federal Register and becomes the law of the land.

OBAMA: Tell me the best part again.

PFEIFFER: You know it, sir.

OBAMA: Tell me again.

PFEIFFER: [sighs] You appointed the Register's Archivist. He'll make a slight mistake in composing the proclamation, adding the digit "2" in the appropriate place, thus repealing the *22nd* Amendment. The 2nd we can do later. How long will you go, sir?

OBAMA: Four terms. At that point the pre-nuptial Vernon Jordan wrote up making Michelle my successor kicks in.

BULLET POINTS

President's Select International Commission on Disarming America

Minutes
January 6, 2013

PRESENT

Joe Biden, Chairman; Vice President of the United States

Hu Jintao, Vice Chairman; President, People's Republic of China

Senator Charles Schumer, Jewish Libby

Mayor Michael Bloomberg, National Scold

Janet Napolitano: Former Director of Homeland Severity

Barbra Streisand, Celebrity Busybody

Piers Morgan, English Gadfly

Tony Morgazzo, President, Brotherhood of Breakers and Enterers

JOE BIDEN: Okay, let's get started. No palimentary crap like, "The Chair recognizes so-and-so," "Who wants to have a movement," or "I second the notion," yada, yada. Just gimme your ideas and I'll run 'em by the Boss.

TONY MORGAN: You'll never get all the guns. So, go after bullets. Order Consumer Affairs to shut down ammunition manufacturers because of high concentrations of lead in their products. Ban importation for the same reason.

JOE BIDEN: That would cost us jobs, gang. Get the same result by requiring producers to sell ammunition only to Homeland Security, law enforcement, and Defense. Homeland Security alone needs 5000 rounds of hollow points for every man, woman, and child in the country.

HU JINTAO: Confucius say, "Outlaw bullets, only outlaws will have bullets."

[puzzled silence]

BIDEN: Did you just make a suggestion, Hu?

SENATOR SCHUMER: I'm not sure, but I think Hu means a ban will result in a flourishing civilian black market in rounds.

HU JINTAO: To limit such actvity, approve China as sole supplier to American gun owners of reasonably priced, reduced-lead, powder-lite ™ cartridges.

BIDEN: Nice. In time, people'll get used to guns that just go "pfhit."

You got a face on you, Tony. What's the problem?

MORGAZZO: Yeah: "in time." But marks still got a lot of real ammo stocked up out there. My guys need protection against unlawful, deadly resistance when they're burglin'.

BIDEN: Mandatory year in the clink for obstructing a felony—that work for you?

BARBRA STREISAND: What about high-capacity magazines?

BIDEN: Covered, Babs. *Gun World, Guns and Ammo*, the rest, USPS has classified "gun porn." No delivery.

MORGAN: You chaps need to disarm your police, like we did our Bobbies.

SCHUMER: Mayor?

BLOOMBERG: Pilot project starts next week. NYPD officers may carry their weapons only in station houses, not on patrol where they're more likely to be used.

BIDEN: Enough for today. I'll issue a statement: "Trust me on this, folks. We ain't takin' guns away from law-abidin' citizens." Course, I won't say anythin' about real bullets.

SCHUMER: Good. Your assurance will assuage the concerns of my three 2nd Amendment constituents who still believe I'm an honorable man.

JOE BIDEN ALMOST ADDRESSES THE NATION

OBAMA: Okay, Joe. I let you carry the ball on this one. Let's hear what you'll tell the country tomorrow night about your gun commission's recommendations.

BIDEN: Straight to the point, Big Guy. You're gonna like it. Here goes:

Hey, howya doin', folks? I bet you're thinkin', "Why's ole Joe in the Oval Office?"

I'll tell ya: the Boss doesn't want his fingerprints on this one. He said to me, "Joe, I need you to lay down the law on guns. I can't, because aside from deciding who to kill with drones, I have a problem makin' big decisions. Use the Oval Office. Sit in my chair. Maybe someday it'll be your chair, God help us. I don't even want to know what you're proposing. Surprise me."

So, here I am with my recommendation. Yeah, that's right, "recommendation." No 2000 page report with chapters, subsections, and the like. Just this one sheet of paper I'm holdin' up. On the sheet, one sentence.

Let's see, 8:04 now. The country can have a national debate about this until midnight. Then the order gets signed by Executive Autopen. The Boss says nobody can actually prove he signed it if the whole thing goes kablooie.

Here's the deal, and I quote: "Anything fires a projectile, any projectile, it's banned."

Clear enough for ya? No handguns, no rifles, no bazookas, no crossbows, no BB shooters, no nerf guns, no slingshots, no water pistols. No exceptions.

Whatever weapons you got now that foul afall of the order—uh, fall afoul of the order—you pile 'em on the curb and the president's new Civilian National Security Corpse will come by and collect 'em. You wanna appeal to the Supremes, go ahead. Guess which branch of government enforces their decrees—or not.

Now, if you're listenin', Piers, press your hand to the screen and gimme five.

God bless America.

Whatcha think, Chief?

OBAMA: Val, feel Hillary out about coming on board as vp. Tell her Joe is a real Number Two and we've convinced him to resign and spend more time with his family.

ANNIE HIDE YOUR GUNS

ABC News Special

GEORGE WILL: Rumor is, the president didn't like Mr. Biden's draft and they had words.

BRIAN WILLIAMS: I was told White House speechwriters rewrote the text. And people are wondering why the president isn't delivering it. Okay, we're on.

Now, live, from the White House, Vice President Joe Biden and, at his feet, live props from the Children against Gun Violence PAC:

VICE PRESIDENT BIDEN: Evenin', everyone.

Yesterday me and the president put our heads together and worked through my commission's recommendations on gun violence. See this? [holds up sheaf of papers] This is what I'm supposed to say. [lays papers down] But I'm gonna be me and use my own words. Whatta they gonna do: pull the plug?

So, why's ole Joe's here, not the Boss? Well, yesterday he says, "Joe, I can't expend capital on this one. Take the blowback for me." Hold on. Hey kids, quit fidgetin' and look up at me adoringly like I showed you.

Anyway, I gotta coupla VP Executive Orders here. Perfectly legal: the Chief's playin' golf, and Article II, Section 1 of the Constitution gives me power when he's incapacitated. Let's get to it.

Order 1: Firearms and ammunition manufacturers, bow and arrow makers, Walmart, Cabela's, gun shops: do your thing, but you can only sell to us Feds and drug cartels.

Order 2: Mandatory turn-in. Everythin'. Hand 'em over or go to jail. And we know who has what: the NSA hasn't been twiddlin' its thumbs the last four years. Confiscated weapons will be used to equip the president's new Civil Service Civilian Army, saving taxpayers a bundle.

You slip somethin' by us, maybe shoot a mugger or home invader mindin' his own business, you're lookin' at hard time.

Order 3: Hunters, register your slingshot or boomerang, you're good to go.

Order 4: Priests and shrinks: record everybody you talk to, send the tapes to the FBI. They'll follow up.

That's it. I'm askin' video game makers and Hollywood to keep the violence down, but only askin'. Not gonna infringe on their First Amendment rights. Hey, you catch *Django*? Did that rock or what? I . . .

JAY CARNEY: Thank you, Mr. Vice President.

CHAPTER 4: BENGHAZI—"OB-LA-DI, OB-LA-DA, LIFE GOES ON"

BENGHAZI: WHAT REALLY HAPPENED

White House Situation Room
September 11, 2012

LEON PANETTA: [to aide] Call the Residence. On speaker.

[First Lady answers]

MICHELLE: What?

PANETTA: Leon Panetta, Ma'am. We need the president in the Situation Room ASAP.

MICHELLE: He's busy playing *Ragnarök II—the Awakening* on his Xbox. His forces are in the middle of a decisive action. Can't you handle the problem?

PANETTA: Uh, no Ma'am.

MICHELLE: Oh for God's sake. [yells] Barack! Pick up! It's Panetta!!

OBAMA: Jeez, Leon. What's so important? I've just breached Rozamin's redoubt; Castle Covenant's ripe for the taking. It'll set the Outliers back on their heels for months.

PANETTA: Trouble sir, Benghazi. I . . .

OBAMA: Ben Ghazi? The Israeli Defense Minister?

PANETTA: No, sir. Our consulate in Libya. Ambassador Stevens and his team are under attack.

OBAMA: Leon, weeks went into planning this siege. You want me to suspend the operation and come down there to do what, exactly?

PANETTA: Sir, only you possess the authority to . . .

OBAMA: Leon, I authorize you to do whatever successfully resolves the situation and accrues to my benefit. Should things blow up in our faces, it's on you. I was out of the loop. Clear?

PANETTA: Yes, sir.

MICHELLE: [in background] Barack! Zulu 4 is in. They want to know if they should proceed to the Chamber of the Gods.

OBAMA: Gotta go, Leon. My people need me. I want good news in the morning.

[next day]

OBAMA: I'll make this quick, everyone. I can get nine holes in if I arrive a little early in Vegas for the fundraiser.

The official story is, the FBI has launched a probe of last night's events in Benghazi. Attorney General Holder promises a full accounting at some indeterminate point in the future, when the incident is forgotten or I've left office, whichever comes first.

DIANE SAWYER: Sir, why don't we ignore Benghazi the way we've done with "Fast and Furious," Solyndra, the Black Panther whitewash, the . . . ?

OBAMA: I get it, Diane.

BRIAN WILLIAMS: I agree. The incident doesn't impact the lives of ordinary Americans. Why even bring the matter up?

WOLF BLITZER: The story's already broken out.

CARNEY: Exactly. So, downplay it. With ten seconds left at the end of the broadcast after, for example, the plight of Yellowstone's wild burros, refer to an incident in Libya that's still being sorted out.

SCOTT PELLEY: What a coincidence! The wild burros story is our lead tonight.

BENGHAZI: HILLARY TESTIFIES

CHAIRMAN ED ROYCE (R-CA): Secretary Clinton, thank you for honoring the subpoena requiring you to testify again under threat of jail time.

CLINTON: Your pleasure.

ROYCE: When you heard about the attack on our consulate in Benghazi, what did you . . .?

CLINTON: Whaaaa?

CLINTON AIDE: Former Secretary Clinton returned from a fund raiser in Mali yesterday, Mr. Chairman. While there, someone threw a grenade at her as she entered a restaurant. She caught it in mid-air, flung it back at the alleged attacker, and covered the body of a Secret Service agent with her own just as the grenade exploded. Secretary Clinton's hearing has been impaired since. [repeats Royce's question in Clinton's ear]

CLINTON: Fatigued after an overseas trip, I suffered a fugue episode as I arrived in the Situation Room that evening, Mr. Chairman.

ROYCE: [voice raised] Ma'am, who gave the order to "Stand down"?

CLINTON: I'm told I was unsteady on my feet and the president asked me to "Sit down."

ROYCE: Did you ignore repeated requests to boost security at the Benghazi compound?

CLINTON: Mr. Chairman, I . . .

[sways, falls forward, smashing her forehead on the table; physician attends]

DOCTOR: [to Royce] Secretary Clinton is okay, Mr. Chairman. She apologizes for being too disoriented to answer your questions coherently, but she insists on continuing.

CLINTON: You wanted to know about Ben Gazarra's problem with the Social Security Administration, Mr. Chairman.

ROYCE: Let's move on. Did a YouTube video provoke the Benghazi attack?

CLINTON: No. It was the result of overmedication.

ROYCE: Why did Susan Rice cover for you on the Sunday talk shows?

CLINTON: Uncovered, Rice loses moisture when simmering, sir.

ROYCE: Madame Secretary, I ask again: who is ultimately responsible for the Benghazi debacle?

CLINTON: Normally, the resident clergyman assumes responsibility for the tabernacle. I thought we were discussing the Consulate. In any case, I accept the blame for whatever happened that I don't remember. Now, excuse me or I'll feint [sic] again.

ROYCE: But, but, where was the president when . . . ?

CLINTON: Whaaaa?

OBAMA WAR ROOM: STAND-DOWN GUY

OBAMA: I thought we had Benghazi under control, Jay.

CARNEY: Not any more sir, given the e mail dump and whistleblowers coming out of the woodwork.

DAN PFEIFFER: We can't stonewall much longer, sir. We have to say something about your involvement.

OBAMA: Okay. How about, I was in the bathroom when it went down. Biden was calling the shots?

PFEIFFER: Seven hours?

OBAMA: Bad sushi?

PFEIFFER: Uh, no, sir.

OBAMA: Let's see: I asked the CIA to call me with an update at 3:00 a.m., then turned in early so I would be fresh when the call came. But I forgot I turned the ringer off.

JAY CARNEY: Lame, sir.

OBAMA: How about a miscommunication? I told guys at the annex to "Stand down," meaning "Take cover, help is on the way," but that order mistakenly went out over military channels and . . .

CARNEY: Uh uh, sir. Even Rachel Maddow wouldn't buy that one.

PFEIFFER: Sir, the AC-130 on station overhead never received orders to support the CIA team when they returned to the annex.

JOE BIDEN: There's the answer, Boss. AC/DC. What idiot deployed the AC-130 to that backwater instead of the DC-130? Everybody knows AC doesn't work in places like . . .

VALERIE JARRETT: Grasping at straws, sir. You told the AC-130 to stand down until surveillance determined the attackers had family members and livestock with them.

OBAMA: I said that? Can you prove it?

PFEIFFER: All on tape, sir.

OBAMA: Oh. Hey, I know. The action leaked over into Friday, Islam's holy day. It would have been culturally insensitive to . . .

PFEIFFER: General Petraeus has informed me he's scheduled a news conference, sir. He suggests you might want to think about standing down.

FROM *BENGHAZI—THE MUSICAL*

Try to remember that night last September
When men were trapped and you turned yellow.
Try to remember that night last September
When they were killed and you were mellow.
Try to remember the rest of September
When it was clear your core was hollow.
Try to remember those days last December,
Your lies unraveled, unlucky fellow.
When you dissemble it´s Bill you resemble,
And if there's any justice in this world you´ll be impeached
And this time Senate Democrats will do the right thing.

CHAPTER 5: TELL US WHAT YOU REALLY THINK

MAYOR BLOOMBERG GUESTS ON CNN'S *STATE OF THE UNION*

CANDY CROWLEY: Mayor Bloomberg, thank you for coming on.

Your Honor, yesterday you said the failed attempt to bomb Grand Central was probably the work of a Tim McVeigh wannabe from Idaho. Today the FBI arrested a Newark man in connection with the case. Can you tell us anything non-discriminatory about the suspect because we don't want our audience to think "Muslim" even though his name is Achmed Azem Hammad.

MAYOR BLOOMBERG: Sure, Candy. But let me clarify something: my sources at the DOJ tell me a hard-core Islamist faction of the Tea Party *is* based in the Northwest.

Anyway, the guy in question often complained property taxes were too high, he could only see a brick wall when he laid his prayer rug down, and his home was due to be foreclosed. Neighbors said he drank Coca Cola to excess.

CROWLEY: Had you known of his plight, you could have deeded him Gracie Mansion, sir. You sure don't need it.

BLOOMBERG: True.

CROWLEY: What is the suspect's political affiliation, sir?

67

BLOOMBERG: When they raided his house, the TV was tuned to *Fox* and a copy of the MCNRA magazine lay on his kitchen table.

CROWLEY: MCNRA?

BLOOMBERG: Muslim Chapter, National Rifle Association.

CROWLEY: I'm told what's-his-name affirmed he owned the SUV that was supposed to blow up, rigged the explosives, and drove the vehicle to the station. How did the authorities get him to admit all this so soon? Was he Mirandized?

BLOOMBERG: Yes, as he was being arrested. Agents warned him repeatedly to stop declaring his guilt and providing information before they read him his rights, but he insisted on incriminating himself over their objections.

CROWLEY: Crazy. Anything you'd like to say to the people of New York about this near miss, Mr. Mayor? Is it simply another case of a clueless idiot fooling around with matches when, as we all know, the real enemy is still lurking in the heartland beyond the Hudson River?

BLOOMBERG: Well, the system worked, Candy. Once the bomb fizzled, we put all the pieces together with remarkable speed. Our ability to act when the danger has passed is so much greater now than it was after Oklahoma City and 9/11.

CROWLEY: Did the president call, sir?

BLOOMBERG: Yes. He's coming to the city to survey the area where the blast damage would have been most severe. Later, we'll evacuate Broadway so he and the First Lady can take in a special performance of *Rock of Ages*. Afterwards, they'll dine at *La Grenouille* to show the American people life goes on, even amidst the most horrible hypothetical carnage.

CROWLEY: Sounds like Manhattan will be shut down while the Obamas are in town. The traffic jams!

BLOOMBERG: Sacrifices are necessary in wartime, Candy. Me, I gave my driver and helicopter pilot the day off.

CROWLEY: Finally, sir: Mets or Yankees this year?

BLOOMBERG: I'm everyone's mayor in this great city, Candy, including people whose boroughs I've never been to. On the question of where my allegiance lies regarding the teams, I'm not going to duck it. I feel strongly both ways.

JOE BIDEN ON *60 INTERMINABLE MINUTES*

BYRON PITTS: Thanks for coming in, Mr. Vice President.

BIDEN: Glad to, Brad. How're Angelina, the kids?

PITTS: Um, fine, sir.

BIDEN: Hey, this interview's on deep background, okay?

PITTS: We're live, Mr. Vice-President.

BIDEN: Whatever. Hit me with your best shot.

PITTS: Is our government broken?

BIDEN: No, Bruce. The country's in bad shape, yes, but the federal government hasn't been this hale and hearty since I became a senator in '73.

PITTS: Would you list some accomplishments of the Obama administration?

BIDEN: Sure. One, under President Obama, Americans don't hafta worry about the Black Plague; two, as we unilaterally decommission our nukes, we gain credibility with Putin, the Ayatollahs, and Kim Young-un. Finally, our immigration policy guarantees everyone landscaping services at an affordable price.

PITTS: Will the president use his "bully pulpit" to help ordinary citizens understand fossil fuels must be phased out ASAP?

BIDEN: Actually, Barry, he uses the bully pulpit to bully people. As to your question: yes, we've had to federalize fuel stocks and set gasoline and home heating oil prices at unaffordable levels, but people need a kick in the pants if we're gonna transition from two-ton gas guzzlers and oil furnaces to wind-powered runabouts and solar heating.

PITTS: Do you lunch with the president once a week as did other vice presidents before you?

BIDEN: Yeah, I do, Bob. I mean, I don't actually join him in the Residence, but I can eat in the White House Mess every Thursday, and the president's a short walk away if he ever wants to see me.

PITTS: How often is that?

BIDEN: Next question.

PITTS: Hypothetical: Israel attacks Iran's nuclear sites. What does the president do?

BIDEN: Won't happen. Contingency plans exist to take out Israel's air force and *Fox News* headquarters if a strike appears imminent. That's classified info, Bret. Can't talk about it.

PITTS: One more: we capture a Tea Partier with al Qaeda ties who's still so upset over the GM bailout he's planted a nuclear device somewhere in Washington. Your advice to President Obama?

BIDEN: First, I confirm they've saved me a spot in the White House Operations Bunker, which is situated 300 feet beneath the East Room and accessible by a secret elevator in the Residence. The bunker's a world-class panic room protected by 10 foot thick concrete/rebar walls and a coded 25 ton triple-tiered steel blast door. Safest place on the planet. Well, against a nuke maybe. But a terrorist *could* introduce some fine-powdered anthrax into the bunker if he accessed the heating vents outside the . . .

PITTS: Your advice to the president about the Tea Party jihadist, sir?

BIDEN: I said, "Look Boss, we gotta squeeze 'im for info, but humanely, to keep the ACLU off our backs. How? Mortarboard the guy."

PITTS: Mortarboard?

BIDEN: Teams of CIA religious scholars in full academic regalia lecturin' him around the clock on the superiority of Shia Islam over Sunni Islam. Until he breaks.

PITTS: If he doesn't?

BIDEN: Then he gets nothin' to drink but D.C. tap water, day in, day out, just D.C. tap water. After three days, he'll sing like a canary.

PITTS: Waterboredom? We'd go that far?

BIDEN: It's in the new interrogation manual Eric Holder ran by Iranian mullahs. They signed off on it.

PITTS: Our time's running short, sir. Any thoughts on helping the victims of Bush's global recession, now in its seventh year?

BIDEN: Yeah. Between you and me, next week the president's gonna announce a new economic strategy we're callin' "The Splurge," deployin' an additional trillion dollars we don't have to fight a futile worldwide War on Poverty. Krugman of the *Times* wrote the book on redistribution of wealth. He'll direct the effort.

PITTS: We'd better stop here. Thanks for your time, Mr. Vice President.

BIDEN: You got it, Brad.

HILLARY, CIA DIRECTOR BRENNAN ON *PBS NEWSHOUR*

JIM LEHRER: Good evening. At his regular briefing this afternoon, White House Press Secretary Jay Carney expressed confidence President Obama was closely monitoring yesterday's invasion of Taiwan by the People's Republic of China from his beachfront compound in Hawaii.

Carney revealed Defense Secretary Chuck Hagel has been in frequent contact with White House Senior Advisor Valerie Jarrett since the crisis began. Ms. Jarrett has issued a statement urging both sides to seek a solution to their differences once hostilities cease.

JUDY WOODRUFF: Also on the *NewsHour* tonight:

*Wisconsin protesters march on state capitol carrying exhumed body of labor icon Cesar Chavez.

*The CIA reportedly sold suitcase nukes in a Kandahar bazaar to lure Mullah Omar out of hiding.

*Joint Chiefs Chairman Martin Dempsey okays burkhas for Muslim women submariners.

*Treasury Secretary Lew cites rising gas prices as proof of booming economy.

RAY SUAREZ: Up first, Special Envoy Hillary Clinton, just returned from Asia, and CIA Director John Brennan.

Mrs. Clinton, the People's Republic is clearly the aggressor in the Taiwan Strait. What counsel did you give the President?

HILLARY: I'll see him at tonight's White House gala honoring America's first black mountain man. I will advise him to honor our commitment to Taiwan by freezing transference of sensitive missile technology to China. He'll consider that a provocation and refuse.

SUAREZ: On another matter, any chance of a nuclear weapons deal with North Korea?

CLINTON: [tearing up] I'm afraid not, Ray. I worked so hard to find a place for the Hermit Klingon in the Global Village. Kim Young-un and I talked and talked and laughed and wept, I stamped my feet, he cursed, we danced and air-kissed, I even threw a lamp at him, but we couldn't get it done.

SUAREZ: What happens now?

CLINTON: One more good cry tonight and I'll be in a better frame of mind when I meet with Supreme Leader Ayatollah Khamenei in Tehran next week.

SUAREZ: Director Brennan, Libya is a mess since the country's, uh, liberation. Did we inadvertently support al Qaeda elements when we intervened to help overthrow Gaddifi?

BRENNAN: That's not quite accurate, Ray. "Intervention" suggests the president actually made a decision. Fact is, as we watched helplessly from the sidelines when things got dicey for the rebels, the president threw up his hands and exclaimed, "Will no one rid me of this Sheikh?"

The generals assumed the president was giving them their heads and proceeded to help the Saudis arm the Libs.

SUAREZ: Libs?

BRENNAN: The president insisted we use the term "Libs" to refer to the rebels. He said it made him feel like they're the good guys.

SUAREZ: Director Brennan, the "President's Commission on Foreign Provocations" reported out yesterday after two years' work. The recommendations?

BRENNAN: The president has an image problem at home and abroad: he appears weak and indecisive. That invites aggressive behavior from people like Kim Young-un, Putin, and Bill O'Reilly. We suggested several ways for him to counter those perceptions.

SUAREZ: Such as?

BRENNAN: Go out to Creech Air Base north of Las Vegas where the Air Force runs overseas drone operations. Bring along pool reporters to tape him remote piloting a drone and dropping a missile on some al Qaeda hotshot in a Pakistani border village. Or, replace the White House basketball court with a firing range and unwind with an M16A4 instead of shooting hoops. Or, wear a string of Taliban ears around his neck at his next press conference.

SUAREZ: And?

BRENNAN: He wasn't interested. Said he'd ride his bicycle without a helmet from now on to show what he's made of.

SUAREZ: Comment on the administration's plan to deal with the pirate plague in the Indian Ocean.

BRENNAN: The president's sending Vice-President Biden to the pirates' lair in Somalia to negotiate the release of hostages, Ray. He's been instructed to stay until there's a breakthrough, even if talks last through midterm elections.

SUAREZ: Final question, Mrs. Clinton: a former aide claims in a new book you considered planting attractive young women on Obama's campaign team in 2008 in hopes of sparking what she said you called an "Obimbo Eruption." Did . . . ?

CLINTON: Don't go there, Ray.

ROPE LINES

CHRIS MATTHEWS: Tonight, Democratic National Committee Chair, Debbie Whassupman Schultz. Welcome, Ma'am. Let's play *Hardball*.

WHASSUPMAN SCHULTZ: Chris, I find "Ma'am" demeaning. Call me Madame Chair, or Chairwoman, or even *Chérie*.

MATTHEWS: Okay, uh, *Chérie*. First up, a small thing: you used to be Whassupman dash Schultz. Now you're just plain Whassupman Schultz. When did you lose your hyphen?

WHASSUPMAN SCHULTZ: I was sixteen, Chris, and Billy Collins and I were making out in his car at Lookout Point. Well, things got out of hand, and . . .

MATTHEWS: Never mind. You wanna make a coupla outrageous claims about Republicans?

WHASSUPMAN SCHULTZ: Sure. Wal-Mart and the Koch brothers plan to lay off 100,000 employees next year to spike unemployment before midterms.

MATTHEWS: Anything else?

WHASSUPMAN SCHULTZ: Rick Perry wants Texas undocumenteds arrested and sentenced to three years hard labor picking cotton for Monsanto.

MATTHEWS: *Muy loco.*

WHASSUPMAN SCHULTZ: Finally, Speaker Boehner's proposing that people of color provide DNA evidence at the polls to prove they are who they say they are.

MATTHEWS: Shameless.

WHASSUPMAN SCHULTZ: Jesse Jackson told me last week he's been hearing the voices of long-deceased African-Americans pleading for retroactive enfranchisement. Oh, if only we still had the House.

MATTHEWS: Moving on, how will Democrats respond if the Supreme Court revisits the healthcare law and declares it unconstitutional?

WHASSUPMAN SCHULTZ: Thank you for not calling ObamaCare the "Pee Pee ACA," Chris. It's a calculated scatological insult unworthy of our friends on the other side of the islet.

To answer your question, the administration will continue to delay implementing the law while the decision is appealed to the International Court in The Hague.

MATTHEWS: Do you believe the president has turned the economy around?

WHASSUPMAN SCHULTZ: Yes, Chris. Last year the economy was blindfolded and wandering about aimlessly. President Obama walked right up to Mr. Economy, grabbed him by the shoulders, pointed him toward the cliff, then shoved him in that direction. I call it leadership.

MATTHEWS: Your district's in Florida. Hypothetical: a massive storm comes ashore and devastates the state. How would President Obama handle the catastrophe versus, say, George W. Bush?

WHASSUPMAN SCHULTZ: I reject your premise, Chris. Obama's pledged to use the great moral authority of the White House to reason with hurricanes and turn them away from land.

After surveying damage inflicted by last year's nor'easter, the president told me, "In my third term, I'll work with Mother Nature to address the root causes of natural catastrophes."

MATTHEWS: Yeah, he gave me the same line in '08. Said he foresaw a time in his administration when planetary forces inimical to man under Bush would agree to share the earth in peace with humanity. [retches]

WHASSUPMAN SCHULTZ: You okay?

MATTHEWS: Yeah, sure. Something I swallowed. What more can we in the knee-pad media do to help Democrats?

WHASSUPMAN SCHULTZ: No double-dip recession talk. Spike homeless-selling-their-organs and people-eating-dog-food stories. And for God's sake, don't reveal we're getting CARE packages from Bangladesh.

MATTHEWS: The administration's robust drone program targeting terrorist leaders, their families, servants, livestock—does it bother you?

WHASSUPMAN SCHULTZ: Democrats cut Democrats slack, Chris. But President Obama promised me this: once he's killed off every conceivable threat to America, he'll declare "World War Free," disband our military, and commission his new Civilian National Security Force to protect his administration from internal threats.

MATTHEWS: What's the biggest lesson Democrats learned from the last two presidential campaigns?

WHASSUPMAN SCHULTZ: Rope lines.

MATTHEWS: Rope lines?

WHASSUPMAN SCHULTZ: After the president's rope line encounter with Joe the Plumber in 2008, McCain locked up tradespeople. We failed to learn the lesson in 2012. In 2014 and thereafter, we'll microtarget professions in rope lines and create scenarios using individuals we've vetted.

MATTHEWS: Ah . . . plants. While cameras roll, the nominee walks the line, shaking hands; he stops, seemingly at random, and has a moving interaction with, oh, Juanita the Motel Maid. Makes all the news shows. Afterward, "Juanita" disappears immediately so *Fox* can't question her.

WHASSUPMAN SCHULTZ: Exactly. Similar encounters will occur every couple of weeks until the election. We've already scheduled Gideon the Jewish OB-GYN, Ahmad the Rug Merchant, and Fulgencio the Miami Dock Worker.

MATTHEWS: Hmm. Could get old after a while.

WHASSUPMAN SCHULTZ: Anticipated. We'll mix in foils occasionally. You'll see our nominees go toe-to-toe with Tom the Hedge Fund Manager, Arnold the Oil Speculator, and Roger the Big Pharma CEO. The plants ask why he's picking on them, our people knock it out of the park.

MATTHEWS: How will your candidates know whom to approach?

WHASSUPMAN SCHULTZ: They'll be the ones holding GOP signs who aren't being attacked by our supporters.

MATTHEWS: Finally, what's your take on the latest sex scandal: former congressman Anthony Weiner backsliding and tweeting nude photos of himself to Sarah Palin?

WHASSUPMAN SCHULTZ: As a female, I am so disgusted by his lewd, unprincipled actions, I'd like to neuter him myself.

As a Democrat, however, I miss his skill in pushing the Republican War on Women and his leadership in making the Internet safe, evidenced by legislation he sponsored to target web predators like himself. I am supporting his mayoral bid in New York because I believe New Yorkers deserve the politicians they elect.

MATTHEWS: Debbie Whassupman Schultz. Come back again soon. Hey, you want to follow each other on Twitter?

WHASSUPMAN SCHULTZ: Don't go there, Chris.

OBAMA AND HAGEL ON
FACE THE NATION

BOB SCHIEFFER: This morning I interview Secretary of Defense Chuck Hagel and President Obama.

[turns to monitor]

Uh, you're smoking, Mr. President? I thought you quit?

OBAMA: Backslid after watching Chuck's confirmation hearing, Bob. And it´s grass not a cigarette, a special blend called "mariguana" because it's grown in female bat dung. I told you this was a "joint" interview.

HAGEL: That's the weed's talking, Bob. I'll kick his butt when he gets unfocused.

SCHIEFFER: Why did you and Secretary Hagel agree to come on this morning, Mr. President? You could have sent a flack to mouth talking points, as you usually do.

OBAMA: I'm here because my numbers are dropping, Bob, and people cut me slack when they see how harmless I look. As for Chuck, appearing with dunderheads raises my stature.

HAGEL: Glad to help, sir.

SCHIEFFER: You've been savaged for choosing Senator Hagel to head Defense, Mr. President.

OBAMA: Reid wanted a doormat in the post; promised if I picked Hagel, the Senate wouldn't submit a budget for another four years. Plus, a dysfunctional Defense Department represents no threat to me.

SCHIEFFER: Senator, why did you accept the offer?

HAGEL: I've played *Call of Duty* on Xbox since it first came out, Bob. Time to get real.

SCHIEFFER: Sir, will you send Secretary Hagel to Russia and Iran to talk disarmament?

OBAMA: Absolutely. Can you think of anyone better than Chuck to give away the store?

HAGEL: I can work with Putin and the Ayatollahs, Bob. As Reagan said, "Trust, don't vilify."

SCHIEFFER: It's been two years since you exposed yourself to the media, Mr. Secretary.

HAGEL: C'mon, Bob. It was just that one time with the blonde from *CNN*.

SCHIEFFER: You mothballed and quarantined the navy's flattops, sir? Why? Was that at the president's direction?

HAGEL: My decision. The World Health Organization declared American imperialism a contagion. We identified the ships as carriers.

SCHIEFFER: Mr. President, the *Times* reports you asked the U.N. to list America as a state sponsor of terrorism.

OBAMA: I did, Bob. Cutting off their foreign markets will sink American firearms and ammunition manufacturers. There's more than one way to skin the 2nd Amendment cat.

SCHIEFFER: Comment on the recent nuclear exchange between Iran and Israel, Mr. Secretary.

HAGEL: I look at the bright side. Sure, the two countries are radioactive slag, now. But they are finally at peace.

SCHIEFFER: Can we stop nuclear proliferation?

HAGEL: Actually, we´re facilitating it to level the international playing field. I've distributed our entire stockpile of nukes to anyone out there who wanted one. It's a logical extension of the president's redistributionist views.

SCHIEFFER: You held none back for ourselves?

HAGEL: No. We've shown we can't be trusted with such power.

SCHIEFFER: You're advocating reconstitution of the Soviet Union and the Warsaw Pact, Mr. President. Why?

OBAMA: The world was never safer than when America was checked by the Soviets.

SCHIEFFER: Last question: what's behind our new alliance with China that's seen the port of Los Angeles become a naval base for the People's Republic?

OBAMA: Concern about a militaristic Japan, Bob. Last thing we need is another aggressive Asian state with world designs.

SCHIEFFER: Thanks for coming on, gentlemen.

PBS NEWSHOUR: GETTING BIN LADEN

JIM LEHRER: Good evening. In an interview on Chris Matthews' *Hardball* last night, President Obama tried to quiet skeptics who believe the raid on Osama bin Laden's compound in Pakistan was a sham staged by the U.S. military. The president also said he is not awed by the power at his command. Here's a clip:

> **MATTHEWS**: Was that really bin Laden, sir, or one of his doubles?
>
> **OBAMA**: Like to show you something, Chris. [unwrapping a handkerchief] This is Osama's right ear. I wanted a finger but they were all gone by the time I requested one. Look at this close-up of Osama from 1997. Check the right ear. Okay, now examine the real thing here. Compare the folds, crevices, and ridges. Clearly identical, yes? No two ears are alike, Chris. The one I'm holding was attached to bin Laden's head. Case closed.
>
> **MATTHEWS**: I'm convinced, Mr. President. Hey, you gonna eat that? Ah, just pulling your leg, sir.
>
> You are the Commander-in-Chief of the mightiest military machine on earth. Are you humbled by the power you possess?
>
> **OBAMA**: Humbled? [snort] Hardly. I've grown in office, Chris. The bin Laden raid, troops in Libya and Syria, DNC shock troops disrupting Tea Party

rallies—I'm actually comfortable using my powers to inflict damage on our enemies and advancing the cause of freedom.

I want you to meet someone, Chris, the man with the "nuclear football." [gestures to military attaché standing out of camera range] C'mon over here, Captain, Major, whatever. Open up the briefcase. [pause] I'm giving you an order, soldier. Now show Mr. Matthews which button I push to take out Orange County. The red one? Put your finger on it, Chris. Go ahead, touch it. Press down and Republicans lose California by thirty points instead of twenty -five. Gives you a little thrill, doesn't it, Chris? Makes you feel like a God?

LEHRER: More of the president's interview with Matthews later in the program.

JUDY WOODRUFF: Also on the *NewsHour* tonight:

*First Lady Michelle Obama orders four peek-a-boo Dior burkhas for next month's trip to Saudi Arabia.

*Maine Senator Susan Collins wins 100 year exemption from federal taxes for state residents. She adamantly denies the boon has anything to do with her decision to switch to Independent and caucus with Democrats.

*New York Times pollsters begin sampling public school kindergartners on presidential preferences.

RAY SUAREZ: Up first, we interview administration officials who watched the bin Laden takedown live from the Situation Room: former CIA Director Leon Panetta, CIA Director John Brennan, Vice President Joe Biden, and former White House Senior Advisor, David Plouffe. Thank you all for coming in.

Director Panetta, Please explain the rules of engagement under which SEAL Team 6 operated that night.

PANETTA: Sure, Ray. The president authorized operatives to use lethal force against bin Laden under two contingencies only: if he resisted or if he failed to defend himself.

SUAREZ: And?

PANETTA: Osama resisted defending himself.

SUAREZ: CIA Director John Brennan, at the time, you clamed bin Laden died while using his second wife as a shield, that she perished as well, and that the youngest son of his third wife was also killed. Later, another official reported the woman was wounded in the leg. Which version is correct, sir?

BRENNAN: Regarding the woman, both, Ray. She was shot in the leg and expired shortly afterward. Some clarifications, however: she was bin Laden's third wife, not his second. And the son who died was actually the fourth born of his first wife, not the youngest of his third.

PANETTA: With all due respect to Mr. Brennan, the "human shield" story never held up, Ray. Close examination of the mission tape reveals the woman had her back to the door while trimming bin Laden's hair when SEALs burst into the room. They mistook her hairdryer for a weapon. Osama wasn't "hiding" behind her.

SUAREZ: Dave Plouffe, former White House Advisor: rumor is President Obama "virtually" participated in the mission.

PLOUFFE: He did, Ray. We knew months ago this would be going down, so the president spent almost every night playing *Mortal Kombat*: *Special Forces* to hone his fighting skills. On the big day, military techs did a systems patch, tying the president's Xbox 360 wireless controller into the squad leader's sensorium. Sort of like a guy at a base in Nevada operating a drone over Afghanistan.

JOE BIDEN: Ah geez, c'mon, Dave. Xbox, for cripes sake. Why jazz it up? I sat right next to him. The Boss played solitaire on his iPad while the firefight went on and on and on.

SUAREZ: Mr. Brennan, in the hours following the action, did the U.S. ask the world's 194 countries to consider taking bin Laden's body for burial?

BRENNAN: Yes, Ray. We sent e-mail inquiries to all governments, but no one answered in a timely fashion. So we took that for a "no."

SUAREZ: Director Panetta, is the administration still opposed to aggressive questioning of terror suspects?

PANETTA: Absolutely. And I can assure you none of the SEALs employed harsh interrogation measures against anyone in the compound who died in the raid.

SUAREZ: Mr. Vice President, what was the mood in the White House when the operation went down successfully?

BIDEN: Real high, Jim, especially the president. Soon's it was over, the Boss called Oliver Stone and asked him to do a movie on the takedown. He liked Cat Stevens as Osama, but insisted he wanted to play himself. Stone balked and the project went nowhere. We didn't have a whole hell of a lot to do with *Zero Dark Thirty*.

SUAREZ: Thank you all.

WALLACE VS. STEWART
ON *FOX NEWS SUNDAY*

CHRIS WALLACE: Jon Stewart, thanks for appearing again on our program.

STEWART: Glad to be here, Chris. Last time, you edited the taped interview to make me look like Kwai Chang Caine being schooled by Master Po. My ratings actually fell off the next week. So the suits at *Comedy Central* told me to take another shot at you, live.

WALLACE: What are your marching orders?

STEWART: Leave you whimpering like Jim Cramer, my friend, make you feel like a fool.

[from jacket pocket pulls out small beaker, removes cover, tosses contents into Wallace's face]

WALLACE: [reeling] Hey, what the hell!

STEWART: Who's the joke on now, Chris?

WALLACE: Are you crazy?

STEWART: Lighten up, Chris. You need a sense of humor if you want to be taken seriously. Hey, it's only water, man. [pointing to label on beaker] See, "H20." Says here right on the . . . [reads] "HCl—hydrochloric acid." Oops. Mislabeled. My bad. Note to self: use cream pie or glitter next time.

WALLACE: But why?

STEWART: [reasonably] Try to understand my position, Chris. A sizable chunk of *The Daily Show*'s core audience hates your guts; they were pissed off when I showed respect and treated you like an equal. That's not who I am. I humiliate right-wingers in a non-partisan way. I had to return to redeem myself.

WALLACE: Your core audience?

STEWART: Yeah. Fox has the Birchers, the neo-fascists, LaRouchers, and unborn rights freaks. My core's a mishmash of animal liberationists, anarchists, human extinctionists, Palinphobes, water cooler thirtysomethings, and fever swampers from the *Democratic Underground.*

WALLACE: I reject your . . .

STEWART: Can we get back to why I'm here? Previously, I called you a "good man." Let me amend. You might be a good man at home with the wife and kids, but professionally, you're a Republican shill.

WALLACE: You believe that?

STEWART: This isn't about what *I* believe, Chris; it's about what I can get my viewers to swallow.

WALLACE: I'll paraphrase something you said last time: "Being a comedian is harder than what you do . . . I put the truth through a meat grinder, coarse setting, then shape it according to my prejudices."

STEWART: I'm usually less direct. I should have said, "I put current events through a process, a comedic process."

WALLACE: Same thing.

STEWART: Hey, back to my agenda. I wanna ask you a question.

WALLACE: Okay.

STEWART: Ever notice Roger Ailes hanging around with a Koch brother?

WALLACE: No, but I've observed him standing around with a Pepsi, brother. My turn now.

STEWART: Devil. You got me. All right, shoot.

WALLACE: I'm going to read something to you, and I want your reaction. This is from *Hamlet* . . .

STEWART: The little village in the Hamptons?

WALLACE: No, the tragedy by Shakespeare. It's a quotation from Act II Scene II. Prince Hamlet is instructing actors he's hired to perform for the court. At one point he says,

And let those that play your clowns, unless one's Robin Williams, speak no more than is set down for them; for there be of them that will themselves laugh, to set on some quantity of barren spectators to laugh too . . .

STEWART: You calling me a clown?

WALLACE: No, that was Shakespeare.

STEWART: How did Shakespeare know about Robin Williams?

WALLACE: Never mind. You understand the quotation?

STEWART: I think so. Unless you're an improvisational genius like Williams, comedians should stick to their scripts and resist the temptation to mug their way through weak routines in pursuit of cheap laughs from an undiscriminating audience. How does the quote concern me?

WALLACE: You just asked four straight questions. My turn again.

STEWART: Damn.

WALLACE: Near the end of our first interview, you said, "I've existed in this country forever. There have been people like me who satirize the political process . . ." You mentioned Will Rogers. Do you compare yourself to Will Rogers?

STEWART: I do. He was a beloved humorist, and so am I. Also, our philosophies are similar. Didn't he say, "I never met a conservative I didn't dislike"?

WALLACE: Not exactly. Finally, let's do a gut check of your political instincts. Hypothetical: the ATF "Fast and Furious/ Gunwalker" scandal leads right to the top. Video emerges of the president examining a Barrett M82 50 caliber rifle before handing it to a Cartel enforcer and saying, "Good hunting." Obama comes to you for advice on handling the blowback. What do you tell him?

STEWART: Pardon yourself before the situation gets out of hand, Mr. President.

WALLACE: How would he justify a self-pardon?

STEWART: In an address to the nation, he'd say, "On behalf of all Americans, I accept this pardon because we can't afford Joe Biden in the Oval Office in these difficult times. And while I'm grateful to myself for the gesture, I am deeply disappointed unanswered questions remain about my involvement in shipping weapons to Mexican drug dealers to promote strict gun control legislation here at home."

WALLACE: Jon Stewart, Counselor to the President. Thanks for . . .

STEWART: [addresses camera while holding up whiteboard displaying Wallace's address, telephone and social security numbers, and private e-mail] Kos Kids, Undergrounders, give the man some feedback.

Don't ever edit me again, Chris.

OBAMA ON *HARDBALL* WITH CHRIS MATTHEWS

CHRIS MATTHEWS: Tonight, Mother Nature shows us who's boss as the Yellowstone volcano blows and Hurricane Madonna struts her stuff in the Gulf. Our guest, President Barack Obama. Welcome, sir.

OBAMA: Good to be here, Chris. Uh, just shake hands; don't squeeze my knee.

MATTHEWS: Sorry. Yellowstone—millions dead and missing, half the population homeless, a looming health crisis; Madonna—Gulf states in tatters.

On the bright side, as Rahm Emanuel might say, a natural disaster is a terrible thing to waste. Will you exploit these tragedies to advance your agenda, sir?

OBAMA: Of course, Chris. Martial law goes into effect at midnight. I've also suspended the 1st, 2nd, and 22nd Amendments to deal with the crises.

MATTHEWS: On what authority, sir?

OBAMA: A codicil in the original Constitution, written in invisible ink. Attorney General Holder discovered it.

MATTHEWS: What's a little known consequence of these disasters, sir?

OBAMA: Caring for proto-citizens who need assistance but are afraid to come forward and be identified as "ill [cough], ill [cough cough] . . .

MATTHEWS: "Illegal"?

OBAMA: That's it. Damn word wouldn't come out. Anyway, I told Congress I need a general amnesty bill ASAP. There's no time to draft a thousand pages to cover all the angles.

MATTHEWS: The Repugs will balk, sir.

OBAMA: Then, by the powers invested in me by me, I'll summarily declare amnesty. So, whoever you are, wherever you are, hang on; if you're here, you're in the clear. And remember to register as an undocumented Democrat.

MATTHEWS: A good time to fast-track cap-and-trade, sir?

OBAMA: It is, Chris. Yellowstone and Madonna are not isolated events. The earth is roiling hot: internally, because of America's underground nuclear testing in decades past; externally, because our cars and smokestacks have elevated the planet's atmospheric temperature. This is the simple logic the deniers reject.

MATTHEWS: Can you do *anything* in the near term to stop eruptions and hurricanes, sir?

OBAMA: Well, I know people expect miracles from me, Chris, but I'm just an ordinary demigod. I did call His office to ask Him to calm the planet; unfortunately, He's in another dimension on business. We're on our own.

MATTHEWS: Any good news to report, sir?

OBAMA: Yes, Chris. We're confident Madonna will destroy every last oil platform in the Gulf.

MATTHEWS: Millions will require federal help. However, you're on record saying we can't afford to spend money we don't have.

OBAMA: And I meant it, Chris. We've squeezed our millionaires and billionaires dry. Now I'm committed to pay-as-you-go.

House Democrats will soon propose a Volcanic Activity Tax, or VAT, to fund relief efforts. We'll use any surplus from the VAT to reduce our debt or create a new entitlement, as the politics warrant. In time, the Hurricane Activity Tax, or HAT, will follow.

MATTHEWS: Finally, sir, a question of a personal nature. I'm not up to speed on the rites associated with your political ministry. Do I wash the dust from your feet, or do you wash the dust from mine?

OBAMA: I'll check with Reverend Wright and get back to you.

BLACK FISTS OF POWER MAGAZINE SCORES INTERVIEW WITH ATTORNEY GENERAL

Chicago (AP)—In an exclusive interview with *Black Fists of Power Magazine* Managing Editor Reverend Jeremiah Wright, America's Chief Law Enforcement Officer continued to dodge responsibility for malfeasances at the Department of Justice even the *Associated Press* and the *New York Times* have been unwilling to ignore.

"I categorically reject any evidence which disproves my assertion I had no knowledge of rogue operations authorized at the highest levels of the DOJ," Holder told Reverend Wright.

The Attorney General also revealed he is disappointed in the New Black Panther Party's "ineffectual incendiary rhetoric" following the Trayvon Martin shooting in Sanford, Florida last winter. "They didn't start the fire; they were supposed to light it, but it never ignited."

The NBPP's failure to spark a race war prompted Holder to sever ties with the group and forge a relationship with its more militant offshoot, Al Sharpton's Even Newer Black Panther Party.

An excerpt from the interview:

> **WRIGHT**: You were charged with Contempt of Congress for stonewalling House Oversight Chairman Darrell Issa on the "Fast and Furious" [aka "Gunwalker"] probe. As Attorney General, you're responsible for arresting yourself. Why hasn't this happened yet?
>
> **HOLDER**: I was working from home when the motion passed. I immediately went to the DOJ to take myself into custody, but my staff told me I hadn't been in all day. The FBI is staking out my office and will inform me when I appear. No word so far.
>
> **WRIGHT**: Will you continue to block the "Gunwalker" investigation?
>
> **HOLDER**: I'm not "blocking" anything, Reverend. I've turned over to the Committee all the documents they requested, more than one hundred thousand pages. Apparently, the Chairman is upset that most of the material is blacked out because of "Executive

Privilege," the long-held doctrine allowing President Obama to ignore our system of checks and balances at his whim.

WRIGHT: So, the "Fast and Furious" imbroglio doesn't worry you?

HOLDER: No. However, God forbid Issa finds out about "Massed and Fissionable."

WRIGHT: "Massed and Fissionable?"

HOLDER: Aka "Nukewalker." ATF agents, posing as disaffected military, have just completed negotiations for the sale of suitcase nukes to Sheriff Joe Arpaio's "Cold Case Posse," an Arizona white supremacist group obsessed with discovering what the media's been suppressing about the president's background. This is off the record, Reverend.

WRIGHT: Mum's the word.

HOLDER: Arpaio thinks he's running a sting. Actually, I'm running one on him. Arrests are imminent.

WRIGHT: So, you'll play the dodge as domestic nuclear Armageddon thwarted by your vigilance. And getting Arpaio and his posse off the president's case is a bonus?

HOLDER: Correct. The miscreants will be held in isolation indefinitely. DOJ attorneys are busy working to discover language revoking the privilege of habeas corpus in exceptional circumstances.

One additional benefit of the sting: Arpaio's plot provides the administration cover to scrap our entire nuclear arsenal, ensuring U.S. nukes never again pose a threat to Americans.

The president's hope and dream is that other nuclear powers will follow his example. If we aren't incinerated by Russia or China after the gesture, he's a shoo-in for another Nobel Peace Prize.

Asked what he would like as his epitaph, Holder replied, "It's good to be the Man."

CHAPTER 6: ATTACK! DOG

OBAMA WAR ROOM: SO, HELP ME, GOD

DAN PFEIFFER: [on phone] Sure, sure, I'll tell him. [hangs up] Charlie Rangel, sir. Said he'd rather you not attend his Harlem fundraiser.

OBAMA: Good grief. Harlem? I'm that toxic? Lame duckdom, here I come.

MICHELLE: Loser talk, Barack. You just gonna hole up in the Residence and watch next year's election train wreck happen?

PFEIFFER: We have options, sir. Our "Split the Vote" pilot program in New Jersey showed promise. The "Independent" pulled almost 6% from Christie in 2010. Suppose we nationalize the strategy for midterms and get the percentage up?

VALERIE JARRETT: Promising. Unknowns are coming of the woodwork to run—and capturing the public's imagination. Let's tap into that dynamic. In every district and every state, we'll encourage selfless, second-tier Democrats to quit the party and launch campaigns as independents.

WHASSUPMAN SCHULTZ: DNC workshops will school the stalking horses to sound centrist or slightly right. While our letter-to-the-editor boiler rooms give them exposure, phony PACS with names like *Right for America* will fund mailings and sponsor ads on their behalf. If candidates attract 10-15% of the vote, some contests come our way.

JACK LEW: I'll alert the IRS to leave these PACS alone, sir.

OBAMA: Debbie, liaise with our MSM familiars. We want the "independents" to get good—but not too good—press. Dan, pass the names to Huffington and Moulitsas: fever swampers are to launch *pro forma* attacks on them. Eric?

HOLDER: Sir, a few threats would give Justice an excuse to get involved.

OBAMA: Okay. Jay, have one of your briefing room plants ask about rumors the GOP fringe is "gunning" for third party spoilers. Then Eric drops the NSA leak investigation and devotes Justice's resources to unearthing right-wing plots. Matthews and the nets will run with that for a month.

JARRETT: We need a fallback, sir. I'll ask eighty of our safest congressmen to switch parties this fall.

OBAMA: Machiavellian! The switchers vote Dem, but Republicans "control" the House and therefore share blame for my failures. Added benefit: the sideshow'll blow the NSA, Benghazi, and IRS fiascos off the front pages.

PFEIFFER: We'll call the party changers the "red mutts," sir. They'll raise holy hell in the Republican caucus. After midterms, back they march to Mistress Nancy.

CARNEY: The other side's energized, sir; it would help if we could depress the vote.

OBAMA: Hmm, depress the vote. The press, the vote . . .

Jay, invite *Times* Editor Jill Abramson and the network anchors to meet with me in the Oval Office tomorrow. For national security reasons, I'll request they treat the midterms as a non-story, like "Fast and Furious" and the Gosnell trial.

CARNEY: Very good, sir. I can almost hear Brian Williams on Wednesday, November 5, 2014: "Elections? We had elections?"

GEORGE SOROS: Limbaugh iss problem in zis regard, zir. Big audience.

OBAMA: I know. George, can your telecommunications people glitch his broadcasts in the run-up to midterms?

SOROS: Ya. Gremlins.

[enter First Lady]

MICHELLE: I'm taking grades 1 through 12 at Sidwell on an Antarctic field trip next spring. Tell Hagel to have a carrier ready for transport. You hear me, Barack?

OBAMA WAR ROOM: BRUSHFIRES

OBAMA: It's finally happened. O'Reilly's obtained copies of my college records and interviewed an old weed buddy. The wingnuts will have an orgasm when they learn I took a course at Occidental called "Bongs Through the Ages."

JAY CARNEY: *The Factor*'s devoting a whole show to the revelations next week, sir. Word is, O'Reilly'll read excerpts from your Harvard Law Review article, "Tart Reform: a New Paradigm for the Oldest Profession."

OBAMA: Good lord! I'll be ridiculed for something I paid somebody else to write. How do we stop this?

DAN PFEIFFER: Posing as a fired *MSNBC* whistleblower, I'll e-mail O'Reilly and set up a meet in Fort Marcy Park tonight, sir. You call in a favor from the Teamsters. Tomorrow morning, joggers'll find old "Fair and Balanced" clutching a note expressing remorse for forging documents meant to discredit you.

OBAMA: Um, maybe something less extreme. John?

BRENNAN: Our Black Projects team has developed a marble-sized nuke that'll fry transmissions in a localized area, sir. I can task a drone to deliver it over *Fox* Headquarters as O'Reilly goes on.

OBAMA: Set it up. But we need a cover story. Dan, order the National Weather Service to warn of severe thunderstorms in the vicinity just before detonation.

BRENNAN: Won't fool anybody, sir.

OBAMA: You're right. Instead, let's give the *Times*, the *Post*, and our network anchors a heads-up on the EMP event. Jay, inform them I want the spike story pulsed—I mean, the pulse story spiked.

CARNEY: Can't forget the blogosphere, sir: The Pajamas guys will out the truth in nanoseconds.

OBAMA: Then I'll shut down the Internet for, uh, national security reasons.

BRENNAN: You agreed to hold off flipping the World Wide Web kill switch unless you were impeached, sir.

JOE BIDEN: I gotta idea, Boss: get in front of the wave. Preempt O'Reilly, and come clean about your misspent youth with a heartfelt statement from the Oval Office.

OBAMA: Might work. Something along these lines:

Let me be perfectly clear. I toked my way through college, but the smoke has long since dissipated, and I am now clear-headed and determined to save the country from modern robber barons such as the Koch brothers in order to see to fruition my healthcare reforms, which are designed to prevent predatory insurers from denying home services to people like Hernando Sosa of Santa Fe, a quadriplegic who died alone last spring after swallowing his dentures, with no one to help him in his final years but an elderly aunt who had lost both feet to diabetes when Kaiser Permanente refused to . . .

BIDEN: Uh, super, Chief. Might wanna tighten it up a little, though.

PFEIFFER: On another matter, Mr. President: in Kentucky, Mitch McConnell seems in fine position to keep his Senate seat. Reid wants our help to stop that from happening.

OBAMA: I'll endorse McConnell and campaign for him. Should tank his support among independents and raise doubts about him with Republicans.

VALERIE JARRETT: But sir, won't Kentucky Democrats stand down because you're pushing for the enemy?

PFEIFFER: Doesn't matter what he does, Val. Democrats in Kentucky are like Democrats everywhere: genetically predisposed to vote against their own interests.

OBAMA: Jay, set up a Mitch McConnell call center in the Situation Room. We'll release a tape of me working the phones. Debbie, arrange for DNC operatives to wave "Barack and Mitch for America" signs at McConnell rallies.

WHASSUPMAN SCHULTZ: Yes, sir. Looking ahead to Election Day: Franken in Minnesota is vulnerable. I'll ask the New Black Panther Party to station, ah, aggressive observers outside polling places in key Republican precincts.

ERIC HOLDER: Assure NBPP leadership that Justice Department lawyers will be on hand to shield their toughs from harassment by local authorities.

OBAMA: Which reminds me: I've overplayed the race card. From now on, I'll employ the victim card to get my numbers up. Any suggestions?

CARNEY: I've arranged for *Media Matters* to claim Hannity is spreading rumors you have another wife and family in Cleveland, attended Madrassa with Mullah Omar, and were born a hermaphrodite. We need people outraged and rallying around you.

OBAMA: Clever. Once we propagate those despicable lies, I'll attend African Methodist Episcopal some rainy Sunday when I can't golf and preach the virtues of forgiveness.

HOLDER: Speaking of victims, sir. Lawsuits were filed yesterday over the alleged shootings at Fort Hood in 2009. One claimant is Federal Police Officer Kimberly Munley, who was allegedly wounded when she attacked Major Nidal Hasan, the alleged gunman.

OBAMA: Damn! Anti-Muslim sentiment will rekindle with Fort Hood back on the front pages. I wonder: could we defuse tensions by inviting Hasan and Munley to the Rose Garden for coffee? Munley would have to wear a burkha, serve the coffee, and remain silent. I'd speak for her.

HOLDER: Hasan would probably decline, sir. They say he doesn't respect women, especially women who shoot him.

OBAMA: What's the status of the investigation?

HOLDER: DOJ's been going through going through Officer Hunley's background with a fine-tooth comb since the incident, sir. I'm confident we'll determine why she resorted to violence that day. Meanwhile, we've identified thirty-five eyewitnesses who are conspiring to claim Major Hasan shouted a Muslim warcry when he shot people.

OBAMA: Wherever the truth leads, Eric.

[enter First Lady]

MICHELLE: Bill Ayers is waiting outside, and he's mad. Says you're behind on royalty payments you owe him for writing your autobiography. Pay the man! You hear me, Barack?

STEVE GRAMMATICO

INSIDE THE DNC: THE

Rubio Delenda Est

Democratic National Committee
MINUTES
September 24, 2013

OFFICERS PRESENT

Debbie Whassupman Schultz, National Chairleader

Mike Honda, Vice Chair, UAW Liaison

Donna Brazile, Vice Chair, Hemispheric-Americans Voting Rights Coordinator

Linda Chavez-Thompson, No Relation to Cesar or Fred

OTHERS

Akio Toyoda, President, Toyota Motor Company

James Clyburn, Emissary, Congressional Black Caucus

Diane Sawyer, Network Lackey

Arthur 'Pinch' Sulzberger, Print Shill, *New York Times*

Eric Holder, Attorney General for Minority Rights

Dennis Kucinich, Director, *Munchkins United for America PAC*

Betty Friedan (1921-2006), Founder, *League of Dead Women Voters*

(Whoopi Goldberg, Channeler)

PROCEEDINGS

Ms. Whassupman Schultz called the meeting to order at 10:14 a.m. after police were summoned to settle a dispute between Mr. Honda and Mr. Toyoda.

On secure video uplink, President Obama spoke from the Kauai Lagoons Golf Club putting green. He warned of the hard road ahead.

AG Holder arrived at 10:23, claiming he didn't remember receiving a memo about the session.

OLD BUSINESS

1. Ms. Whassupman Schultz announced *Planned Parenthood* had submitted the winning design for the new Democratic National Committee logo that pokes *Fox News* in the eye.

We Abort. You Decry.

2. General Holder notified all 18,000 U.S. municipalities to eliminate pre-registration as a requisite for voting.

"The requirement is a violation of the 1965 Voting Rights Act," Holder said, "disenfranchising our homeless citizens, who can't know in which community they'll be living on Election Day."

Regarding the Supreme Court's recent 5-4 decision to strike down the Act, Mr. Holder remarked, "I appreciate the Court's input, but I choose which laws to enforce."

3. Ms. Chavez-Thompson confirmed friendly Federal magistrates in Pennsylvania and Ohio have agreed in advance to extend

metropolitan area poll hours until midnight on Election Day, 2014, so that derelicts caught up in late sweeps by ACORN press gangs may exercise their franchise.

4. Ms. Whassupman Schultz again expressed concern about growing public awareness of influence peddling by Congressional Democrats.

The Committee previewed a video scheduled for showing at House and Senate party caucuses next fall. It opens with former Congressman William "Cold Cash" Jefferson discussing integrity, ethics, and how not to get caught. Barbra Streisand closes with a cautionary tune inspired by *South Pacific's* "You've Got to Be Carefully Taught."

You've Got to Be Carefully Bought

You've got to wiggle your bum
Like a worm.
You've got to land those big fish
Term to term.
You need to show them
You'll never stand firm,
So you can be carefully bought.

You deserve to be bought—
Take your share.
All your colleagues are bought,
It's quite fair.
Yes, demand what's your due,
Who'll glean a clue
As long as you're carefully bought?

You better grab the dough
While you can.
You know it's the reason you ran.
Snag it in cash,
Mr. Government Man;
Stash it with forethought
Or poop hits the fan,
And your cunning might all come to naught.

> Now, if you're found out,
> You must claim
> That it's all a political frame.
> Just brazen it out,
> And show no one your shame.
> There's a chance you'll stay carefully bought.

NEW BUSINESS

1. Ms. Whassupman Schultz queried Mr. Sulzberger on the status of the DNC newsletter, the *New York Times*.

Mr. Sulzberger said the paper is hemorrhaging money and readers. He is disappointed by the poor response to a current promotion: dinner at La Grenouille with Paul Krugman for new subscribers who purchase a three month subscription.

Sulzberger also revealed he is in talks with *Globe Magazine* regarding a merger. "The *Times* gets an instant shot of credibility if the deal happens."

Regarding a balanced profile of Newt Gingrich in the *Times*, Mr. Sulzberger said, "Normally, we'd spike such a piece, but we're broke. The edition sold out as a collectors' item. We hawk more newspapers or we'll wind up a Saudi billionaire's trophy rag."

2. Ms. Brazile recommended firing DNC Internet trolls striking for Carpal Tunnel coverage. "Let's outsource their work to Internet boiler room drudges from Pakistan," she suggested. Tabled.

3. Ms. Whassupman Schultz read a poem she penned for the Party's upcoming fundraising appeal.

> Last year went well; the Pubbies caved.
> We've gotten mostly what we've craved:
> To gut our econ, sound retreat,
> Color red our balance sheet,
> Show lesser countries we'll self-screw

> to keep a lid on CO2,
> And borrow money (since we're broke)
> to give to Gaia's poorer folk.
>
> We've brought our country to the brink
> And shown that Democrats don't blink;
> Ahead: more change! Tricked-up reform!
> And by these measures Earth transform.
>
> We'll cool the planet, save the whales,
> Tell our kids tall climate tales.
> And when we're through and temps are pleasing,
> We'll warm to threats of global freezing.

4. Ms. Sawyer will channel Betty Friedan next month for *20/20*. Tentative title for the segment: "Who Speaks for the Dead?"

5. Ms. Brazile wondered how Party candidates might make more effective appeals to diverse ethnic groups.

Mr. Clyburn recalled Senator Obama receiving positive reviews for "talking Appalachian" at a Shenandoah Valley church supper in 2008.

Subsequently, Obama hawked his redistributionist philosophy to Italians, Jews, and Poles in their own vernacular.

The Committee agreed to consider hiring ethnic speech coaches to help candidates pitch the Party's socialist message to targeted audiences next election season. Program code name: Marxist Dialectics.

Motion to adjourn. Unanimous.

OBAMA WAR ROOM: WORK-RELATED

DAN PFEIFFER: Unless the labor picture brightens and voters forget your ineptness and corruption, sir, we'll lose Congress in 2014. Key initiatives like gutting Defense, forcing the richest 75% to pay their fair share, and passing an immigration bill with an amnesia rider are on the block.

OBAMA: It'll help that my new Bureau of Labor Statistics staffed by fired IRS personnel will be in place to fudge numbers this fall.

JAY CARNEY: Little more than a year to fool voters into thinking the economy's turned the corner, sir.

JOE BIDEN: Too iffy, Chief. Hey, whyant we thinka somethin' bad that's bound to happen soon, then be proactive? Gets us out of our crouch.

JACK LEW: He has a point, sir. Um, China. They might dump our T-bills anytime. So we give them Manhattan as a "Special Administrative Region" like Hong Kong if they continue to prop us up.

OBAMA: Probably run the borough better than Bloomberg. But, no. Be like giving the island back to the Indians for some beads. Any other ideas? George?

SOROS: Mind games, zir. Next week I haff ten tousand tugs wearing Palin 2016 T-shirts assaulting White House.

OBAMA: Good. Make it so. Jay, alert the alphabets; I want tape of GOP hooliganism aired live. Jack?

LEW: Regarding unemployment, sir. You're spending so much we can't print money fast enough to keep up. Let's create thousands of union jobs with a crash program to build an additional half-dozen mints.

OBAMA: Mints! Jack knows I love my confections. Six new mints it is. Schedule prime-time groundbreakings for mid- to late September. Marine One will fly me to each after a round of golf at a posh nearby track.

LEW: Ah, financing them, sir?

OBAMA: Commerce, scale back ammo purchases next fiscal year to seven billion rounds, half your original target.

PENNY PRITZKER: Oh, shoot.

LEW: In the near term, sir, add third shifts to operating mints.

OBAMA: Smart. Means an immediate need for engravers, machinists, electricians, and the like. Paper mills and ink producers will increase their hiring, too.

LEW: The armored cars we use to transport freshly printed bills now—big, heavy gas guzzlers? Junk 'em, sir. Buy GM back and task them to build a fleet of solar-powered, bullet-resistant vans.

SOROS: North Korea hass excellent counterfeit stock, zir; zey can tide us over till new mints are up und running.

OBAMA: Good idea. Jack, you and George work out a deal with the Norks. Seal it by offering Kim Young-un a "shipload-of-arms-allowed-to-pass-unmolested-to-Iran" card. Joe?

BIDEN: Ya still need more bodies workin', Boss. Whyncha order Commerce to recall census workers and get an early start on the 2020 count?

OBAMA: Problem is, every trick in the book only lowers the last jobs report before midterms down to maybe 6%. I want it at 3% or less. So come on, everyone! Suggest something radical.

PFEIFFER: Well, sir, we could cut the rate to zero by hiring all fourteen million officially unemployed to locate and register the seven million who've stopped looking for work. We'd offer excellent salaries and benefits.

OBAMA: Hmm. Then I can truthfully say I created nine million good jobs. But what do we do about the nine million when they finish their assignment and the seven million they found who stopped looking for work?

LEW: We hire all sixteen million as Labor Department information specialists. Their job: identifying the nation's twenty million underemployed.

VALERIE JARRETT: The underemployed, once we've identified them?

LEW: We award them federal grants and tax breaks to start small businesses. We promise government will be the primary purchaser of their goods and services. Failure is impossible.

OBAMA: Ah, then we mandate they hire the folks we hired to find them. Oh, man, the way we're going, a year from now, we'll be dealing with a labor shortage. Can we hold Bush responsible should that happen?

[enter Michelle]

MICHELLE: They'll be shutting down half of Washington when I motorcade to Whole Foods in thirty minutes to get some arugula. Better tell your people to leave early to avoid the gridlock. You hear me, Barack?

OBAMA SOLILOQUY*: WATCHING PAUL RYAN ADDRESS THE DETROIT ECONOMIC CLUB

I

Ooooh, he speaks, the Pubs' Orion!
Expel your foul discharges—phew!

Could glares steal breath, Master Ryan,
Right now you'd be turning blue!
Huh? Big spending cuts are needed?
Oh, Fed tax rates mustn't rise?
And these "facts" I've not conceded?
Why? They're falsehoods, damn your eyes!

II

In the past we've had discussions—
"Paul, thanks for coming!" I must bear
Rants on market repercussions,
Treas'ry futures, budget snares.
"Our job outlook's pathetic; rarely
Has it been this bad, I think.
Want a deal to face this squarely?"
Want emetics in your drink?

III

Aww! So sad your Roadmap folded,
All those hours and effort spent!
I confess, we push-and-polled it
Till we hastened its descent.
Poor old Grandma was affronted
When you shoved her off that peak.
The best you had I blunted.
(Is his time up yet? The geek!)

IV

Jeez, I'm starved! My chef Cristeta
Waits inside our hotel suite

With live lobsters (Don't tell PETA!)
And the finest cuts of meat:
Marbled Kobe, umm, oven-roasted grouse;
Rocky Oysters, *Poulet, Veal Fondue.*
If this rube attains the White House,
They'll be serving Shepherd's Stew.

V

While I feign concern, compassion,
Truth and honor's what he touts.
Well, get real, they're out-of-fashion
In a country filled with louts.
I'm the Boss man, Chief Tirader,
The epitome of cool.
Ryan's a dreary green eyeshader;
He says, "*Govern*"; I say, "*Rule.*"

VI

Ho, Bernanke! Print more money!
Yes, I'll spend us out of debt!
Better not try to stop me, sonny;
You'd have reason to regret.
I hear you prize your honor; your rep, too.
Everyone says that you don't faze.
Well, wait'll you see what Wolf and Williams
Dump on you in coming days.

VII

Hmm, maybe I'll pose a gun rights question
That boxes you in real tight.

Make you seem like Charlton Heston
To the middle and left of right.
Photoshop you shooting a moose
With a silly grin on your face;
Standin' there with your thirty ought six
Won't please anyone 'cept the base.

VIII

Wait! I'll ask a pawn at *WaPo*
To follow you to the loo;
Take a stall and tap his right foot,
Then report he saw your shoe.
Or a maid who needs her green card,
Who can tell what she might say
When a *Times*man trolls for canards
On the congressman's recent stay?

IX

Just don't panic! Who's the master?
I am the King; I run the show.
If it seems I face disaster,
I can fabricate a foe
And a crisis which is breaking
On the day the Houses vote.
Oh, I'm up. *"Thanks, Paul, for making . . ."*
There! Nice'ties made. Now, speak. By rote.

*This piece is a parody—*not* an exact parody—of
Victorian poet Robert Browning's "Soliloquy of the
Spanish Cloister," published in 1842.

Browning (1812-1889) is best known for his dramatic monologues, in which a speaker (not the author) unwittingly reveals himself to be quite different from his public persona.

"Soliloquy of the Spanish Cloister" is a variant of the dramatic monologue.

BIDEN UNLEASHED

Washington (AP)—At a hastily called press briefing yesterday, Vice President Joe Biden blasted the *New York Times* for reporting a top secret document on American missile defense was made public accidentally.

"I expect better of the *Times*," Biden told reporters. "It makes us look like the gang that couldn't shoot straight. Instead of covering for the administration reflexively, they shoulda checked with us first. We woulda sworn 'em to secrecy and told 'em it was a *quid pro quo* with Iran and North Korea, not a security breach.

"See, the deal was, we 'inadvertently' make public the technical details of our anti-missile program, they agree to sit down and talk about nuclear disarmament.

"Ayatollah Khamenei, Kim Young-un," Biden continued, "we outfoxed 'em, 'cause we had already made the missile defense info available to the U.N. Select Committee on U.S. Disarmament, on which Iran sits. So we didn't give up a thing to Iran or North Korea."

In other remarks, the vice president expressed frustration at the administration's unexpected difficulty in dispersing Stimulus IV's $800 billion dollars.

"Ain't easy bein' green, lemme tell ya," Biden said. "Sure, everybody wants some dough re me, but we're doin' this right and vettin' people: no change in your pocket unless you been in our pocket, or promise you will be."

Mr. Biden revealed the president is also concerned about the slow pace of spending. "The Big O says to me, 'Joe, I'm puttin' you in charge of gettin' rid of Stimulus IV money by fall because Stimulus V is comin' down the track, and I want the last train unloaded and out of the station before the next one arrives.'"

I said, 'Don't worry, Boss. When I run the railroad, I'll get 'er done. Anything left over, I'll use as filler for the California sinkhole."

OBAMA WAR ROOM: MICHELLE MA BELLICOSE

[White House exercise facility]

MICHELLE: Well, come in, people. Lew, Carney, get over here and spot for me while I press 250. Everybody else, pull up a mat and sit so we can start.

JOE BIDEN: Huh? Why's the Boss in the corner in his PJs staring out the window?

MICHELLE: He's stressed out. I'm running things until his therapist clears him to continue denying there are scandals. Anybody got a problem with that?

DAN PFEIFFER: No Ma'am, but what set him off?

MICHELLE: Yesterday he had to lay up on the first par 5 at Burning Tree and couldn't choose between a 6-iron and 7-iron. Told his playing partners he wanted to sleep on it. At dinner, a steward asked what flavor parfait he preferred for dessert. He never decided. Midnight, he was still muttering, "I like the strawberry, but the peach appeals to me, too."

VALERIE JARRETT: Deteriorating decision-making skills. It started right after he took office in 2008 and has gotten progressively worse. I mean, the CIA knew where bin Laden was hiding since mid-2009. He couldn't pull the trigger. I had to use his autopen to sign the order authorizing the SEALs' raid on Osama's compound.

MICHELLE: Hmmph. He didn't have a problem deciding on those chili dogs for lunch in public today and stepping on my daily nutrition bulletin in the process.

Well, to business. Nancy, some of your members defected to the enemy on guns, taxes, Benghazi, and the IRS and NSA. I'm not happy.

PELOSI: Noted. Leadership's scheduled a confab tonight with the recalcitrants in Rayburn B113.

PFEIFFER: But that's the carpenters' workshop in the sub-basement.

PELOSI: Correct. SEIU enforcers will restrain these people while I clip off their pinkies. A Smithsonian preservationist agreed to shrink the fingers and create a digital necklace for me to wear when I'm lobbying my caucus. I'll tell them, "These little pinkies voted 'nay.'"

By the way, I asked Anthony Weiner to come, too.

MICHELLE: Weiner? Why? He's been out of office since . . .

PELOSI: Anthony embarrassed the party and got off easy by resigning. I've waited long enough for my pound of flesh.

MICHELLE: Pound?

PELOSI: Figure of speech. Anyway, call it an extreme circumcision. I'll display the appendage in a jar of formaldehyde on my desk with a label reading, "Gentlemen, this is what happens when you think with your . . ."

MICHELLE: I get it. Hey, you're leaving?

PELOSI: Call me if Waterwalker over there gets back on his game. [exits]

VALERIE JARRETT: Typical jab. She doesn't fear the president. Nobody fears him.

MICHELLE: Well, I'm not Barack. Kathleen, order the FDA to ban Botox for women over 70 because of a possible link to the onset of megalomania.

SEBELIUS: Good idea. Means less face time for her with the media.

MICHELLE: Let's move on. Harry, what's your plan to marginalize and frustrate Senate Republicans?

REID: Senate Democrats will vote to designate the late Robert Byrd as the Senate's first posthumous Emeritus Senator, with limited floor rights. Disney's Imagineers just delivered a Byrd automaton for use in the Senate chamber. It's programmed to say, "Those amendments are out of order," and, "The rules permit reconciliation," and, "The Founders would be livid at Republican tactics."

PELOSI: You know, we'd get a lot more done with a Stepford president.

PFEIFFER: Some bad news: Senator Joe Mancin [D-WV] is threatening to change parties.

MICHELLE: Debbie, assign a DNC covert operator to break into his condo this weekend and leave an ear of corn under his pillow, shucked. And a note: "Stay in our crib—or else."

WHASSUPMAN SHULTZ: An off ear he can't refuse.

MICHELLE: Jack, where's your report on bringing the world together through American largesse.

LEW: Here, Ma'am. I'm calling the proposal, "Tax Americana." Ten trillion distributed abroad over the next five years. Half raised from new taxes and raids on pension funds, the other half from my printing presses. The world will love us.

BIDEN: Maybe. Right now, though, we better start showing the world some moxie. Iran just laughed off our warning not to do it again after they sank our carrier in the Persian Gulf.

MICHELLE: True. John, inform Putin the president will be displeased if Russia invades Poland. Carney, at today's briefing, demand Assad return murdered Syrian dissidents' bodies to their families. Lew, straight talk to China: they buy more Treasuries or we'll print so much currency, the T-bills they now own will become worthless. Unfortunately, we still need their financing to become insolvent.

BIDEN: Looks like Palin's getting set to run against the Boss in 2016, Ma'am. We gotta blunt her impact without turnin' women off.

MICHELLE: Covered. I'll be on the ticket with Barack. Joe, we're moving you over to Veterans' Affairs. Also . . .

[enter Attorney General]

ERIC HOLDER: Sorry to interrupt, Ma'am. Just got a text from Brennan at CIA. Says an anonymous caller claimed a Somali, Nadif Osman, will bring down International Airways Flight 227 tomorrow evening as it approaches New York. He'll board in Hamburg wearing C4 plastique shoelaces and detonate in seat F124. A man named Osman *is* booked on the flight, but he's not on our watchlists.

MICHELLE: Hmm. Anonymous caller. No red flags. That puts the "threat" at the low end of the probable cause threshold, Eric. Without correlating the name to your predicate, we can do nothing. So, we give this guy the benefit of the doubt.

HOLDER: Of course, Ma'am. But on the off chance he does try something and passengers attack and thwart him, ACLU attorneys will be on the tarmac to advise Mr. Osman of his rights the moment he disembarks.

[in corner, Obama's cell rings. He answers]

MICHELLE: Barack, I thought I confiscated all your toys. Who is that?

OBAMA: Chris Matthews, dear. He wants to know what I'm wearing. Should I tell him?

YOU HEAR ME, BARACK?

CHAPTER 7: PRES. TIDIGITATOR VS. THE RODHAM

PBS NEWSHOUR: A WHISTLEBLOWER AT STATE?

JIM LEHRER: Good evening. In an extraordinary display of compassion, President Obama spent the afternoon on Louisiana's coast comforting pelicans that had lost their mates following another well blowout in the Gulf.

He also quaffed a quart of seawater to quash rumors Gulf water is unsafe to drink. Aides claimed the small tar ball he coughed up later was harmless.

JEFFREY BROWN: On the *NewsHour* tonight:

*Homeless pet population explodes as the Bush Recession lingers into year six.

*Disney World to relocate to Martha's Vineyard for First Family's stay in August.

*And finally, *Washington Post* Associate Editor Bob Woodward talks with Judy Woodruff about his high-level informant in the State Department.

LEHRER: Forget the lineup, Jeff. Let's get to the Foggy Bottom mole. Judy, you start.

WOODRUFF: Thanks, Jim. Carl, I assume you're revealing this information because your source is no longer at State. Correct?

WOODWARD: Uh, it's Bob, Judy. Yes, that's so.

WOODRUFF: How long did you cultivate this individual?

WOODWARD: For a year, up until early 2013. Without getting specific, I'd rendezvous with the woman the first Thursday of every month at 6:00 p.m. in the women's restroom at a Starbucks half a block east of the State Department.

We'd occupy adjoining stalls and confirm identities by tapping out a predetermined code with our feet, after which she pushed into my stall a carry-on bag stuffed with copies of top-secret memoranda, policy drafts, and audio tapes and transcripts of strategy meetings.

WOODRUFF: Her code name?

WOODWARD: "Deep Tote."

WOODRUFF: You'd been meeting with the source until early this year. What happened?

WOODWARD: This is as sensitive as "Deep Throat," Judy. I'll take her identity to my grave. The only thing I'll say is, she had some health problems prior to testifying before Congress that crucial information about security at the Benghazi consulate never reached her desk.

WOODRUFF: What's the president's state of mind lately, Mr. Bernstein?

WOODWARD: It's Woodward, Judy. Bernstein and I don't speak anymore. The president is frustrated and angry; he believes he's lefted the ship and received no credit.

WOODRUFF: "Lefted" the ship?

WOODWARD: The president can't bring himself to say, "righted" the ship. Anyway, he's short with his staff and often refuses to take urgent calls from Chuck Hagel and George Clooney.

WOODRUFF: Will Martha's Vineyard be completely evacuated this summer to allow the First Family privacy?

WOODWARD: Ugly rumor, Judy. Friends of the Obamas who maintain homes on the island may stay.

WOODRUFF: You brought along the audio of a "War Room" meeting last summer at the Vineyard. How did you obtain that?

WOODWARD: From someone who wants to get on my good side, Judy. Anyway, the First Lady chaired until the president arrived.

WOODRUFF: Let's listen while we roll the transcript on screen:

> **MICHELLE**: I don't care what question you're asked: keep saying "paying their fair share" every time you open your mouths.
>
> **VALERIE JARRETT** I commissioned the Huffington Post to poll 30 billionaires on the issue. Eighty percent favor our position that, in principle, but only in principle, they should be paying more. The networks lead with those numbers tonight.
>
> **DAVID PLOUFFE**: Jay, Ask HuffPo to release internals only to the DNC. Defer press inquiries to the vice president. Joe, you say you can't comment.
>
> **BIDEN**: About what?
>
> **MICHELLE**: Never mind. Any way we can avoid looking like royalty while we're here?
>
> **JARRETT**: I'll arrange a small oil spill off Oak Bluffs. Reporters situated some distance away will film you and Barack rescuing lifelike seabirds from the muck. Also, they'll photograph the president clearing wild arugula near the compound.
>
> **MICHELLE**: Good. Dave, hire local handymen to throw up a shack nearby and stock it with poor people

from Haiti. Ask Habitat for Humanity to come in and renovate. Barack and I will pound nails with them for the cameras before we head to the beach.

[enter the president]

OBAMA: Hey, who called this meeting?

MICHELLE: What happened with Tiger?

OBAMA: It was Charles Barkley, not Tiger. I always feel better about my game when I play with Charles.

PLOUFFE: Sir, our political situation is dire: the "Fast and Furious" cover-up appears to be unraveling; D.C. District Court has cleared the way for construction of a mosque in Lafayette Park; the FBI is arresting CIA agents; and Russian troops just invaded the Aleutians.

OBAMA: So?

PLOUFFE: Your presidency is at risk, sir, and our territory has been violated. I called Sarah Palin in Wasilla and she said she could see the Russians from her house. You need to act.

OBAMA: Fine. Can't take ten minutes off. Tell Holder to fall on his sword; inform the CIA their agents may use reasonable force to resist arrest; on the mosque, release a statement that I have strong opinions on the project.

JARRETT: The Russians, sir?

OBAMA: Oh. [punches button on red phone] Vladimir? Listen, I am very sorry for whatever we did to provoke your aggression.

Certainly, I'll include Russia on my next World Apology Tour.

Absolutely. No problem. Thank you. [hangs up] That went well. He'll bring up the invasion next time the Security Council meets.

PLOUFFE: Nicely done, sir. By the way, where's the officer with the launch codes? Nobody's seen him in a week.

MICHELLE: The guy with a suitcase who followed us everywhere? I sent him back to the Pentagon.

OBAMA: But . . .

MICHELLE: Face it, Hoss. Under no circumstances would you ever retaliate with nuclear weapons against anybody for any reason. Morally, you're comfortable having America stand down. Am I wrong, Barack?

WOODRUFF: Amazing. Thanks for sharing with us, Mr. Woodstein. One last thing: what's the subject of your next book?

WOODWARD: The corrupt media.

WOODRUFF: Don't go there, Bub.

HILLARY TO CHALLENGE OBAMA FOR NOMINATION IN 2016

Washington (AP)—In a stunning announcement this morning on *The Today Show*, former Secretary of State Hillary Clinton told host Matt Lauer she will challenge Barack Obama for the 2016 Democratic presidential nomination.

[transcript]

LAUER: Thanks for coming on, Madame Secretary. Let's get right to it: will you seek the presidency in 2016?

HILLARY: Yes, Matt. Our country's heading in the wrong direction way too fast. We must slow down if we wish to delay our collapse by a couple of decades. So I'm reporting for duty. I will battle the president for the nomination.

LAUER: But he can't run for a third term. The 22nd Amendment prohibits . . .

HILLARY: Get real, Matt. When has the Constitution stopped him before? Obama's a megalomaniac. It's up to Democrats to rein him in. He runs again, he's toast, and we'll lose the House and Senate, too. Meanwhile, my numbers are in the stratosphere, mainly because people like you have generously ignored my disastrous tenure at State.

LAUER: [blushing] Well, it's what we do, Ma'am. Won't a challenge open you up to a disloyalty charge?

HILLARY: I offered the president an option to avoid a primary battle. He rejected it.

LAUER: What option?

HILLARY: Replace Biden on the ticket with me. I'd rally the troops. We'd win and, at the least, retain the Senate. Then Obama does the mother of all end runs around the Constitution and names me co-president. In January, 2016, we take the oath together and deliver dual inaugural addresses.

LAUER: Wouldn't Republicans . . .

HILLARY: We own the DOJ, Matt. Holder could stonewall indefinitely. As for the courts stepping in? Don't make me laugh. The other day I heard the president say, "How many divisions does Scalia have?" We'd be good, Matt. No balance, no check.

LAUER: Why did the president reject your proposal?

HILLARY: He balked at some minor details: my portfolio as CP to include oversight of Justice, State, Defense, Treasury, Homeland Security, and Health and Human Services. He'd get Agriculture, Veterans' Affairs, whatever's left.

LAUER: Oh.

HILLARY: I also wanted him to support my play to take back my Senate seat and replace Reid as majority leader in the new Congress, guaranteeing unprecedented cooperation between the Senate and the White House.

LAUER: Indeed. How would a shared Presidency work, anyway?

HILLARY: I'd operate in the Oval Office weekdays and during crises. Air Force One and The Residence: my perks. The Obamas could stay in the Lincoln Bedroom when I wasn't hosting donor sleepovers. We'd work out some sort of timeshare arrangement for Camp David.

LAUER: That's a little . . .

HILLARY: I retained Bob Bennett to write a political pre-nuptial codifying the deal. When Obama balked, the window closed.

LAUER: So, how will you run your campaign?

HILLARY: I'll focus on women and men who like to be dominated by women. That's more than half the electorate. I'll talk about whipping the country into shape, beating inflation, thrashing our enemies. I'd be an Amazonadominatrix: females will admire my strength; males will desire and fear me.

LAUER: Assuming you won the presidency, would you offer Obama a role in your administration?

HILLARY: No. He takes too many vacations.

LAUER: What about . . . Bill?

HILLARY: Bill, Bill, Bill. Always comes back to him, doesn't it? Even when he philanders, he's so hound-dog likable, he sucks up my oxygen. Pity's gotten me this far. Time to push him aside and show some fire in the belly.

LAUER: Forgive me, Madame Secretary, but if you turn on the First Black President, aren't you forgetting the, uh, the . . . ?

HILLARY: The African-American vote? No, Matt. I'm good there. My history in the civil rights movement predates Obama's birth. I never told anyone this before, but I was on the balcony of the Lorraine Motel when Dr. King was felled by the sniper.

LAUER: You were?

HILLARY: I had taken some time off from Wellesley to follow him and join the struggle. I saw the sniper's gun barrel an instant before he fired and threw myself in front of Dr. King to take the bullet. I was too late.

LAUER: I didn't know.

HILLARY: Reverend Jackson thought it would be best if I left before the media arrived. I hitched a ride to California and a few days later marched with Cesar Chavez in Sacramento. These memories are burned into my brain, Matt. They've stayed with me long after film and eyewitness accounts discredited them.

LAUER: I'm troubled, Ma'am. You'd force me and my colleagues to choose between you and Obama.

HILLARY: Know this, Matt: any expression of support by friendly media for Obama 44 will deeply offend Clinton 45. Soros is in my corner. The other day he said, "Highness, give me za verd, und I buy Disney, GE, ZBS, und ZNN, zen I clean house." Choose your horse, Matt.

[End transcript]

HILLARY WAR ROOM: GOING FOR BAROKE

HILLARY: I took one on Benghazi for the team. Now Obama pays. I announce my candidacy for 2016 next week.

HOWARD WOLFSON: What's your rationale for opposing Obama's try for a third term, my Liege?

ANN LEWIS: No rationale is necessary, Howard. This is about a woman's right to choose.

HILLARY: Correct. The decision to contend is between me and my spin doctor. I do wonder whether I should have stayed in the public eye by remaining Secretary of Stasis.

WOLFSON: Um, he asked for your resignation, Ma'am.

PAUL BEGALA: You'll alienate the black vote if you attack Obama, Mistress.

HILLARY: How do I campaign without criticizing him?

LEWIS: Go positive, your Majesty. Commend his Muslim roots, his resolve to take out terrorists even if it means obliterating their families, his "Buy American" initiative encouraging drug cartels to shop here for their arms needs.

WOLFSON: Praise his work ethic on the golf course, his faith in Putin's honor, his courage in shutting down North Dakota's oil fields to save the Sprague Pipit songbird, his cleverness in making more room beneath the bus for those in disfavor by special ordering 14 foot Michelin tires for the vehicle.

HILLARY: Wonderful! I'll appear generous while planting doubts. He rejects my "compliments," he looks petty. Serpenthead?

JAMES CARVILLE: Exalted One, task our media loyalists to push this meme: under Obama, the poor may be obese and own Xboxes and SUVs, but their children are still going to bed without iPads.

HILLARY: Works for me. Anyone else?

HUMA ABEDIN WEINER: Highness, announce that on Day One of your administration you'll pardon Obama for crimes he committed as president. Waive the standard contribution to your library.

HILLARY: So magnanimous of me!

Huma, you're leaving already?

HUMA: I'm due at Langley to help the CIA plot the Brotherhood's return to power in Egypt, my Grace.

HILLARY: Oh, okay. Everyone, Reverend Al's through with Obama and is joining our team.

SHARPTON: As the inimical Popeye might say, resist we musk, or the foul ordure of the Obama regime will Kaiser Permeate the very fabric of our national travesty the Geek Fakes are weaving as we speak.

[silence]

HILLARY: I can't imagine Jesse Jackson expressing the thought any more plainly, Al. For the time being, you can help us most by remaining quietly committed to the president's reelection.

LEWIS: Invite Reverend Wright to offer the benediction at your first fundraiser, M'Lady. Then blast him and his venomous anti-Americanism. Show voters that Obama may be unwilling to stand up to Wright, but you're not.

HILLARY: Hijacking his Sister Souljah moment. I like it! Now, everyone, as you know, George switched to us as well, and I'm sure you're wondering why. I'll let him tell you.

SOROS: Obama iss veak horse, Eminence. You, you are strong horse, haff big haunches, hams like . . .

HILLARY: We get it, George. You haff—have suggestions?

SOROS: For Pennsylvahnee primary, I fund new pro-Obama 527—"Citizens for Confiscation uff Guns." Za group's pitch: "Obama. Our only hope to repeal 2nd Amendment."

Und I offer gas coupons to Democrats in primaries you vin. Ve make billion bumper stickers: "Hillary rule, free tank of fuel."

HILLARY: Marvelous! Axelrod will scream bloody murder, but as Putin said when the Ukraine complained about Russian intimidation, "Crimea River." Moving on, how do we neutralize Oprah? Mr. Clean?

CARVILLE: My grandma would cut off the ends, sprinkle salt over the slices, and put 'em in a pan with possum innards.

HILLARY: Oprah, not okra, Jimbo. Paul?

BEGALA: I'll supply the *Enquirer* with photoshopped images of Perry and Oprah hunting together at his Texas camp.

HILLARY: Good idea. But forget the *Enquirer*; they abide by standards. The *Washington Post* will run them without asking questions.

LEWIS: Exalted One, you must propose something substantive about what you'll actually do as president.

HILLARY: I'll promise to rid the planet of war, disease, and famine, but I won't say how unless I'm elected. I'll open my campaign with a thirty second spot depicting a *Road Warrior* world if I lose.

BILL CLINTON: Honey, we got to make you seem like regular people, not some ice queen who . . .

HILLARY: Did I ask for your opinion?

BILL CLINTON: No, Ma'am.

HILLARY: He's right, though. What can I do to appear, well, ordinary?

WOLFSON: Appear on a trash TV talk show, Sensei. Discuss your marriage frankly. Disclose affairs with unnamed males in your Secret Service detail. The Agency can't comment. In one stroke you'll squash some ugly rumors and thrill millions of women who've waited for tit for tat since Monica.

HILLARY: Inspired! This we can do now. Howard, book me, Bill, Lewinsky, and Paula Jones on Springer for a throw down. Make sure the set has plenty of lamps near at hand for hurling.

What about exhibiting my soft side?

LEWIS: Pledge to adopt infants representing every ethnic and racial group in the world, Ladyship.

HILLARY: Oh, the humanity! When I'm elected, we'll house them in the renamed "Eisenhower Executive Orphanage Building." I'll be the model for working mothers everywhere who want it all.

BEGALA: Out of the box, you'll need some encouraging poll numbers, my Queen. I'll task the *Times* to run a poll with this question: "Given President Obama's incompetence, narcissism, and arrogance, would you be more likely or less likely to vote to give him a third term?"

HILLARY: Other ideas?

WOLFSON: Mistress, fire us all. Finish the campaign with no staff or advisors. You'll look decisive, self-reliant.

BEGALA: Howard, are you out of your . . . ?

SANDY BERGER: I'll sneak into Axelrod's office and stuff a copy of Obama's 2016 campaign plan down my jockeys, your Magnitude. If I'm caught and Axelrod asks me what's in my pants, I'll just say I'm glad to see him.

BILL: Good 'un, Sandy.

HILLARY: Shuddup, Bill. Who let Berger in here?

HILLARY ON *THIS WEEK*: STATE OF THE SECRETARY

GEORGE STEPHANOPOULOS: Our guest this morning, former Secretary of State Hillary Clinton. Welcome, Madame Secretary.

HILLARY: Good morning, George. Remember, one question about Benghazi and I'm outta here.

GREGORY: Yes'm. Rumors abound that during your tenure as Secretary of State, you and President Obama clashed often. True?

HILLARY: Yes, George. We were rarely on the same page. In fact, I considered having State secede from the administration.

STEPHANOPOULOS: Wow.

HILLARY: My staff was riddled with spies who regularly undercut me and reported directly to the West Wing. Sometimes, the stress caused me to fall down, hit my head, and forget things. That usually happened before I was called to testify before some committee or other.

STEPHANOPOULOS: The Secret Service is pledged to protect you from harm, which must include distress caused by disloyal underlings. Did the Agency monitor the Department to investigate threats to your emotional well-being?

HILLARY: They did, and we conducted a purge of White House moles. But we didn't get them all. I never felt Foggy Bottom was really mine.

STEPHANOPOULOS: What would pulling State out of the administration have accomplished?

HILLARY: I don't play well when I'm answerable to others, George. Secession guaranteed a clean break. I figured, absent accountability, my relations with the White House and Congress would improve. And if some House chairman with an attitude called me to testify, I'd tell him to pound sand.

STEPHANOPOULOS: Did you discuss this with Bill and Chelsea?

HILLARY: Chelsea was supportive. I planned to make her my ambassador to Washington while I groomed her to succeed me as Head of State. Bill would have been posted to Zimbabwe to keep him out of trouble. Maddie Albright had agreed to be his Number Two and bird dog him.

STEPHANOPOULOS: Ah, his *chargé d'affaires*. And your title?

HILLARY: "Secretary for Life," subject to a show-of-hands ratification by Department careerists. Call it a "Diplomats' Free Choice Initiative."* My first foreign trip: New York, to visit my summer home in Chappaqua.

STEPHANOPOULOS: So, why didn't you pull the trigger?

HILLARY: It came down to practicalities. George. State had no independent source of income. The planes I used to cart my entourage all over the world belonged to the president. Fly commercial? No way. I decided to wait until Air Force One was available.

STEPHANOPOULOS: Of course. Thanks for coming on, Madame Secretary.

OBAMA WAR ROOM: STUCK

OBAMA: Hillary made it clear in our meeting last week she's coming after me in 2016.

DAN PFEIFFER: Not too early to start moving against her, sir.

OBAMA: Agreed. Begin spreading rumors about her weight, health, proclivities, hairdos, face jobs, whatever. She'll pay a price for challenging me. The gall of the woman, pointing out my tanking poll numbers and her stratospheric reputation.

VALERIE JARRETT: You never told us what, if anything, she wanted.

OBAMA: Offered to replace Dumbo here as VP immediately. Said she'd rally the troops, get me over 50% again even with ObamaCare hanging around my neck.

BIDEN: Nasty, Boss. Next time I see her, I'm gonna give her the fing . . .

OBAMA: Shuddup, Joe. Vice presidents should be seen, not flipping the bird.

Anyway, there's more. After she replaced Joe, I was to name her CP—Co-President. We'd repeat the inauguration, taking the oath together. I'd put my hand on the Bible; she'd repeat Justice Roberts' words.

JARRETT: Nothing seems like a deal-breaker.

OBAMA: Wait for it. She wanted me to give up practically the entire presidential portfolio. I'd be the one going to funerals. Oh, and Huma was to replace Kerry as Secretary of State.

JARRETT: You could've agreed, sir, then reneged after she was on board.

OBAMA: Uh uh. Said if I accepted the proposal, she'd retain counsel to write a contract binding me to her terms.

PFEIFFER: You were right to reject . . .

OBAMA: In retrospect, yes. But I might have bitten the bullet if not for one other condition: Bill to be named Special Envoy to the World, leading the fight against U.S. hegemony. That particular prerogative I will never give up.

CHAPTER 8: THE CHIEF EXECUTIVE BROADCASTING SYSTEM PRESENTS . . .

LIVE, FROM THE SITUATION ROOM, THE CHIEF EXECUTIVE BROADCASTING SYSTEM PRESENTS *THE CEBS NIGHTLY NEWS WITH JAY CARNEY*

CARNEY: Good evening. On our broadcast tonight:

*When the bow breaks—Saudi King Abdullah issues obeisance dispensation to President Obama for upcoming audience.

Sharia, Baby—Islamic reprise of 60s rock classic hits No. 1 on Iranian charts.

*Finally, former congressman Dennis Kucinich to star in Alfred E. Neuman biopic.

Those stories and more later, but first we talk live with the president of the United States, Barack Obama. Welcome, sir. Thanks for coming on.

OBAMA: My pleasure, Chris.

CARNEY: Uh, I'm Jay Carney, sir. Your Press Secretary?

OBAMA: Oops, honest mistake, Jay. When you hugged me, I thought I was on *Hardball.*

CARNEY: Let's address foreign policy tonight. Mr. President. Czechoslovakia and Poland indicated today they're against the new START treaty you're pressuring the Senate to ratify. What's their problem?

OBAMA: They're still ticked because I broke my promise to them on missile defense several years ago, Jay.

CARNEY: You did what you had to, sir.

OBAMA: Exactly. With the Bear awake, we couldn't have protected them in the long run, anyway. Actually, it's to our advantage to let Eastern Europe fall into the Russian orbit again. So I'm giving away the store with START to embolden the Rooskies.

CARNEY: *Embolden* them? Please explain, sir.

OBAMA: A lot easier to downsize our military if we aren't resisting Russian expansionism, Jay. In fact, the only way to check a new Russian Empire is to encourage one resembling the old Soviet model.

CARNEY: Are you saying we should welcome the reconstitution of the Warsaw Pact, sir?

OBAMA: Absolutely, Jay. We also stand aside when Putin gobbles back up the post-Soviet states. Why? In a flash, Russia becomes big, bloated, and hidebound again. More territory to defend, obscene military budgets, restive populations. Meanwhile, we're sitting pretty on the sidelines watching it all go down.

CARNEY: I think I understand. Instead of becoming a sleek new superpower, Russia morphs into the Soviet Union 2.0., a lumbering, doomed giant.

OBAMA: Correct.

CARNEY: Let me play devil's advocate, sir. Wouldn't this strategy forfeit our leverage with Putin and get us nothing in return?

OBAMA: Letting Russia assume our responsibilities as a counterweight to China and Iran, that's nothing?

CARNEY: Our European allies, are they on board, sir?

OBAMA: Not exactly, Jay. And I don't care. Here's where I agree with Republicans: Old Europe has been a drain on us since World War II. About time another superpower looked out for those failed states. Why not Russia?

CARNEY: So, you'd encourage Putin to extend Russia's sphere of influence to the Atlantic?

OBAMA: Yes, and here's how: U.S. sponsorship of the first "World Peace Conference" at Camp David. On opening day, I'd deliver another of my signature orations, this one an international riff on the late Rodney King's "Can't we all just get along" plea.

CARNEY: Forgive me, sir, but everybody knows by now your speeches are full of ground round and curry, dignifying frothing.

OBAMA: Ouch. Actually, *this* address has substance. I'll label NATO a relic of the Cold War and call for its disbandment.

CARNEY: Makes sense, sir. No NATO, no confrontation when Russia moves west.

Mr. President, what's the status of the economic initiative you're rumored to be working on with Putin? Word is, it'll ease the transition to Russian hegemony on the Continent.

OBAMA: We're close, Jay. We've agreed to prop up the ruble by manipulating Western currencies. Russia guarantees delivery of natural gas to our former allies, except in time of war or international tension. Best deal we could get.

Oh, and Putin wants our backing for what he's calling the Greater European Co-Prosperity Sphere.

CARNEY: Nice ring to it, sir.

MICHELLE: We'll swing by Moscow so he can to sign on to the pact next month at the end of his "Golf on Every Continent Holiday World Tour."

CARNEY: Golf in Antarctica?

OBAMA: The U.S. Army Corps of Engineers guarantees McMurdo Country Club will be ready when I arrive. Greens might be slick.

CARNEY: Sir, some actions you've described to me may appear to others as signs of weakness.

OBAMA: Jay, if no one considers us a threat, why would anyone threaten us? Fact is, we are the world's foremost importer, with over 300 million voracious consumers. Anything jeopardizes our economy, the whole world goes belly up. So, mess with us, and fifty countries are on your case.

MICHELLE: By the way, I want to visit Costa del Sol one more time before the Russians take over. You hear me, Barack?

LIVE, FROM THE CABINET ROOM, THE CHIEF EXECUTIVE BROADCASTING SYSTEM PRESENTS *THE CEBS NIGHTLY NEWS WITH JAY CARNEY*

CARNEY: Good evening. Our lineup tonight:

*The economy resurgent—unemployment drops to 18.4% as all signs point to a robust recovery.

*Border wars—federal marshals raid Arizona police station to free undocumented border jumpers detained by Arizona officers.

*Finally, Michelle Obama has chosen sculptor Leif Bjornson to add the president's image to Mount Rushmore.

More on those stories a bit later. First, a live interview with President Obama. Thanks for taking the time to talk with us, sir.

OBAMA: My pleasure, Marv. It's a great opportunity for me to speak directly to the American people about college hoops without the media filter.

CARNEY: Uh, sir, I'm Jay, Jay Carney, your Press Secretary? You're speaking with Marv Albert later tonight.

OBAMA: Ah, just messin' with ya, Jay. Shoot. [to Secret Service detail] Easy, guys.

CARNEY: Sir, despite your arguments to justify making America a former superpower, polls show voters still believe we're headed in the wrong direction. What do you say to those people?

OBAMA: I say, "You don't understand"; I say, "I'm on your side"; I say, "Limbaugh, Beck, Levin, Coulter, Hannity and the rest of the loony right are deliberately misrepresenting what I'm really all about." Because if that got out, Jay, their audience would be gone in a flash.

CARNEY: Please explain, sir.

OBAMA: The knock on me is I seek redistribution of wealth—you know, "From each according to his ability, to each according to his need." The right's been pushing that canard since before I became president.

In fact, the opposite is true. I'm not interested in redistributing wealth. I want to *destroy* it. Why? To force Americans to become leaner, harder, and more self-reliant so they'll be better prepared for the hardships which lie ahead.

CARNEY: You don't want everyone's quality of life to be equal?

OBAMA: Yes, I do. Equally *hard.* You see, Jay, the only way Americans will understand government is not the answer is to *make* it the answer. To paraphrase Marx, the sweetest sound of all is the crumbling of your countrymen's certainties.

CARNEY: Karl Marx?

OBAMA: Groucho. Jay, civilizations are like people: they're born, reach maturity, age, then die. One thing great cultures have in common before they become terminal: abundance. Look around you. Our country is so rich its poor are obese. An ominous sign.

CARNEY: I think I understand. Before you were elected, Americans were fat and happy, oblivious to history bearing down on them like a bullet train. Now we're all spooked, we're wondering if the economy's going to implode, if the North Koreans will lob one at Manhattan.

OBAMA: Exactly, Jay. To weather this existential crisis, stave off the long, slow slide into oblivion, perhaps even emerge from the experience revitalized, we must become hungry and fearful, like the least of the nations that envy us now. As the sage opined, "Strive to be one of the many; being one of the few, eschew."

CARNEY: God bless you, sir.

OBAMA: It was a quotation, Jay. Know the author?

CARNEY: Uh, Sun Tzu?

OBAMA: David Carradine. Remember, Caine in *Kung Fu*?

CARNEY: Sure. So, you're promoting a nanny state to wreck the economy in order to spark a new American Revolution?

OBAMA: Essentially, yes. In the Forestry service, they call it a "controlled burn." Devastation, but from the ashes, growth. Couple hundred years, we take our place on the world stage again, stronger than ever.

CARNEY: Sir, I must say, you're talking straighter to the American people than any president has since Lincoln. Why now?

OBAMA: The polls, Jay.

CARNEY: "America chooses decline." Sir, are Pelosi and Reid on board?

OBAMA: Yes, except the part about our resurgence. Philosophical differences there.

CARNEY: Some will call you a visionary, sir. But extremists in both parties will make trouble for you.

OBAMA: What happens, happens, Jay. "In dreams begin prosecutions." Fitzgerald.

CARNEY: F. Scott?

OBAMA: Patrick.

[enter First Lady]

MICHELLE: Hey, I need the Cabinet Room in five minutes for my Alinsky breakout session. You hear me, Barack?

LIVE, FROM THE WHITE HOUSE MOVIE THEATER, THE CHIEF EXECUTIVE BROADCASTING SYSTEM PRESENTS *THE CEBS NIGHTLY NEWS WITH JAY CARNEY*

CARNEY: Good evening. On our broadcast tonight:

*Voters heard—Congress unanimously passes tern limits, setting seasonal daily bag at ten.

*Gimme shelter—Hovel-ready projects to provide corrugated cardboard dwellings for urban homeless.

*Finally, Gray Lady Gray—the *New York Times* to boost circulation with Sunday photo feature, "Op-Ed Beauties—Babes of the *Times*."

Those stories and more later. First, former presidential advisor David Axelrod joins us unwillingly from Chicago shortly after former Illinois governor Rod Blagojevich's reported disappearance following his pardon by President Obama. Welcome, sir.

AXELROD: Thanks for forcing me to come on, Jay.

CARNEY: "Hovel-ready" homes for inner-city street people. Whose idea was that?

AXELROD: Mine, actually, Jay. I told the corrugated cardboard CEOs, this is a windfall for you, and I expect a hefty donation to the DNC. You decline, I reach out to the Chinese drywall barons and offer the same deal. They came around.

CARNEY: Any word on Blagojevich, David?

AXELROD: Who?

CARNEY: Never mind. Rumor is the Obamas will spend the entire summer on Martha's Vineyard. True?

AXELROD: Yes, Jay. With state-of-the-art communications, the president can avoid his responsibilities wherever he is.

CARNEY: Millions of Americans are suffering while he parties. Doesn't it look bad?

AXELROD: No. Sequestration's affected the Obamas, too. They're serving wagyu burgers instead of *wagyu* steaks at White House barbecues. Also, Mrs. Obama gave her sushi chef the day off last week after she cancelled the Air Force's morning Bluefin Tuna flight from Tokyo.

CARNEY: You've said publicly the First Couple must live like regular people in Washington.

AXELROD: Yes. I told the Obamas to cut back on restaurant outings that shut down entire cities; eat in with a few dozen friends and watch films in their simple thirty seat theater like ordinary Americans on a budget; and postpone commissioning a new presidential yacht until the president's third term.

CARNEY: Ooh, bet he balked there.

AXELROD: The "common man" meme is necessary if we're going to repeal the 22nd amendment limiting the president to two terms, Jay. He has to seem like a regular guy.

Next week, he and vice president will begin painting the North Portico.

CARNEY: Painting, as in ladder and brush?

AXELROD: Correct. There's more. For his meeting with the Canadian prime minister in Ottawa in late September, the president's booked on Jet Blue, economy class, into Detroit. After a layover, he'll fly to Ottawa on a ten seat "puddle jumper." I advised him to bring a snack.

CARNEY: His entourage is huge. How are they all going to fit into a small plane?

AXELROD: All are travelling on Air Force One. Remember, they're not the ones with a PR problem.

CARNEY: I imagine the First Family will take fewer vacations to exotic locales from now on and visit Camp David more often.

AXELROD: Afraid not, Jay. Camp David's been shuttered until the president's numbers hit 50%. I've always felt the retreat looked like some Russian Czar's country dacha. That won't play right now.

CARNEY: Pretty gloomy.

AXELROD: Well, here's something positive: next month we're running a "Meet-President-Obama-for-a-Thursday-lunch-on-the-Truman-Balcony" national lottery. Anyone who's been in the U.S. at least a week is eligible.

CARNEY: This is good news?

AXELROD: Yes. Blows Biden's regular Thursday lunch with the president out of the water. Joe can buy a ticket like anyone else if he wants a shot at keeping his spot.

CARNEY: I see. Let me quiz you on several unrelated matters. Word's out the First Lady is converting the Eisenhower Executive Office Building to condos for her relatives. Is this so?

AXELROD: It is, Jay. The president complains he can't take a step without tripping over one of her cousins in the Residence. When the issue of the EEOB comes up, we say, "historic restoration" and leave it to the press corps not to report the rest.

CARNEY: How's the president's blind trust doing?

AXELROD: Very well, and thanks for asking, Jay. I'm always telling him moving his portfolio to gold just before being elected in 2008 was prescient. Who says he doesn't understand the market? There's a reason he got into Punahou.

CARNEY: Gold took a big hit recently, sir.

AXELROD: I heard his portfolio managers got him out of gold a couple days before the bottom dropped out. Luck of the Irish.

CARNEY: Irish?

AXELROD: We'll, his name *is* O'Bama.

CARNEY: Finally, Iran. Our sources tell us the Iranians already possess one Hiroshima-level bomb which now sits atop a missile aimed at Tel Aviv.

AXELROD: The president is aware of the intelligence, Jay. I can assure the American people our forces in the region are prepared to act the instant the Commander-in-Chief issues orders.

CARNEY: Giving the lie to wingnuts who say he hasn't the moxie for preemption.

AXELROD: That's right. We will not hesitate to attack Israel's air force should Netanyahu decide to hit Iran before diplomacy has run its course. Which could take decades. Centuries, even.

CARNEY: Dangerous times. David Axelrod, please come again. *Inshallah*, as the president is fond of saying.

AXELROD: *Inshallah*, to you too, Jay. And get used to it.

CHAPTER 9: SHILLS

WIKILEAKS DOCUMENT DUMP TARGETS LIBERAL MEDIA

Washington Times — Off-the-record exchanges and thousands of confidential e-mails dating back six years reveal high-profile journalists aiding and advising President Obama since he announced his candidacy in early 2007.

The material was originally discovered by a cleaning lady at *CNN*. Surfing on Wolf Blitzer's computer during her 4:00 a.m. break, Emalina Ortiz inadvertently opened a window to "BO-WeServe"—a private forum for journalists supporting Obama's campaign and, later, his administration's agenda.

Shocked by what she read, Ortiz impulsively copied the archives to a flash drive she carried on her keychain and mailed it to WikiLeaks' Julian Assange, a man she had heard Blitzer describe in his broadcasts as "a hero, someone who is not afraid to shine a light into the sewer to see what's floating around down there."

Spokesmen from the *New York Times*, the *Washington Post*, *ABC*, *CBS*, *NBC*, and *CNN* blasted Assange for exposing communications linking Obama's rise and governance to support from and tutelage by some of the biggest names in journalism.

In a brief phone interview, *Times* Executive Editor Jill Abramson railed: "The cheeky sumbitch actually asked me if I wanted to break the story. Advised me to run it with a 'Who watches the watchers?' angle. What the hell's the matter with Assange? He knows the drill: we're leaked *to*, not *on*. Only the *Times* destroys reputations with impunity and immunity. He crossed a line coming after us."

A sampling of the e-mails:

From: billkeller@TheTimesSheIsaChangin.com

To: OhMama08@IMD1.net

Date: September 19, 2007

Subject: Iraq

Stop waffling on Iraq, Senator. Raise the ante. Pledge to airlift out the entire American presence to Okinawa within two days after your oath. It'll be the Berlin Blockade in reverse, a shining example of American ingenuity. How does "Operation Iraq Excursion" sound?

From: kcouric@seebs.com

To: OhMama08@IMD1.net

Date: May 1, 2008

Subject: Hillary

Hillary's a pit bull, Senator; you're a poodle. You schmooze with a glass of Zinfandel; she throws down a shot and a beer. Change perceptions, sir. Go to a bar in Trenton, play setback with the locals, get falling-down drunk. And if you order a bitters, don't cling to it.

Also, Bill's been quiet. Get under his skin so he pops. How about a 3:00 a.m. Oval Office ad with a Hillary lookalike yelling at someone just off camera, "I warned you! Starting Monday, all the interns will be male."

From: Wblitzer@CdoubleN.com

To: OhMama08@IMD1.net

Date: August 24, 2008

Subject: Energy

Engineer a spike in gas prices before the election, sir. The Saudis will curtail production on request. They'll want a *quid pro quo*. Promise you'll support the construction of a major mosque somewhere in Manhattan.

Also, McCain's getting mileage from the goofy $300 million "better car battery" contest he's proposing. Trump him: offer $500 million tax-free to whoever discovers how to turn seawater into gasoline. God forbid someone actually does it.

To: OhMama2012@IMD1.net

From: Bwilliams@ZenBC.com

Date: August 18, 2009

Subject: Democrats' Resistance to Jettisoning Public Option

Pelosi and Reid are playing power games, sir. Short term, push back; long term, throw them under the bus by usurping their roles.

Run for your old Senate seat next year. Grab Emanuel's House seat as well.

Once elected, use presidential influence to replace Reid as Majority Leader and Pelosi as Speaker. Then, citing Executive Imperative, waive the rule you must be on the floor to vote.

A guy in Legal says nothing in the Constitution prevents you from holding multiple offices and chewing gum at the same time.

Yes, the wingnuts will scream "power grab!" So what? Use the Trinity analogy to muddy the waters: explain you'd be, simultaneously, one politician in three persons and three politicians in one person. Let the Constitutional theologians sort it out.

From: CgibsonAB@Sea.com

To: OhMama2012@IMD1.net

Date: November 1, 2009

Subject: Iran

You are a wuss on Iran, sir. Everybody just laughs when you say, "All options are on the table." The only things on the table are your elbows. Time to get tough.

Pistachios are a major cash crop for the country. Levy a 30% tariff on their pistachio exports to the U.S. Kick 'em in the nuts.

From: Dmilbank@wishywashypost.com

To: OhMama2012@IMD1.net

Date: November 23, 2010

Subject: TSA

The TSA is ticking everyone off, sir, and you're paying the price. Reduce public frustration by allowing every tenth passenger an aggressive pat down of a gender-of-their-choice TSA agent.

Scrap the air marshal program to cut costs. Instead, order DOJ lawyers to deputize and brief passengers before takeoffs on rules of engagement with suicide bombers.

In Part 2 of *New WikiLeaks Document Dump Targets Liberal Media*, BO-WeServers discuss the people's right to remain ignorant.

DAN RATHER TAPPED TO HEAD NEWSPAPER RELIEF AGENCY

Washington, D.C. *(Reuters)*—To preserve the nation's access to free, filtered information, President Barack Obama named Dan ("Kenneth, what is the frequency?") Rather to head the administration's Newspaper Relief Agency.

Mr. Obama introduced Rather as America's first "Dead Tree Press Czar" at an unannounced briefing last night in the White House sub-basement. As DTPC, Rather will dispense no-string grants to failing liberal newspapers.

In a statement, the president said, "Democratic house organs and their veteran journalists must not be allowed to disappear simply because they've lost the public's trust. The science is settled, and the time to act is now." For his part, Rather insisted the NRA would not cost taxpayers a dime:

> The NRA has no budget. George Soros will fund the agency's operations from some loose change he found in his tux. My job is to assess the needs of publications like the *New York Times* and assign federal paper pushers to run them at a loss indefinitely. Mr. Soros wants what the president and I want: to preserve the storied tradition of print journalists committed to getting the story right and turning it left.
>
> Selected newspapers will actually see a dramatic increase in circulation even as advertisers desert them and revenue falls. No watching the bottom line anymore, so we'll tell 'em, 'Give it away.' Starting next week, a free copy of the *Washington Post* will be delivered to every home, college dormitory room, and occupied cardboard box in the metropolitan Washington area. People might be scrounging for scraps in trash bins, but they'll have access to Krugman, Dowd, and Robinson.

Asked to explain the criteria by which newspapers are chosen for resuscitation, Rather replied cryptically, "My Uncle Bill, a West Texas cowman tough as an armadillo wearing a Kevlar vest, once told me, 'Dan, when you got live fish in the barrel, bonk the puny ones and chum 'em up for the others 'fore you go back to the bait store.'"

Speaking on condition of anonymity, *Times* publisher Arthur 'Pinch' Sulzberger told reporters he's thrilled Mr. Obama and Mr. Soros are "pulling my nuts out of the fire." Sulzberger praised Obama's choice of Rather to lead the agency, saying, "For g-d-fearing newsmen like me, it's Festivus in April. Dan's a guy who understands you put your story out there before the truth can get its pants on.

"My goal is not to inform our readers but to shape their opinions," Sulzberger continued. "We're on the same page as the NRA: as long as the *Times* continues fabricating, distorting, and omitting news in service to this administration, we'll be all right. Well, except for Douthat, our token op-ed conservative, and the ombudsman. They're toast. David Brooks, we'll keep. He shows promise. I think Jayson Blair deserves another shot, too."

A spokesman for Mr. Soros acknowledged the financier's participation in the relief effort and previewed for reporters a thirty-second spot that will begin running this week in New York, Chicago, and Los Angeles.

In hunting garb, Soros is shown striding on the African savannah. He spots a bull elephant about to charge, raises his CZ-550 big game rifle, and drops the beast with one shot. Then, looking straight into the camera, he says, "My name iss George Soros, und I am za NRA."

IN AN ALTERNATE UNIVERSE: ANCHORS AWAY [SIC]

SCOTT PELLEY: We've never been used this way before. The White House called today and gave me a list of stories they do not want covered tonight. Told me to remember the *AP*.

BRIAN WILLIAMS: Once upon a time it was collaborative. Now, they don't even trust us to spin anything correctly. Rachel Maddow was just appointed *Nightly News* Managing Editor. And she reports to Jay Carney.

BOB SCHIEFFER: During the third presidential debate, I was "directed" to ask Romney if he had any concerns about a Mormon in the Oval Office who is subject to his church's elders.

WILLIAMS: Candy Crowley told me she was ordered to set Romney up or she'd be a stringer in Nairobi.

DIANE SAWYER: Wasn't so long ago they rolled over in the morning, kissed us, and said they still respected us. Now, well. They trash Woodward just for fun. The right is right: Obama's an egocentric narcissist who doesn't know he's in over his head.

PELLEY: Or worse: he knows exactly what he's doing.

WOLF BLITZER: I've come to realize the president's a bully at home and a cupcake abroad. I'm tired of sucking up to him.

JIM LEHRER: Same here. Look, we're all progressives, but it's way past time we put patriotism before ideology and journalistic integrity before bootlicking. So, what do we do?

PELLEY: We get our reputations back. Instead of shaping the news on our evening broadcasts and specials, we start reporting it and let the chips fall.

WILLIAMS: Yes, like Bret Baier does on *Fox News* and Hume before him. I'm in. I'm doing a live interview with the president when he returns from his trip to the Far East. I'll ask why he took half Washington's population on his Asian sojourn.

PELLEY: Watch your back, Brian. Someone spotted Olbermann lurking around Rockefeller Plaza. These days, the worst person in the world is anyone with a job. I wouldn't go to the restroom without an escort.

SAWYER: I'll do a *20/20* segment on "All the President's Men." First up: Axelrod and his honorary membership in Russia's Politburo.

Another thing: *ABC* did Speaker Boehner wrong when they withdrew their invitation to him to appear on *This Week*. I'm on *The View* next Thursday to talk about the politics. I'll invite Boehner to come along as my companion. After everybody walks off the set, he can say whatever he wants.

BLITZER: Three House Democrats told me they were waterboarded by Emanuel until they promised to vote "yes" on ObamaCare. All lost their seats and are mad as hell. I'll interview them on *The Situation Room*.

PELLEY: Biden's my guest on *60 Minutes* this week. He gets the Sarah Palin treatment. Jim, what about you?

LEHRER: Hmm. I'll assemble a panel of experts to explain the role of mortgage derivatives in the . . .

ALL: Jim!

LEHRER: All right, all right. Barney Frank is scheduled to come on next week to discuss his former role as Ranking Member of the House Financial Services Committee. Instead, I'll lead with the Fannie Mae and Freddie Mac debacle and trap him into going toe-to-toe with surprise guest Paul Ryan over who's to blame.

PELLEY: Ryan's a tough cookie, Jim, but Barney will cut him off whenever Ryan starts to hit home.

LEHRER: No problem. I'll have Frank on a satellite feed. He gets his say, and when it's Ryan's turn, Barney's picture blanks out and his mic fails. He'll interrupt and filibuster into dead air while Ryan takes chunks out of him.

WILLIAMS: Just reflecting a little. Back in 2007, I slipped up one day and stated publicly, "Good news is not news." Those were the days when we thought a journalist's highest calling was keeping Bush's poll numbers down.

BLITZER: So Obama gets in and we spend our time operating on the principle bad news is not news in order to keep his numbers up. Ladies and gentlemen, we have been flaming hypocrites. Time to make amends.

SAWYER: Agreed. Back to good old-fashioned reporting, not spinning.

BLITZER: Join hands. Let's remember what Benjamin Franklin wrote in 1776: "We must, indeed, all hang together, or most assuredly we shall all hang separately."

[Williams' cell rings]

WILLIAMS: Hello. Starting when? Who? Figures. Thanks, Bill. [hangs up] One of my sources in the upper echelons. They got wind about this meeting. Beginning Wednesday, *NBC Nightly News* is on a two minute tape-delay. It begins.

JESSE JACKSON, 'PINCH' SULZBERGER CHANNEL ROBERT FROST ON *A PRAIRIE HOME COMPANION*

Washington Times—An anonymous source has provided the *Times* an audio tape of a special *Prairie Home Companion 2012* election night special that was never broadcast.

In a note accompanying the tape, the source identifies himself as an employee of Prairie Home Companion Productions. He claims the show was recorded on election eve, when it was widely expected President Obama would lose his bid for reelection.

Transcript follows:

Tuesday, November 6, 2012

Garrison Keillor Presents

A Prairie Home Companion Special Election Night Poetic Commentary

Reverend Jesse Jackson and *New York Times* Publisher Arthur 'Pinch' Sulzberger

Invoke the Bard of New England

With the Frost There Comes a Thumpin'

First Reading

"Sobbing in the 'hood on Election Evening"

(Apologies, "Stopping by Woods on a Snowy Evening")

Recited by the Reverend Jesse Jackson

These exit polls portending woe
Don't mean that I'll be eating crow.
I warned him, made it crystal clear
The race was always his to blow.
His counselors must think I'm seer
Because I said he'd lose last year
When all he prized was Kobe steak
And flailing at that little sphere.
My urban base is stunned awake;
What will the new Man give—or take?
As is my wont, I'll school the bleep
And show the world he don't know Jake.
The road is twisty, hard and steep,
And Sharpton's sniffing 'round my sheep,
But I'll remain atop the heap,
But I'll remain atop the heap.

Second Reading

"The Gray Lady Shaken

(But Not Stirred)"

Recited by Arthur 'Pinch' Sulzberger, Publisher, *New York Times*

(Deepest Regrets, "The Road Not Taken")

Two men contest for the nation's good.
Just one's entitled to take the prize
And rule the land as I think he should,
Using the law, as I hope he would,
To help our side screw the other guys.
But the wrong man won, with votes to spare,
Did so even though we rigged the game,
(Quite a lot more than we usually dare)
To get what we believe is our fair share,
While doing our best to shrug off shame.

Now, I have a decision to weigh:
Steer it straight or more leftward tack.
I've given it thought; honor's in play.
So many contend we've gone astray,
Setting a course from which we can't turn back.
I shall be shaping news till I die,
Even if through a paywall fence.
What counts, how well we spin and lie,
Spotpick the "what" and omit the "why"
To ensure our readers' ignorance.

SOUTH PARK FOLLIES

DIANE SAWYER: After the blowback last time, I can't believe *South Park* did another episode satirizing Islam. How do we report it without offending Muslims?

BRIAN WILLIAMS: The same: remain neutral. Say, "In other news, *Comedy Central* pulled this week's *South Park* episode to avoid a *fatwa* issued against network executives. Next on our broadcast, etc."

SAWYER: But there's no context.

SCOTT PELLEY: Context is *Fox*'s thing.

SAWYER: Parker and Stone haven't learned anything. Mocking Islam is insane. As for us when it comes to religion, we tread carefully, except for Catholicism and Judaism.

What's your lead tonight, Brian?

WILLIAMS: A former priest who claims he facilitated an affair between two Cardinals during the papal election. All refused requests for interviews to present their side of the story.

SAWYER: Damning. Ours is an *exposé* of Catholic adoption services. The records show a disproportionate number of children placed in America go to couples who are in the top 25% of income.

The agencies deliberately discriminate against people who can't support the child. Can you imagine?

WILLIAMS: And they call themselves Christians. Sorta like Fannie Mae or Freddie Mac saying, hey, no American dream for you: we're not going to help you buy a house you can't afford.

What's up at *CBS* tonight, Scott?

PELLEY: "Celibate Nuns: A Vanishing Breed."

SAWYER: I'll say. Who's on *Meet the Press* Sunday, Brian?

WILLIAMS: Round table: Ahmadinejad, Kim Young-un, and Putin will argue that freedom of speech is overrated.

SAWYER: Who's on the other side?

WILLIAMS: There's another side?

CHAPTER 10: ASK ME NO QUESTIONS

OBAMA WAR ROOM: WHAT IF THE PRESIDENT GAVE A NEWS CONFERENCE AND NOBODY CAME?

JAY CARNEY: You haven't had a prime time news conference in quite a while, sir. Now, with Texas seceding and unemployment at 23%, well, whispering's started you're afraid to face reporters.

OBAMA: Hey, I've done plenty of one-on-ones recently: Rachel Maddow, Scott Pelley, SpongeBob Squarepants, Charlie Jones at KJIV TV in Idaho Falls . . .

DAN PFEIFFER: Not good enough, sir. You need to show the national media some leg. Fortunately, Carney's press corps bunnies still don't understand you loathe them.

VALERIE JARRETT: They think it's unrequited love.

CARNEY: And they're desperate for face time on national TV. Today, the correspondents made an offer: consent to do a nighttime presser, and they'll ask the questions we give them and pledge not to follow up.

JARRETT: Jay, those *are* the ground rules now.

CARNEY: I reminded them, and they came back with this: one presser in exchange for three "escape-from-the-pool-so-the-president-can-play-golf-in-peace" passes.

JOE BIDEN: The Carney Man's right, Boss. I know you don't wanna breathe the same air as those boobs, so how 'bout some kinda compromise?

MICHELLE: Listen up, Barack: conduct the first presidential telepresser from Camp David. Correspondents gather in the East Room, as usual, but they address questions to your image on a monitor. A feed from Aspen Lodge shows you sitting in a wing chair by a blazing fire, confident and in command of the answers you're reading from a teleprompter off camera.

OBAMA: I like the visuals, dear. But I want the media at another level of remove.

Jay, set up worktables instead of chairs in the East Room. Before the questioning begins, instruct participants to place their laptops on assigned tables, with screens facing my monitor and displaying reporters' photos. They exit and assemble in the briefing room.

JARRETT: I see where you're going with this, sir. The news conference starts, and cameras pan the venue. Your live image on the giant monitor in front dwarfs the ghost-in-the-machine faces on the laptops. You call on a reporter; the camera zooms in on his laptop photo while his disembodied voice asks a question piped in from the press room. You answer looking like Zeus on Olympus.

BIDEN: Man, I dunno. What journalist with a shred of self-respect would go for that?

PFEIFFER: Attention paid to them by this president on national TV trumps self-respect.

CARNEY: Jake Tapper and Ed Henry will balk.

OBAMA: They're getting on my nerves. When I fly to Oslo next week, throw them off the plane—after it's airborne.

CARNEY: Sir, the news conference. Let's do it this Fri . . .

OBAMA: No, Thursday. The White Sox are playing the Mets Friday night.

CARNEY: So, you open with a twenty minute statement on Bush's culpability for North Korea's invasion of South Korea. Then take a question on the solar home heating mandate and another on our progress in ensuring that civil authorities will never run out of ammunition. Close by bantering a little with Helen Thomas's doppelgänger. They'll eat it up.

MICHELLE: I won't go to Camp David unless our chef comes too. You hear me, Barack?

CARNEY MAN

JAY CARNEY: Several announcements before I begin today's briefing. I've been working with former Press Secretary Bob Gibbs to become more abrasive and condescending. Please bear with me while I redefine my relationship with you all.

Now, new rule starting tomorrow: one question per correspondent to be submitted a week in advance. No follow-ups. Next, I want a better tone from you people. Dis me and I'll come down on you like ten tall buildings. You may consider that a threat.

Okay, I see Madeleine's visiting us from the Great Beyond. You go first, girl.

HELEN THOMAS: It's Helen Thomas, Ray. Will you ask the Secret Service to eject us if we press you on the administration's evasions and lies?

CARNEY: No, and the question offends me, Muriel. Security! Escort Ms. Albright to the time-out room. Um, Jack?

JAKE TAPPER: I'm Jake, Jay. You just told Helen no one would be ejected from the briefing.

CARNEY: I said the Secret Service wouldn't do it. You'll notice the men dragging Helen out now are wearing SEIU tees. They're volunteers, ordinary thugs giving back to their country.

Next, uh, Captain?

MAJOR GARRETT: Uh, Major, Jay. So, you won't be answering questions for a week. What do we do in the interim?

CARNEY: You'll attend mandatory seminars by Professor Gibbs, such as, "Don't Ask, 'Cause We Won't Tell," "Innocuous Correspondents' Questions for Dummies," and "Dodge Ball."

Let's wrap up. You there, Mick.

MARK KNOLLER: Mark. Jay, Attorney General Holder said he personally Mirandized Osama bin Laden's dead body. True?

CARNEY: Eric Holder's job is difficult, and we should all be grateful for his efforts to run the truth to ground and then kick it in the head so it stays down.

KNOLLER: Has the president ever talked with the AG about how the DOJ planned to find those the White House hasn't authorized to leak highly sensitive information?

CARNEY: The president talks with many people every day.

KNOLLER: C'mon, why won't . . . ?

CARNEY: You got your answer, Mike. Now, back off or get out. One more. Rachel?

SPEAK SOFTLY TO ME

The White House
Office of the Press Secretary
For Immediate Release
Press Conference by the President
Fort Belvoir Golf Club Locker Room
1:03 p.m. EDT

THE PRESIDENT: Good afternoon. As you can see, we're trying something different today. You're in the White House Briefing Room looking at a monitor, and I'm here at the club. Jay thought things would be more pleasant if he put some distance between me and all you bird dogs.

Anyway, I just finished eighteen holes and figured I'd do another presser to light a fire under McConnell and Boehner. Also, I have several announcements to make before I evade your questions.

First, the putt I made on #3 had to be at least forty feet and I . . .

JAY CARNEY: Sir.

THE PRESIDENT: Oh. Sorry, Jay.

You're all aware Republicans refuse to raise taxes on entrepreneurs who selfishly exploit the system to create non-green businesses for profit. My pleas to House Speaker Boehner to punish these start-ups—uh, I mean upstarts—for chasing and catching their dreams instead of saving the planet have been rebuffed. I am still hopeful we can resolve this issue my way in a bipartisan fashion.

Next Wednesday I'll be conducting a televised "Conversation with Older Americans" in senior centers and convalescent homes across the country. Attendance is mandatory for those on Social Security, except for individuals not expected to live through November 2014.

160

The program begins with a Steven Spielberg short film, "Ryan's Hauteur," about a prideful Republican's obsession to kick the canes down the road and watch old folks topple over.

Finally, I'm happy to report talks with Iranian fanatics on the proposed "Iran-U.S. Mutual Defense Pact" are complete. Iran has agreed to come to our aid if we're attacked by a non-Muslim state, and we'll come to their aid if they're attacked by a Jewish state. I consider this arrangement a personal matter and will not be submitting it to the Senate for ratification.

That concludes my prepared remarks. Unfortunately, there's no time left for me to take questions, so . . . [mugs] haa, just messing' wit' y'all.

[looking at list]

Let's see. Chuck, Chuck Todd, *NBC News*. Hey Jay, how far could you chuck Todd if I ordered you to? Never mind. All right, hit me, Chuck.

Q: Thank you, Mr. President You said the other day Social Security checks might not go out if Republicans continue to obstruct your efforts to make the IRS an arm of the Democratic Party.

THE PRESIDENT: Chuck, Chuck, Chuck, that's the least of it. Inmates will be released from maximum security prisons and violate old ladies in the street; seniors will be removed from nursing homes and deposited with relatives; nuclear submarines will be scuttled at sea; toilet paper will become more valuable than gold; and the Almighty will descend from heaven and judge the wicked. I'll assist Him.

All these things Republicans unleash on us if they don't give in, especially on confiscatory gun control and taxation. There's nothing I can do, aside from ensuring Fort Belvoir Golf Club remains a sanctuary.

Okay, now we'll go to, uh, Carlos Estrada, *El Paso Times*. Where is he? Go ahead, Carlos. Remember, no shouting.

Q: Thank you, Mr. President. Sir, communities all along the Rio Grande are pleading for more agents to patrol the border. Governor Perry of Texas said recently you won't act because you don't like him or his state. True?

THE PRESIDENT: No, Carlos. In fact, this morning, I asked Homeland Security to order Border Patrol clerical personnel in the El Paso office to spend one afternoon a month in the field. Proving, I might add, that despite what Boehner and McConnell say, I support lower Texas.

Q: But questions remain, sir, about your commitment to the integrity of our . . .

THE PRESIDENT: I know, I know. Let me tell you something. Last week I directed the Department of Justice to file an *amicus* brief supporting Oregon's claim that Washington State is unlawfully diverting the Columbia River to water Washington croplands. As I have said repeatedly, and as my action demonstrates, I oppose illegal irrigation.

Next, um, Sunni Uplands, *Berkeley Free Press*.

Q: Thank you, Mr. President. Do you approve of Attorney General Holder's handling of the "Fast and Furious" debacle? Is he following your orders?

THE PRESIDENT: I haven't spoken to Eric Holder since last fall, Sunni. He may well be doing what I want. Otherwise, I won't comment on the investigation until the DOJ Inspector General clears me of any impeachable offense.

Now we'll go to Rachel Maddow, *MSDNC News*

Q: Sir, should Justice Elena Kagan recuse herself when the Patient Protection and Affordable Care Act comes up before the Supreme Court again this fall?

THE PRESIDENT: This may surprise some people, but my answer is yes. I want a clean vote, which I believe will favor the government's position. A lingering controversy over the decision serves no one.

Q: You're surprisingly sanguine about the outcome, sir. Would your attitude relate to Senator Reid's statement today that he's discovered additional "no" votes in the trunk of his car voiding the Roberts and Alito confirmations?

THE PRESIDENT: No connection, Rachel.

Last question, um, Weather Guy Al Roker. Where are you, Big Al? Am I going to get wet if I play another nine? Remember your *Depends* today?

Q: You're good until 5:00, sir. And yes sir, I did; that's the straight poop.

Washington is buzzing about a strange scene which took place at the Whole Foods Market on P Street this morning: a half dozen Vatican Swiss Guards in full regalia accompanying the First Lady into the store. Can you explain?

THE PRESIDENT: Miscommunication, Al. Secretary of State Kerry overheard Michelle telling me the other day that she needed to go to Whole Foods to get some Swiss chard. Things just snowballed from there.

JAY CARNEY: Thank you, Mr. President.

LET'S PLAY SOFTBALL

CHRIS MATTHEWS: Tonight, we're in the White House with President Barack Obama.

OBAMA: Hello, Chris. Hey, you ever see someone about your ADHD problem?

MATTHEWS: Too busy.

I criticized you pretty harshly a while back, Mr. President, and you were angry with me. But you came on anyway. I'd like to kiss and make up.

OBAMA: [to SS agents outside camera range] Kneecap him if he gets closer than two feet.

MATTHEWS: Sir, rumor is you cut your Asian trip short to conduct emergency meetings with your economic advisors.

OBAMA: Not true, Chris. I returned earlier, but for a more important reason than rescuing our economy: word reached me about an NBA lockout next season and I wanted to nip that possibility in the bud.

MATTHEWS: What's going on?

OBAMA: Hush-hush summit at Camp David last weekend with team owners. Colin Powell and Al Sharpton were my lead mediators. Kobe Bryant and David Stern represented their constituents.

MATTHEWS: Any luck, sir?

OBAMA: We kept the owners locked up in Laurel Lodge while the other principals went at it elsewhere. Sharpton and Bryant hashed things out in Dogwood while Powell and Stern went head-to-head in Rosebud. The four met and agreed on terms. All concerned parties will meet Saturday in the Conference Room.

MATTHEWS: Participants?

OBAMA: Me, my mediators, the Commissioner, owners, player reps, lawyers, team mascots, and beer vendors

MATTHEWS: The program?

OBAMA: I'll host a nationally televised bilateral ceremony in the Presidential Cabin, Aspen Lodge. The opposing parties agree to terms and declare a truce, guaranteeing a full season beginning this fall. People may not have jobs, but they won't be denied their pro basketball fix while I'm president.

MATTHEWS: A real coup, sir. Um, are you aware the *AP*'s reporting today that you asked Bill Ayers to serve as a Cabinet-level children's advocate? Odd, since Ayers has been on your case lately.

OBAMA: Sure, Chris. We knew weeks ago the *AP* was taking an interest.

Well, you won't be hearing any more from Bill about me. He's charged with ensuring kids use their school-day down time wisely by teaching them how to improvise explosive devices.

MATTHEWS: A useful skill, sir.

OBAMA: He'll also browbeat principals nationwide to provide a drop-in call center where kids can come when they're free and phone area residents to remind them to vote for the Democratic candidate of their choice

In addition, Bill's also developing mandatory K-8 units on topics such as, "Students' Responsibilities to the State" and "How to Inform on Parents, Relatives, and Teachers." I've seen galley proofs of his new children's reader, *Does Your Daddy Love Obama, Does Your Momma*? Bill's confident he'll have public schools radicalized by 2016. Kids will be eating their parents' livers when he's done with them.

MATTHEWS: Two courts have ruled you abused your power by making recess appointments to the NLRB. Recess is the only way Ayers gets through. You'd defy the ruling?

OBAMA: No, Chris. Ayers' position is an educational matter. His base of operations will not be in Washington but an elementary school in Chicago. I'll appoint him one day next week during the school's, uh, recess period. Let's see Mark Levin's Landmark Legal Foundation challenge that.

MATTHEWS: Ah. Sir, the FCC suspended *Fox*'s broadcast license. Why?

OBAMA: Unlike *CBS*, *NBC*, *ABC*, and *CNN*, Roger Ailes refused my request for air time to address the country's K-8 pupils, depriving future voters of their First Amendment right to be propagandized.

MATTHEWS: Why'd he fuss over a lousy fifteen minutes?

OBAMA: Actually, Chris, I'm spending a half hour every Tuesday morning talking to kids in their classrooms.

MATTHEWS: Live?

OBAMA: God no. Tuesday's a golf day. As is every day. Unless it's raining. Then I tape segments for *Tuesdays with the President*. We have ten in the can already.

MATTHEWS: About what?

OBAMA: I'll chat with youngsters on topics relevant to them, such as, "Child Labor laws and Household Chores," "Gender Bias in Allowance Allocations," and, "The Previous Administration's Continuing Failures." The First Lady's taped one entitled, "Pet Nutrition: Animals Are People, too."

MATTHEWS: If teachers ignore you and continue their lessons?

OBAMA: A no-no. DNC Chair Whassupman Schultz will seed every classroom with informers, from steeped-in-the-womb progressive moppets to pre-pubescent Teamster wannabes. The balkers won't be happy with their schedules next year.

MATTHEWS: Why are you devoting so much time to kids?

OBAMA: I've lost the adults, Chris. Adolescents too, most likely. Unemployment, the national debt, sheer incompetence, scandals. According to our pollsters, however, children up to around twelve remain innocent and trusting.

MATTHEWS: So, they're your fallback constituency, a captive audience monitored by loyal Democrats and their union bosses. But sir, they can't vote.

OBAMA: Not now, Chris. Soon. Americans who've attained the age of reason yet are denied the vote represent the largest class of disenfranchised citizens in our country. We're going to correct this injustice before the next election.

MATTHEWS: Won't get through Congress, sir.

OBAMA: We're laying the groundwork for passage, Chris. When classes resume after the holidays, a reconstituted ACORN will establish APSCO chapters in every K-8 school in America.

MATTHEWS: APSCO?

OBAMA: Association of Preteen School Community Organizers. Sort of an ACORN children's auxiliary.

MATTHEWS: The goal?

OBAMA: To demand Congress pass an amendment to 1993's Motor Voter Law allowing K-8 kids to register and vote in their buildings. While Speaker Boehner laughs himself silly, Justice will file a writ with the Ninth Circuit Court of Appeals arguing the earlier legislation encompasses these rights.

MATTHEWS: Should fly with the Ninth. And Roberts will probably be your fifth vote with the Supremes. So, what then?

OBAMA: APSCO representatives from each grade will be granted release time to register their schoolmates. On Election Day, they'll escort the newly enfranchised to voting machines in the cafeteria.

MATTHEWS: You seem sure the kids will vote Democratic, sir.

OBAMA: They're just kids, Chris. Teachers will help them mark their ballots.

MATTHEWS: The return of Civics to the curriculum. Almost outta time, sir. How about I say something brief, you respond in a couple words?

OBAMA: Okay.

MATTHEWS: "Fast and Furious."

OBAMA: Past and spurious

MATTHEWS: Benghazi.

OBAMA: Loved him in *Road House.*

MATTHEWS: IRS.

HOLDER: I'm from the government and I'm here to . . . Hey, open the door!

[enter First Lady]

MICHELLE: Interview's done. *Cosmo*'s here to do a spread on you. No nudity. You hear me, Barack?

OBAMA WAR ROOM: DODGE CITY

OBAMA: Crisis after crisis. Will it ever stop? Tell me again why I wanted another term.

JOE BIDEN: You gotta finish the job makin' everybody in America equally miserable, Boss.

JACK LEW: Speaking of which, there are troubling instances of prosperity despite your best efforts to squash the recovery, sir. I recommend IRS audits to ferret out winners.

OBAMA: Make it so. Nobody should profit when people are suffering.

LEW: Is that wise, sir, with four congressional investigations of the IRS going on now?

OBAMA: No problemo. Tomorrow I'm renaming the Internal Revenue Service the American People's Collection Agency. APCA will start out with a clean slate. Order their tax exempt unit to crack down on non-progressives. Here's something they can add to their questionnaires: "How long after conception did each member of your organization feel pulled to the right?"

CARNEY: Sir, we have to get our media sycophants to come home. Make yourself more available.

OBAMA: Jay, when did I hold my last solo prime news conference?

CARNEY: I can't recall, sir. You've only done a handful since 2009.

OBAMA: A handful. Maybe six. Okay. Begin reruns next week. Space them out so they last until midterms next year. I need a breather.

BIDEN: Smart, Chief. Questions are always the same and so are your nothingburger answers. Nobody´ll notice been there, done that. Meanwhile, you´ll appear engaged.

CARNEY: By the way, sir, my Q and A tussles with reporters are getting to me. From now on I´ll make a two minute statement in the press room at noon. It´ll list on the schedule as my, uh, daily brief.

DAN PFEIFFER: Benghazi, Boston Marathon, DOJ snooping, Iran, Mali, Syria, double-dip recession, tax hikes, unemployment, deficits, ObamaCare horror stories—sir, maybe it's best you get out of town until it all blows over or people accept things as the new normal.

OBAMA: Go abroad through 2016? I don't . . .

PFEIFFER: Remember, you can´t be criticized when you´re on foreign soil.

VALERIE JARRETT: Barack, you´ve done more damage to the country in one term than you ever dreamed possible. Take a break, wind down. We can manage the decline until you get back.

OBAMA: Well, I *could* do a global golf goodwill tour, set a goal to play in every country in the world with a track. That should take about four years and give the lie to people who say I have no agenda.

BIDEN: I wouldn't leave yet, Boss, not while even Stewart and Leno are takin' shots at you. We need a major distraction.

PFEIFFER: A war between Egypt and Israel would shift focus away from you, sir.

OBAMA: True. Valerie, this is your area.

JARRETT: I'll reach out to Hillary, ask her to tell Huma to get a message to the Egyptian military: please provoke a serious but non-nuclear response from Israel. We'll intervene to force a truce in three days. Be sure they understand: we'll make up their losses, and then some. Maybe an additional half-dozen F-16s.

OBAMA: Sweeten the pot. Throw in one nuclear-tipped cruise missile preprogrammed for Tel Aviv.

JAY CARNEY: Whatever we do, we'll still get hammered for losing Egypt, sir.

OBAMA: No we won't. I'll fly over with Chris Christie when hostilities cease and survey the damage. Does FEMA possess international capabilities?

PFEIFFER: FEMA doesn't even have local capabilities, sir. Uh, why would Christie agree to go?

OBAMA: I'll ask Springsteen to do a live benefit for the Egyptian military while we're there. Christie'll host. Jeez, I hope he doesn't bear hug Bruce.

BIDEN: Hey, Chief. You still hot to make Susie Rice Roving Ambassador to the Middle East in addition to U.N. Ambassador? The Repugs are still harpin' on Benghazi, saying' she was either a dupe or a liar.

JARRETT: Well, she´s not a dupe, she was out of the loop; she´s not a liar, she was singing with the choir. And Jay, set up a meet with Sharpton, Jackson, the CBC, the *Times* editorial board, E. J. Dionne, and Maddow. Time to push the racist meme again.

BIDEN: Nice thinkin´, Val. McCain, Graham, they been all over her like, uh, like white on Rice.

OBAMA: "Like White on Rice?" Joe, you´re leaving tomorrow to attend Queen Elizabeth's funeral.

BIDEN: She´s not dead yet, Chief.

OBAMA: I want you to be on hand, just in case.

OBAMA PRESSER: IT'S THE BUDGET, BUSTER

The White House
Office of the Press Secretary
Transcript: President Obama Press Conference
East Room
8: 03 p.m. EST

PRESIDENT OBAMA: Good evening. Let me be perfectly clear: I'll make a brief statement, then take one pre-screened question.

JAY CARNEY: [from side of room] Sir, you agreed to five unscreened questions.

OBAMA: Oh, right. Everyone, a follow-up counts as a separate question. Don't screw your colleagues.

As I have said repeatedly since attending Basuki Elementary in Jakarta, America's national debt is unsustainable. My budget confronts head-on what that scrawny fella from Indiana called the new "Red Menace" during last year's campaign.

Like New Jersey's Fat Man, I understand the realities. You heard it here: OMB's first draft for FY 2014 came in at $8.7 trillion. "Unacceptable," I told them. After weeks of chainsawing through the bloat, OMB Director Sylvia Mathews finally delivered my $3.73 trillion budget.

I see some heads shaking. Look, the final product does indeed represent a savings of almost $5 trillion off the initial proposal. Extrapolating from similar budget scenarios each cycle through FY 2018, and taking into account hyperinflation and debt servicing, we stand to chop about $60 trillion in spending over the next five years. In so doing, we'll keep the deficit monster at bay a while longer.

If my budget is adopted as is, we'll continue to maintain our slow and steady spiral towards insolvency, which will happen around 2030. But if it's tampered with in any way, we risk returning to the time before FDR when "individual responsibility" was code for "Stand on your own two feet."

I promise you, no going backwards on my watch.

Okay, let's start the questioning with, uh, Jack Tripper.

Q: Jake Tapper, sir. *CNN*. Word's coming in that thousands of Muslims stormed Trafalgar Square and demanded the dissolution of Parliament and Queen Elizabeth's abdication. Your reaction?

OBAMA: I urge Prime Minister Cameron to listen to the people and begin an orderly transition to a government responsive to the desires of unassimilated British Muslims. Uh, wait a sec. [reads message on BlackBerry]

Before I say anything more, I'll want confirmation Tripper's report is accurate. CIA Director Brennan is monitoring *MSNBC* as I speak to determine what is going on across the pond. We'll keep you informed. Um, Artie Crapsinger?

Q: Martin Crutsinger, sir. *Associated Press.* A rumor's floating around you plan to chop $22 billion from Homeland Security and give it to Organizing for America to promote education in flyover states like Wisconsin. True?

OBAMA: Yes, Artie. Terrorists aren't interested in Nebraska. DHS is wasting money protecting the vast red wasteland—I mean, heartland. Yesterday, I told Homeland Security I was halving their allocation and charged her with safeguarding urban Democratic strongholds in the lead-up to November, 2014. Next question, hmm, oh, Henry?

Q: Ed Henry, sir, *Fox News.* Experts say exploitation of a newly discovered 200 billion barrel oil field in North Dakota could drive the price of gasoline down to $1 a gallon eventually, threatening your push to plug-in hybrids like the Chevy Volt.

OBAMA: I've just declared the whole area a national monument, Ned.

Q: Sir, if the field extended into Manitoba and cheap fuel from Canada floods the nation, would you raise federal gas taxes to thwart predatory underpricing?

OBAMA: No, I wouldn't, not in these difficult times. The EPA has anticipated "oversupply" scenarios. They've ordered refineries to develop costly new eco-friendly formulas for all grades. If necessary, they'll be mandated to keep pump prices hovering at $4 or more a gallon without a tax hike that would hurt the middle class. Last question goes to, um, Will Flora.

Q: Bill Plante, sir. *CBS News.* Wisconsin Governor Scott Walker said today . . .

OBAMA: Hold on, Phil. My cell's vibrating. Only three people know this number. Gotta take the call.

[steps away from the podium, whispering, unaware the mic is picking up his voice]

Hey, Sonia. How ya doin' girl? No, actually not a good time, but whassup? Another PPACA challenge? Damn. Kennedy will go with the wingnuts. I see 5-4. What? Six for a quorum? I didn't know that. Uh huh. Okay. I'll arrange it.[hangs up, dials] Michelle, set up four cots in the Residence. Kagan, Breyer, Sotomayor, and Ginsberg will be staying with us for a while. How long? Until Scalia retires. Gotta go. [hangs up]

CARNEY: Thank you, Mr. President.

DO NOT MARCH DOCILE TO OBAMA'S BEAT*

Do not march docile to Obama's beat.
Lord, help us thwart the charl'tan's goal;
Rail, rail against the gall of his conceit.

My friends, all is not lost, though time is fleet.
We must take back from him that which he stole;
Do not march docile to Obama's beat.

Wise men who stood on deck and bore the heat,
And tried to steer the country 'round the shoal:
Rail, rail against the gall of his conceit.

Cowardly men who took their pleasures neat
And bowed and scraped and did as they were told:
Do not march docile to Obama's beat.

Misguided men who worshipped at his feet,
Those drunk on rule or cozened by the dole:
Rail, rail against the gall of his conceit.

Needs must, we gather on the streets
And fight to save our country's soul.
Do not march docile to Obama's beat;
Rail, rail against the gall of his conceit.

*A takeoff of the Dylan Thomas poem, "Do Not Go Gentle into That Good Night"

CHAPTER 11: "YOU'VE GOT YOUR TROUBLES, I'VE GOT MINE"*

Roger Greenaway and Roger Cook

OBAMA WAR ROOM: SELLING IT

OBAMA: Maybe I should become less visible. The appearance on *Saturday Night Live,* that two week stint on *The View,* guesting on *The Simpsons* and *South Park*. People must be getting tired of seeing my mug whenever they turn on the TV.

JAY CARNEY: Actually, sir, better to do more media, not less. Use overexposure as a club.

OBAMA: You mean, bore them until they support my agenda just to get me out of their living rooms?

VALERIE JARRETT: Makes sense, sir. Despite your reputation for eloquence, you've a knack for putting people to sleep when you speak, especially on economic issues. Exploit that talent.

I advise weekly, prime-time Oval Office addresses devoted to topics such as auction-rate securities and collateral debt obligations.

JACK LEW: Go on Letterman, Ellen, and ESPN, sir. Pontificate professorially on credit default swaps and randomized market algorithms. Appear on *Jeopardy!* : "Mortgage-backed Derivatives for $200, Alex."

OBAMA: Book 'em, Jay! But to make Americans yell "Uncle!," I need my own gig.

MICHELLE: Host a syndicated financial game show modeled after Pat Sajak's. Jack can develop the concept. Call it *Wheel of Fortune 500*.

CHRIS MATTHEWS: Another possibility, sir: a recurring role on a soap. With everything else, no one escapes you. I'll ask a *Days of Our Lives* producer I know to write you in as a popular black president held hostage on a remote Hudson River Island by a smitten gay hedge fund manager incensed by rumors of your affection for a hunky blond MSNBC news personality who . . .

JARRETT: Can it, Tingles.

Sir, compete against your predecessors on "Survivor: Camp David." Enlist their cooperation by including a parachute jump for Bush 41; a brush-clearing contest for 43; an "Excursion to Hooters" reward for Clinton; and an Israeli-Palestinian peacemaking challenge for Carter

OBAMA: Wait, we can't forget Limbaugh. He'll see through our scheme to numb the populace into acquiescence.

ERIC HOLDER: Order the FCC to shut Limbaugh down, sir. His First Amendment rights must be weighed against the societal costs of his rants. We can expect Sotomayor's and Kagan's support when Limbaugh's challenge reaches the SCOTUS.

LEW: He won't bother. He'll go satellite, like Imus.

OBAMA: Doesn't matter. Such transmissions traverse public atmosphere, which is under the regulatory authority of my new Satellite Oversight Board.

HOLDER: There's always a drone strike.

JOE BIDEN: We're overreactin' here, Boss. All we gotta do is marginalize Limbaugh. He has, what, 600 outlets? Appropriate the other 11,000 stations and debut "The Barack Obama Show" opposite him. He's dead meat!

JARRETT: Joe comes up with something now and then, sir.

OBAMA: Head-to-head with Rush? All right, I'm in. Hmm, catchy opening music. How about Melissa Etheridge's "I'm the Only One" to remind listeners that, well, I am.

[Mimicking announcer] "And now, coming to you live from the Oval Office, the Potentate of Progressivism, the Lord of Leftists, the Duke of Demagoguery, Barrracck Hus-SEIN Obaaaama."

DAN PFEIFFER: Make the call-in number 1-800-Alinsky, sir. No screener necessary; just take calls originating in Cambridge, Berkeley, and Madison. A real cross-section of the American public.

OBAMA: Okay. No streaming or commercials. Free membership for "Hussein 24/7" members. Half-hour tape delay in case the teleprompter goes down or I want a smoke. Matthews and Maddow sub for me every other day. I need my links time.

CARNEY: Provide public service announcements at breaks, sir: "Witness Arizona police tasering a Hispanic child at an ice cream parlor? Call our hotline at the Justice Department." Or, "Spot a CEO in first class instead of coach? Secretary Lew wants to know."

OBAMA: Nice. I'll issue a directive mandating three hours daily paid leave for federal employees who want to tune in to the program. Call it "The Radio Free Choice Act."

MICHELLE: By the way, keep Monday nights free next month. We're going on *Dancing with the Stars*. You're always dancing as fast as you can, so you'll be the professional, and I'll be the *ingénue* with the beautiful bare arms. I'll lead. You hear me, Barack?

TELEPROMPTER FAIL

The White House
Office of the Press Secretary
Presidential News Conference
8:03 p.m. EDT

THE PRESIDENT: Good evening. I'm winging this one tonight with just notes because some boob loaded the wrong talking points into my teleprompter. I am not responsible for any screw-ups.

Several announcements:

Today, federal marshals delivered George W. Bush to The Hague for his war crimes trial next month. Attorney General Holder has cooperated fully with the tribunal. My message to the world: until the day I leave office, former American presidents are not above international law.

Next, I intend to sign the "Voting Booth Transparency Act" if it actually reaches my desk. If not, I'll impose it by fiat, which is legal according to a lost Amendment just discovered by Attorney General Holder.

Beginning in November, this long-overdue updating of the "Freedom of Information Act" (FOIA) rips away the veil of secrecy surrounding the act of voting. Citizens must mark and sign their ballots before witnesses, and this information becomes part of the public record.

Your friends, relatives, neighbors, union bosses, and SEIU thugs have a right to know if you voted the way they wanted you to or the way you promised you would. The days of isolated cubicles and anonymous marks on generic ballots are over.

At this time, I'd like to recognize Prince Nouria El-Aziz, my new White House Counselor on U.S./Islamic relations. [pointing]

He's the fellow in traditional Saudi dress standing against the wall next to Valerie Jarrett. [El-Aziz bows to the president; Obama bows back]

His Majesty, King Abdullah Bin Abdul-Aziz, honors me by assigning one of his 403 nephews to be his eyes and ears in the West Wing.

Now, uh, normally, I'd take two planted questions, ramble aimlessly in response, then leave.

However, the other day I received this letter from Miss Pearson's third grade class at Wilson Elementary in Boston:

[looks at sheet]

"Dear Mr. President, Some of us kids think you filibuster the first couple of questions at your press conferences to run out the clock. Others believe you're naturally long-winded. Would you settle the argument? Thanks, Billy Jankowski, Class Secretary."

In fact, Billy, you kids pegged me: both sides are right. So, tonight I think I'll shake things up by taking four questions, none of them planted. And, of course, no teleprompter.

I'll begin with, uh, [looks away, stabs finger at seating chart] Farid.

Q: Thank you, Mr. President. Farid Moradi, *Tehran Times*. Any progress in reining in Israel's nuclear weapons program?

THE PRESIDENT: Some good news. Michael Moore, my Special Envoy to the region, tells me the Iranians are so focused on building an atomic bomb, they've cut back on mischief-making in Iraq and Afghanistan.

To encourage such behavior, I've offered to share "clean nuke" technology with Iran, and the Mullahs appear receptive. This could be a breakthrough. After all, neutron bombs are good for the environment.

[stabs chart again]

Damn! Uh, Jake.

Q: Jake Tapper, *CNN,* sir. Smuggled tapes out of Iran show protestors having their eyes gouged out, fingernails pulled, and their genitals shocked with electric cattle prods. Does this bother you?

THE PRESIDENT: Jake, I will not denigrate the culture of another country's secret police. I did ask our intelligence agencies to provide evidence Iran was waterboarding. By all accounts, they prefer jet skiing, surfing, and parasailing. I don't care what they do, as long as it's not waterboarding.

Um, Martin.

Q: Martin Crapslinger, *Associated Press.* Sir, despite your best efforts, pockets of prosperity continue to exist out there. Are you going to get the IRS involved in ferreting out the winners who are not bearing their fair share of the suffering?

THE PRESIDENT: Martin, let me be frank: I will not tolerate businesses which profit at the expense of their competitors. Such behavior President Bush condoned, even as our economy sped through the last turn at 110 mph, spun out, rolled over, and sailed off the cliff into the chasm, from which my team and I are winching that baby back onto the road.

One more. Uh, Jay.

Q: Jay Nordlinger, National Review. Care for a little language, sir? Your speech mannerisms are making pundits yearn for Bush 43. How will you counter the widening perception of a presidential fluency gap?

THE PRESIDENT: I reject your premise, Jay, whatever it is. But let me be unspeakably clear: for too long, as I've said repeatedly, I've been criticized for my so-called verbal eccentricities, and yes, my advisers want me to converse like a regular guy, so I'm trying to change, but make no mistake, change isn't as easy as some folks think, it won't happen overnight, and I will not be held hostage to anyone's expectations.

Incidentally, I'll continue to say "Pockeeston" because I like the way the word rolls off my tongue. And if you hear me using the expression, "press corpse," don't assume it was an error.

JAY CARNEY: Thank you, Mr. President.

OBAMA WAR ROOM: DON'T STOP THINKING ABOUT CAMPAIGNING

OBAMA: So I told them, *"Zero Dark Thirty* is a farce; they made me a footnote. I need you guys to tell the real story."

Anyway, Lucas will produce and Spielberg will direct *Barack CoJones and the Devil's Lair,* with Denzel Washington playing me and Cat Stevens as Osama. Chuck, order SEAL Team Six released from their official duties during production to play themselves. Release date: October 2014.

KATHLEEN SEBELIUS: I'll announce healthcare waivers for Paramount, Lucasfilm Ltd., and Amblin Entertainment tomorrow morning, Mr. President.

DAN PFEIFFER: We should beef up your *macho bona fides* in the short term, sir, to keep Republicans intimidated.

VALERIE JARRETT: Tie it into family values. Visit your destitute brother in Africa and give him a few bucks. Then go into the bush without the Secret Service and kill a lion with a spear. Gutsier than Palin shooting a moose with a 30-06 at two hundred yards.

OBAMA: I'll do that once I force Netanyahu to risk national suicide for a shot at peace.

JARRETT: The vice president arrived, sir—I think.

[enter Biden wearing surgical gloves, mask, and scrubs]

OBAMA: What's with the getup, Joe? You look like you're attending an autopsy.

BIDEN: This outfit? My driver sneezed on the way over; and I saw a gate guard wipin' his nose. Maybe some contagion's goin' down. So I went right to Medical and got protection. We might hafta quarantine Washington, like FDR did in '55.

OBAMA: I'll, uh, think about it.

Joe, you're heading my Select Commission on "Kicking the Can down the Road on Iran." Where are they at right now?

BIDEN: [checks wall map] Same place as yesterday.

OBAMA: The bomb, Joe.

BIDEN: We estimate they'll have two Hiroshima-level nukes by Labor Day. Our forces in the region remain on alert and are prepared take out Israel's air force if an attack on Iran appears imminent.

JARRETT: That would certainly give the lie to wingnuts who say you don't have the guts for preemptive action, sir.

BIDEN: Hey, I gotta tinkle, Big Guy. Gimme a minute. [leaves]

PFEIFFER: Sir, now's the time.

OBAMA: I know, I know. This better work, Dan. Man's driving me crazy: calling every five minutes, waylaying me after meetings. This morning, I caught him in the Oval Office addressing the nation.

[Biden returns]

OBAMA: Joe, a special assignment for you.

BIDEN: Whassup, Boss? Wahmeeta go to Russia, straighten Putin out? Or plug my tripartite plan for D.C. to the *Post*? How 'bout a budget debate with Ryan Paul on *Meet the Press*? Just say the word.

OBAMA: None of those, Joe. Actually, I'm appointing you roving ambassador to Smalltown, USA. You'll be my, uh, what's that title I'm giving him, Dan?

PFEIFFER: *Ijit*, sir. Rhymes with widget.

BIDEN: *Ijit*?

OBAMA: It's a Native American honorific, Joe—Ojibwa, I think. Means, "simple, plain-spoken man." You'll start in Oregon and work east through election night 2014, visiting every hamlet and telling folks my plans for the country. Joe, historians will acclaim you the Obama Administration's Village *Ijit*.

BIDEN: I'm on it, Chief. I'll leave tomorrow, report in daily.

OBAMA: Godspeed, Joe. Watch your topknot out there.

Ah, he's gone. Val, tell the switchboard to shunt his calls to State. What's my schedule today?

JARRETT: You're meeting a delegation of Comanches at ten, sir. You'll present a federal eminent domain order giving back the tribe's ancestral West Texas homeland--Governor Perry's turf, incidentally. Afterwards you leave for an aerial survey of damage to golf courses in the storm-ravaged South.

PFEIFFER: Regarding your approval ratings among Hispanics, *Majestad*: they're looking at Rubio and Cruz and slipping away from our *hacienda*. Could be trouble for you in '16.

OBAMA: Time to crank up the rumor mill. Jay, ask Maddow to find a genealogist who'll swear the Rubio family's roots are Italian, not Cuban. Tell our National Council of La Raza and Reconquista contacts to push the meme. As for Cruz, let's muddy his heritage waters: release a blizzard of press releases spelling his name C-r-u-i-s-e.

JAY CARNEY: *Si, Padrone*. I'll alert the *Times* and the alphabets what we're about.

PFEIFFER: *Presidente*, Hispanics will flock to your banner if we expel *gringos* from Arizona and California and cede the states to Mexico. *Quid pro quo*: Mexico allows *Norte Americanos* reeling from the Obama economy to cross the border in search of work.

JARRETT: Naming that refitted navy minesweeper after Cesar Chavez didn't have much impact on Hispanics, *Caudillo*.

OBAMA: Get the Vatican on the horn. I'll put Chavez in for sainthood and tell Pope Francis I want it fast-tracked.

PFEIFFER: Sir, Christie appears to be getting ready to take you on next go-round. We should knock him down a peg.

JAY CARNEY: I'll commission a poll with this question: "Does Governor Christie's inability to control his weight make it more likely or less likely you'll vote for him?"

PFEIFFER: Sir, Barney Frank and his sister, Ann Lewis, are here to advise you on the housing crisis.

OBAMA: Right. Headsets on, everyone. Ms. Lewis will provide simultaneous translation.

FRANK/LEWIS: Good news, sir: foreclosures are increasing. Bad news: not fast enough. Unless we act now, no catastrophic economic event to rally the nation around you and the Party occurs before November 2014.

OBAMA: Damn! Can we accelerate the timetable for fiscal Armageddon?

FRANK/LEWIS: One possibility, sir: mandating home ownership by every citizen over 21.

OBAMA: Okay. Jack, tell banks to start lending again as if their charters depended on it. Dan, advise Fannie and Freddie to open the spigots wide, and stonewall the Inquisitors on the House Financial Services Committee.

LEW: Sir, HUD will need your Civilian National Security Force to evict non-compliants from their apartments and cardboard boxes and force them into homes.

OBAMA: Not enough units are ready. Is Blackwater still hiring out mercenaries?

[enter Michelle]

Oh, Jay, Michelle has something to say to you. She speaks for me.

MICHELLE: You're not working out, Carney. So, back to Biden you go. Word is he's leaving tomorrow on a long trip. Better get home and pack.

OBAMA: Chris Matthews, aka Tweety, will be my new Press Secretary, everyone.

MICHELLE: I still don't like the way he looks at you. Keep the door open when you're alone in a room with him. You hear me, Barack?

REPORT: FIRST LADY FILES SUIT OVER SOTOMAYOR NOMINATION

Washington (AP)—In an interview with Katie Couric this afternoon, Michelle Obama revealed she is suing the president for breach of contract over the nomination of Sonia Sotomayor to the Supreme Court in 2009.

Over hamburgers on our second date in 1990, Barack and I pledged that whoever became president would nominate the other for the first opening on the Supreme Court. Even then I knew every promise he made came with an expiration date [ht: Jim Geraghty, NRO], so I recorded the conversation, just in case.

When Barack nominated Sotomayor, I was sure we'd settle the matter. I assumed that after reminding him of our pact, he'd pull her name and nominate me. I expected Jewish and Hispanic support, as my first cousin's father-in-law was a rabbi who operated a bodega in Spanish Harlem.

The problem was, Hispanics supported him in 2008 and wanted payback. Mr. Silver Tongue confessed he was under enormous pressure to nominate one of their own. Eventually, I came around. We couldn't afford to alienate that constituency and stay in the White House for eight years or more.

I agreed to take the second appointment. I warned him there'd be no dog-and-pony show, no hearings. I'd designate one "Meet the Nominee Day" at the White House; senators would call my office to book short interviews.

He bypassed me again in 2010 and nominated Elena Kagan. My attorneys advised me to sit tight until the next opening. When Ruth Bader Ginsburg hinted she might retire before 2016, I decided to act. I *will* have her seat.

Asked about her thoughts on joining the Court, the First Lady issued a warning: "Damn tradition! No way am I going to answer the door and get coffee for old white guys. Neither should Elena. I'll demand Alito resume those duties. Thomas and Scalia fuss, I'll sue their behinds for gender discrimination, take it to The Hague if I have to.

Mrs. Obama continued, "Once I'm seated my primary goal will be to invalidate the 22nd amendment limiting First Ladies to two terms. It is an anachronism unworthy of a living Constitution."

OBAMA WAR ROOM: BRIDGE OVER TROUBLED WATERS

JAY CARNEY: Sir, word from the Senate on your American Jobs Act. Majority Leader Reid is complaining of constipation. Says he's been pushing since yesterday, but he can't pass the bill.

OBAMA: *Merde*! After I did all the heavy lifting. Damn do-nothing Congress.

VALERIE JARRETT: Good thing you're leaving the country next week, sir. No one can blame you if the measure tanks when you're abroad on official business.

OBAMA: Where am I off to?

DAN PFEIFFER: You'll begin your working tour of Scotland's golf courses on Monday, sir. Meanwhile, the First Lady and several dozen close friends and family members are already aboard the presidential yacht, Alinsky, *en route* to the Galapagos for a holiday.

OBAMA: Message her confirmation we'll rendezvous a week from Friday on the *Côte d'Azur*. When do I return home?

CARNEY: Um, we want to be flexible, Mr. President. Tell him, Poll Boy.

CHUCK TODD: Recent surveys indicate hiring spikes and an uptick in consumer confidence while you're away, sir. It's as if some great weight were lifted from . . .

OBAMA: Enough, Chuck. Add Ireland to my itinerary, Dan. Inform Michelle I'll join her on the Riviera October 1st. Eric, do you have the "Gunwalker" thing under control?

HOLDER: I believe I can stall the investigation until after you finish your third term. All bets are off if the Republicans find out about "Nukewalker."

JOE BIDEN: Hey Boss, hot off the wires: Maxine Waters slapped you upside the head today on *Good Morning America.*

OBAMA: Second time this week she's taken a chunk out of my hide. Why?

JARRETT: Word is she's ginning up a rift with you to distract attention from a new investigation into charges she owns a bank we've been propping up.

OBAMA: Oh for the love of Pete. Would she stop harassing me if I pardoned her?

ERIC HOLDER: You can't, sir. The probe is a Congressional matter involving ethics, not criminality.

OBAMA: The Ethics Committee took two years to deal with the last complaint against her. She won't let up on me until they rule on this one, which may not happen in my lifetime. I'd talk to her, but she scares me more than [whispers] Michelle.

JOE BIDEN: Here's a thought, Boss. Make her an offer she can't refuse: she resigns her seat and becomes your Special Envoy to Africa. Big staff, her own plane. She could put it on her mausoleum.

OBAMA: You're thinking Roland Burris, Joe. Still . . . Val, reach out to the lady and feel her out on Joe's suggestion. Tell her I'll throw in the Medal of Freedom.

DAN PFEIFFER: On another matter, sir: early days yet, but Rand, Christie, and Cruz are shaping up as your biggest threats in 2016. And Gingrich is making noises again.

OBAMA: I don't want to be on a stage with any of those guys. Brian, I never had a chance to ask you, but what happened in that first debate you moderated last election? Romney walked all over both us.

WILLIAMS: [defensively] I did my job, sir. The problem was *Politico*'s Harris. He was a lightweight, let himself get pushed around. Next go round I'll have Hoffa and Trumka as co-moderators. Somebody dodges a question or comes after us like Newt did, they'll break his legs.

BIDEN: Hate to be a contrarian, Chief, but Perry worries me.

OBAMA: Hmm. Texas is experiencing a rash of wildfires. How can we play the situation to our advantage?

PFEIFFER: Designate the whole state a national disaster area.

OBAMA: Don't you mean, "natural" disaster area?

PFEIFFER: No, sir. In the heat of the moment, who'll notice the substitution of "national" for "natural"? If Perry gets the nomination, we'll run ad after ad declaring that Texas was officially declared a national disaster and had to be bailed out by the federal government.

OBAMA: Good. Now, policies. Let's assess our progress. Big Oil: suspend drilling operations indefinitely over safety concern—check; Big Insurance: continue to implement ObamaCare until the industry collapses, paving the way for single payer—check; Big Pharma: price controls on all drugs to discourage research which would produce medicines prolonging life—check. What'd I leave out?

PFEIFFER: Big Farma, sir. When we control corn, soybeans, and wheat, everyone on earth will be eating out of our hands.

OBAMA: Jack, make sure our new stimulus forces funds on any agricultural entity with more than two tractors. They take government money, we own 'em.

LEW: Never get through the House, sir.

OBAMA: Congress is out of the loop on this one, Jack: TARP now means, "**T**reasury **A**ssets **R**equested by **P**resident."

LEW: We need more revenue since so many millionaires have moved to Costa Rica, sir.

OBAMA: Add a third shift to the mints to print additional greenbacks. Alert the IRS to find a loophole in the tax code allowing a surtax on registered Republicans.

What other pies can we get our finger into?

PFEIFFER: How about Hollywood, sir? Most feature films flop. The film industry could use the steady hand of government to right things.

OBAMA: Agreed. Jack, find some loose change and buy 51% stakes in the major studios. Then merge those entities into one film company called, um, DC Productions, run by the FCC in the public interest. Look into a federal takeover of Big Porno, too.

CHUCK HAGEL: [entering, breathless] Mr. President, Mr. President, Iran has launched a chemical attack on Kuwait, fired missiles at our carrier group in the Gulf, and set Iraq's oil fields ablaze. How should we respond?

OBAMA: I'll mull this overnight, maybe decide tomorrow.

PFEIFFER: Um, sir, after Benghazi . . .

OBAMA: Okay, okay. Get me Ayatollah Khamenei on a secure line right now.

Ayatollah! It's Barack. Uh, Obama. U.S. president? Peace be with you as well, sir. Yes, of course, until it isn't.

Yes, the girls are fine.

Listen, we've gotten word that . . . Oh, it was a crop duster that went off course? And those are weather balloons in the Gulf, not missiles? But Iraq . . . Ah, Greenpeace suicide bombers are blowing up the oil wells. I understand, sir. I'll tell our people to stand down.

It's a misunderstanding, everyone. He gave me assurances.

[phone rings]

CARNEY: The First Lady calling from the presidential yacht *Alinsky*, sir. On speaker.

MICHELLE: [agitated, speaking to someone in background] I don't care if they're endangered. Tell the Ecuadorians I promised a staffer I'd bring back a tortoise for her daughter's show-and-tell.

Hello, hello, am I coming in?

OBAMA: Yes, dear. Loud and clear.

MICHELLE: I just had a thought: get the Atlantis out of storage for our anniversary on October 3rd. This year, I'm in the mood for a romantic dinner above the earth and under the stars. You hear me, Barack?

SMOKE-FILLED RUMBA

DAN PFEIFFER: The delegation is here, sir.

OBAMA: All right. Bring them in. Let's get this over with.

[enter Clintons, DNC Chair Whassupman Schultz, Reid, Pelosi, Jesse Jackson, George Soros]

HARRY REID: Debbie, tell the president what you told us.

WHASSUPMAN SCHULTZ: It's finally happened after five years, sir: you're getting blamed for the state of the economy. In a telephone survey of 1000 people, 10% said they would hold their noses and vote to give you a third term; 10% complained the aides were mean, the kids never visited, and the home smelled like disinfectant; and 80% wept when they conceded they had voted for you last November.

OBAMA: Bad, yes, but still time to . . .

NANCY PELOSI: Tell him the rest, Debbie.

WHASSUPMAN SCHULTZ: The survey was limited to Democrats in Ms. Pelosi's district, sir. Of those who were deeply upset with you, 40% say they would switch parties if you ran again in 2016.

PELOSI: Obviously, they're good Democrats, sir. They've simply had it with you and unlikely to support your contention that the Framers meant the 22nd Amendment to apply only to Caucasians.

OBAMA: So, you want me to stand down and back Hillary in 2016?

WHASSUPMAN SCHULTZ: God no, sir. It'd look like we pushed you out. Poof goes the black vote. Yes, blow off the two-term limit and run, but welcome her primary challenge.

VALERIE JARRETT: Ah, I understand. He's supposed to lose gracefully, then stump for Hillary in places like Harlem, Watts, and Liberty City, where his approval rating is holding steady at 97%. I'd pass, sir.

HILLARY: Billy Jeff here broke trail for you in the 90s, Barack. "First Black President," and all. You owe us.

BILL CLINTON: True dat, man. Who's your Daddy? Hillary, she's family, bro. You cut her back in '08. She was bangin' till you come along. Wasn't right, turnin' on a sister, way you did.

HILLARY: We didn't go looking for those pictures of you campaigning for Gus Hall when he ran for president on the Communist Party ticket in '84, Barack.

BILL: Or that tape of your "Community Activists—Today and Tomorrow" speech in Havana in '88.

HILLARY: We sat on that material last time, and we'll do everything we can to keep it from seeing the light of day this time—if you work with us.

BILL: Ya got game, man, but you are so over. Pump your brakes, bro.

OBAMA: Jesse, I can't believe you're with them.

JACKSON: I'm going to be Secretary of Reparations in Hillary's cabinet, Mr. President. I'm begging you, be part of the solution to save our revolution, and I'll make restitution by spurring redistribution. Hey Carney, that's not for attribution.

WHASSUPMAN SCHULTZ: Hillary is the wife of the Man from Hope, sir. Keep hope alive.

OBAMA: You're asking a lot. Joe, this affects your plans for 2016. Any questions for Hillary?

BIDEN: Ma'am, do you think the rain will affect the rhubarb?

HARRY REID: As Orwell might say, sir: "Winning is losing."

BILL: With you as nominee, the Repugs get energized. They'll put their squabbling aside and coalesce around their candidate. A nightmare scenario for us.

GEORGE SOROS: Ya. You vill loose, und za party vill loose. I vill be oopset. It's *my* party, und I vill cry if I vant to, cry if I vant to . . .

WHASSUPMAN SCHULTZ: George is heavily invested in our success, sir.

OBAMA: What's in this for me?

REID: You don't face voters in a general election. You go out head held high, dignity intact.

PELOSI: The country's hungry for Clinton II, sir. When Hillary wins, the GOP splinters and the Tea Party goes third party. It'll take ten or twenty years for them to get their act together.

HILLARY: Meanwhile, I'd appoint you U.N. Ambassador, Federal Reserve Chairman, Disney CEO—whatever you want. How does Chief Justice of the Supreme Court sound?

WHASSUPMAN SCHULTZ: In 2024 or 2028, whenever she's decided she's had enough, you run to succeed Hillary, Mr. President, a fresh face again, with years of unaccountability behind you.

OBAMA: You seem positive Hillary would trounce me in the primaries.

WHASSUPMAN SCHULTZ: Well, we'd need your help to ensure it happens. For example, keep Biden on the ticket; play golf more often with Boehner; hold weekly self-pitying press conferences; announce everywhere you go a nuclear waste repository is under consideration for the community.

REID: The idea is to damage yourself in the short-term with petty stuff no one will remember a decade later.

PELOSI: Use our media advantage to exploit your unpopularity, sir. That "anyone-seen-with-you-loses-his-seat" thing works both ways. Invite Republicans from tossup districts to Putin's state dinner next month.

OBAMA: Clever. A riff on "Keep your enemies close." Michelle and I pose with the marks so Soros-funded PACS can run ads showing Joe Redstate hobnobbing with me.

WHASSUPMAN SCHULTZ: Bingo. The subtext: "Obama can work with this guy." Kiss of death.

PELOSI: Along those lines: I'm radioactive, too, Mr. President. I'll appear in a series of ads praising vulnerable Republicans. They'll squeal like pigs, but it's a free country—for now.

WHASSUPMAN SCHULTZ: With your assistance, sir, we might be able to take back the House. I have 100,000 clueless Democrats ready to move from safe districts to tossups before midterms. They'll register to vote, live in trailer parks until Election Day. Afterwards, Teamsters will transport them back home.

Code name: "Operation Hope and Change Your Address."

MICHELLE: I've never been prouder of our unions. Say yes, Barack.

OBAMA: Okay, I guess I'm in. However, I still think I could win the nomination without even trying.

HILLARY: No, you wouldn't, because there's a failsafe. When I declare my candidacy, I'll "discover" Bill's been foolin' around with an airline stewardess. We'll divorce, he'll join your campaign out of pique.

BILL: Huh? You never . . .

HILLARY: Shuddup, Bill. You'll do what you're told. Whoever you're for always goes down. Law of nature.

OBAMA WAR ROOM: DESPERATE TIMES

OBAMA: Ryan's the one who's giving their caucus spine in the budget fights. He still won't budge?

VALERIE JARRETT: No, sir. His family, release them?

OBAMA: Not yet. Wait another day or two. Give Mrs. Ryan formula for the baby, though.

DAN PFEIFFER: Pelosi called. Says she has a bag of parliamentary tricks that'll temporarily block House Republicans from passing legislation.

OBAMA: Get her on the horn.

Hey Nancy, how ya doin'? Look, if you're able to stall Boehner's tax bill, Reid will push the Senate to swallow his plan. As long as you don't . . . Well, yes, I remember our discussion. [sighs] Yes, I agree to your terms. [hangs up]

PFEIFFER: What did you promise her, sir?

OBAMA: On my next overseas trip, we'll install a booster seat in Air Force One's co-pilot chair, and her grandson will pretend to fly the plane.

JARRETT: Not too bad.

JOE BIDEN: I hate to mention this, Boss, but I've busted my butt pushing your agenda in the Senate, and . . .

OBAMA: I keep my word, Joe. I'll notify the Secret Service that tomorrow morning, from 4:30 a.m. to 4:45 a.m., I'll be temporarily unable to function as president because I'll be unconscious, sleeping. You'll take the helm. Try not to start a war.

PFEIFFER: The Reid bill, sir? It would help to get some Republican senators on board.

OBAMA: Hmm, on board. Val, reach out to Collins and Murkowski. Tell them I respectfully request their appearance at 8:00 p.m. aboard my presidential yacht, *Alinsky*, docked at the Gangplank Marina, 600 Water St SW.

JAY CARNEY: Um, there is no presidential yacht anymore, sir.

OBAMA: Wrong, Jay. I slipped the order for a new one into the shipbuilding procurement bill last year. A surprise gift to Michelle for our anniversary.

Jay, tell Research and Destroy I want updated folders on those senators by 5:00. Tonight, I'm going on a shakedown cruise.

BIDEN: Schumer will try to sabotage the majority leader, Chief. Reid might lose votes in *his* caucus.

OBAMA: Invite Senate Democrats over for a private briefing tomorrow afternoon.

JARRETT: Sir, they're tired of listening to you tell them . . .

OBAMA: Not me. I'll ask Max Baucus in for lunch and drinks beforehand; he'll speak for the Reid plan at the meeting.

PFEIFFER: Sir, at the best of times, he goes on and on. And now that he's retiring . . .

OBAMA: Once they're assembled, the Chief Usher locks the doors. Only those who agree to vote "yea" for Reid may leave. Call it, "Baucus the Caucus."

BIDEN: Good thinkin', Boss. But how do we get Reid's bill through Boehner's House.

PFEIFFER: Pelosi demands a vote on Reid. Boehner agrees because he has the "nays." Nancy submits the tally to the CBO to score, using the party breakdown from 2007 as a baseline. The numbers now favor us. She runs the bill over to the Senate. A courier puts it in your hands minutes after passage. You sign. Done.

OBAMA: Hmm. "Tote the Vote."

PFEIFFER: Uh, oh. A text from Pelosi, sir. She's upped the ante. Wants an August timeshare in the Residence while you and the family are vacationing on Martha's Vineyard.

OBAMA: Damn! Say yes, but she brings her own sheets. Val, how bad are my latest numbers?

JARRETT: A majority now thinks you're to blame for the debt crisis, sir. If the election were held today, you'd lose to Rand Paul by twenty points.

OBAMA: Must be because I'm not getting my message out. Jay, starting tomorrow, schedule press briefings for me on the hour, around the clock. Joe will stand in for me because I'll be busy handling crises. Right now, I need a break. Everybody wait here.

[enter First Lady ten minutes later]

BIDEN: Uh, Ma'am. You seen the Big O?

MICHELLE: In the Rose Garden, chain-smoking and crushing ants.

PFEIFFER: Ants?

MICHELLE: He watches them, then crushes the ones heading either left or right. Those meandering aimlessly, he leaves alone. Some kind of simpatico thing. I'm worried about him.

BIDEN: Problem is, Ma'am, all these scandals poppin' up have paralyzed him. He strategeries pretty good, but at crunch time, he can't bite the bullet and make a decision. Can you help?

MICHELLE: Maybe. [opens window, yells] Hey. Get back in here right now. The dinnerware people arrived. I want you to choose a pattern. You hear me, Barack?

OVERHEARD AT A HOLLYWOOD WATERING HOLE

BILL CLINTON: Jeez, Harry. She's got me on a short leash. I think one of my agents is one of *her* agents. He follows me everywhere 24/7. When I go into a stall in the men's room, he checks me out over the door with one of those periscope thingies. He's taping every move I make. I mean, I want to party with some wild ladies before I dry up. I can't breathe.

HARRY THOMASON: She's got the mojo now, Bill. Price you pay. Maybe when she's president, the pressure eases. Tell you what. Promise her you'll redouble your efforts to elect her and you won't refill your Viagra prescription for the duration. In return, demand to be named ambassador to Sweden right after her inauguration.

CLINTON: Might work. You know, she said something odd the other day. Got a bad feeling when I heard it. Went to the salon with her, and the stylist asked her what her pleasure was, and she looked hard at me and snarled, "Bob it." What was that about?

THOMASON: Watch your back, man. Your front, too.

OBAMA WAR ROOM: STORMY WEATHER

OBAMA: A huge spike in Federal hiring last month and I'm still getting grief about rising unemployment? Ridiculous. And why isn't Thursday's stock market plunge gone from the news cycle by now?

JOE BIDEN: The answer's always the same, Boss: *Fox News*. And some of our poodles in the media are takin' a cue from them and startin' to strain at the leash.

DAN PFEIFFER: Joe's right, sir. We must recommit to "preserve, protect and defend" your administration from criticism.

OBAMA: Let's start pushing back. Chris, you're our go-to media lackey. How would you neutralize *Fox* and squelch the alphabets' nascent insurgency?

MATTHEWS: Ignore *Fox*, sir; their ratings go up whenever you mention them. And don't attack the anchors; cultivate them. I recommend a soft, tactile approach: a hug for Diane, say; an arm around the shoulder for Brian; maybe a pat on the bum for me . . .

MICHELLE: Watch it, Tingles.

JACK LEW: Network sympathizers we've got, sir. We need better HUMINT from the parent companies' upper echelons, and leverage to intimidate them.

OBAMA: Right. Hey, you know how the Soviets assigned political officers to military units to enforce the party line. We'll riff off that. I'll order FCC lawyers to monitor General Electric and Disney board meetings for hate speech.

MATTHEWS: "Hate speech"?

LEW: Another expression for "dissent" in Obama's America, Chris.

VALERIE JARRETT: Those corporations employ high-powered legal talent, sir. They'll file challenges as soon as the FCC acts.

ERIC HOLDER: My best attorneys are working Guantanamo cases now, Mr. President. I'll reassign them to keep a boot on the opposition team's throats.

WHASSUPMAN SCHULTZ: A related matter, sir. The Internet trolls we're running out of the DNC just formed a union. They want to be paid by the word, and they want benefits. They've threatened to stop posting on lucianne.com, americanthinker. com and *National Review*, among others.

Worse yet, they're prepared to man a virtual picket line around the *Daily Kos* and *NPR*. We suspect they're Breitbart-inspired Astroturf.

OBAMA: Where's the outrage? All right, Debbie, you and Pfeiffer handle negotiations. Nickel a word, excluding articles and prepositions. Last, best, and final. Bonuses for longevity at high-traffic conservative sites. Get banned, get docked. Health benefits limited to carpal tunnel issues, but only with two doctors' affidavits. Forged, acceptable. Dan?

PFEIFFER: A dirty trick wouldn't hurt, sir. A tech guy I know says he can hack *Fox*'s control room and plant a twenty-second porno clip in the middle of O'Reilly's show.

OBAMA: I didn't hear that.

JOE BIDEN: We oughta take Jake the Tapper down a peg, too. My people'll photoshop a picture of him hookin' up with Janeane Garofalo in some East D.C. dive.

OBAMA: Meanwhile, I'll personally challenge the "demigod to demagogue" meme Hannity's been pushing. Jay, call Lorne. Tell him I'll host *Saturday Night Live* next week.

CARNEY: Are you sure, sir? They mocked you recently.

OBAMA: Not to my face. In person, the cast will pull their punches out of respect for the office I'm diminishing.

CARNEY: Lorne is sure to . . .

OBAMA: Non-negotiable condition: Bill Maher's people write the show. Maddow and O'Donnell present "Weekend Update."

BIDEN: Hey Chris, you and Olbermann make up yet after the set-to you had?

MATTHEWS: I tried. Bought him dinner the other day at the Seafarer's Grill on Connecticut Avenue. He took one bite of his red snapper, then stormed out, yelling, "This is the worst poisson in the world!"

HOPING*

I am hoping Ezra Klein
eats a copy of the Constitution
and tells us if it's binding
and I am hoping
60 Minutes winds down
and I am hoping
Chris Christie doesn't explode
and I am hoping
Old Media
requests end-of-life counseling
and I am really hoping
Rachel Maddow screws up
and forgets to spin a story

I am hoping *Nova*
reports a major extinction event
involving NPR and PBS
and I am hoping
Brian Williams
does not get more unctuous
and I am hoping

someone finally interrupts Bill O'Reilly
and I am hoping Saudi Arabia
changes its mind about
endowing the "Al Jazeera Chair"
at Columbia University School of Journalism
and I am really hoping
journalists like David Gregory
are treated like ordinary citizens
when they break the law

I am hoping Diane Sawyer
takes the time one day
to differentiate between
profit and profit margin
and I am hoping that Al Sharpton
interviews Dennis Miller
and I am hoping
Chris Matthews
joins an anger management group
and I am hoping Eliot Spitzer
turns down the offer
to host a show
on the Playboy Channel
and I am hoping
George Will and Charles Krauthammer
agree to appear
on the same panel
and disagree
and I am really hoping
for a sign
that Jay Carney is embarrassed
to be part of the Obama Administration

I am hoping Helen Thomas
reincarnates and finally makes good on her threat to
lie down in front of an Israeli tank
and smirk

and I am hoping
Iowahawk and Scott Ott
share a Pulitzer prize
for political harpooning
and I am hoping Ray Suarez
schedules his next surgery in Cuba
and I am hoping the *IRS*
looks in the mirror
and is ashamed
and I am really hoping
a new Eric Sevareid
emerges at *CBS*

I am hoping Paul Krugman
stops mailing it in
and I am hoping to hear Eric Holder
utter the words "administration of cowards"
at a news conference
and I am hoping the FCC
abandons its plans
to monitor thought waves
and I am hoping
the *New York Times*
continues to offer new subscribers
lunch with Maureen Dowd
at the Four Seasons
and I am really hoping liberalism
is classified as a delusional disorder
in DSM-V

I am hoping Dan Rather
becomes easier to swallow
than a ripe *habanero* chili pepper
and I am hoping
the *Washington Post*
shills one day
for a Republican

and I am hoping "Fast and Furious"
bubble ups into Matt Lauer's field of vision
and I am hoping Oprah
chooses Rules for Radical Conservatives
for her book club
and I am really, really hoping
that more Americans realize
what an extraordinary human being Tony Snow was

*This and the following piece were inspired by Lawrence Ferlinghetti's *"I Am Waiting,"* from *A Coney Island of the Mind* (1958)

STILL HOPING

I am hoping *Media Matters*
condemns the president
for urinating on the Constitution
and I am hoping
that one day
Bill Maher makes me laugh
and I am hoping
to meet someone
who has actually watched *Hardball*
I am hoping
Debbie Whassupman Schultz
finally says something intelligent
and I am really hoping
Adam Carolla
appears on *The View*
and kicks butt

I am hoping Hollywood
produces this generation's version

of *The Green Berets*
and I am hoping
Glenn Beck escapes captivity
and exposes his double
and I am hoping
Wolf Blitzer
messes up one morning and shaves
and I am hoping George Soros
is down to his last million
by year's end
and I am really hoping
Michelle Obama announces
she'll still love America
if her husband is impeached

I am hoping the Keystone pipeline
will not be built
on condition
that it never carry oil
and I am hoping "pork barrel"
doesn't disappear from the lexicon
because it offends CAIR
and I am hoping
for the day
when humor is color blind
and I am hoping John Roberts
upbraided Elena Kagan
for not doing the right thing on the PPACA
and recusing
and I am really hoping
Madonna declares
she's mad as hell
and she's not gonna shake it any more

I am hoping Hillary Clinton
goes back to Chappaqua
and plays happy homemaker

and I am hoping that neutral moderators
host future Republican debates
and I am hoping for GM
to admit the Volt
was not grounded in reality
and I am hoping Michael Moore
acknowledges his Sumo wrestler son
and I am really hoping
the Taliban
permit us to leave Afghanistan
with dignity

I am hoping Massachusetts scotches plans
to create the Kennedy Memorial Senate Seat
and I am hoping Maureen Dowd
writes something nice about somebody
and I am hoping to hear a joke
about a priest, a rabbi, and a mullah
walking into a bar
and I am hoping the AMA
trashes ObamaCare
and I am hoping
Camp David
is not renamed Camp Malcolm X
and I am really hoping
Paul Ryan steps up
and saves us

I am hoping the AP
characterizes as scatological
the administration's
Friday night document dumps
and I am hoping the AARP! AARP!
quits woofing submissively
when Kathleen Sebelius says "Heel"
and I am hoping the president
orders his launch codes officer

to start following him around again
and I am hoping Dan Rather
wraps up his career
like a tortilla
at a street stand in Juarez
and I am hoping
Bob Beckel
continues to keep a lid on it
on *The Five*
and I am really really hoping
Democrats come to their senses
before they take us all off the cliff

CHAPTER 12: MACHINATIONS

OBAMA WAR ROOM: MISDIRECTION

DAN PFEIFFER: Boehner's office just called, sir. He's changed his mind. Says you can address a joint session next Friday at 2:00 a.m.

OBAMA: Cheeky bastard. All right, accept. Eric, order Federal marshals to round up and escort legislators to the Chamber. Encourage them to be rough with Republicans.

JAY CARNEY: Our dirty tricks team affixed a wireless speaker under Joe Wilson's seat, sir. We'll trigger it to replay "You lie!" four minutes into your remarks.

BRIAN WILLIAMS: Afterward, our technicians will enhance the audio, pinpoint the source, and nail him. Wilson will deny, but voiceprint analysis confirms it's his voice.

OBAMA: And another firestorm. Man never learns.

JOE BIDEN: Lotta voters throwing the Kool-Aid back in our faces, Boss. I wonder if a speech toutin' investment in urine-powered cars and prefabricated bamboo homes will help your numbers.

OBAMA: Anyone with a better idea?

CARNEY: Do a 180, sir: experience a "Come-to-Jesus Moment" before the whole country, announcing you've finally realized you're a socialist ideologue.

OBAMA: Ouch! Who would believe I had this . . . epiphany?

VALERIE JARRETT: After baring your soul, entreat Paul Ryan to take over immediately as OMB Director.

OBAMA: Lemme think about that.

JARRETT: You could proclaim support for the flat tax sir, effectively eviscerating the IRS. Millions of NObamas would bless you; Grover Norquist might suffer a stroke.

OBAMA: Hmm. So *really* slash spending, except for Defense; dissolve the NLRB; open up drilling in Anwar and the Gulf; and join Republicans in the fight to overturn ObamaCare?

PFEIFFER: That's the idea, sir. You'd lose the base, of course, but independents and disaffected moderate Democrats would come flocking back when your actions sparked an economic boom.

BIDEN: Sounds logical, Chief. With unemployment down to 5%, the Dow at 20,000, and gas at 99 cents a gallon, voters will demand repeal of the 22nd Amendment so you can run for a third term. On January 21st, 2016, return to the tried and true policies that got us to where we are right now.

OBAMA: Allowing me to spend my last four years adhering to the principles which guided me through my first four. One step forward, two steps back; or is it one step backward, two steps forward?

JARRETT: Sounds tempting, sir, but if you decide to go for a third term as a right winger, you *will* be primaried.

PFEIFFER: Not necessarily a bad thing, Val. An internal contest might revitalize us all.

BIDEN: So, who'd the primary opponent be? Cuomo the Younger [snort]? Nader the Undead? Hillary?

PFEIFFER: Not Hillary. She'd beat him. No, I think you, Mr. Vice-President.

BIDEN: Me?

PFEIFFER: Why not? Next to you, the president always looks good. When he wins the nomination, he'll graciously offer to keep you on as veep.

OBAMA: Wait! Wait! Wait! Enough! I'd go crazy if I spent the next couple of years trying to flank Perry, pretending to care what's happening in flyover country. No. The economy's down but not out yet. My job's not done. We remain on course.

PFEIFFER: We can't depend on foreign policy screw-ups, natural disasters like Sandy, and terror attacks to distract voters from the harm you're doing to the country, sir.

OBAMA: Well, then, let's create our own diversions. George?

SOROS: I pay couple pointy-head Kos Kids to tattoo swastika und American eagle on shaved skulls, guest on *Hardball*, und threaten uprising unless president impeached.

WILLIAMS: Clever. The other anchors and I could use the appearance as a pretext to go after anyone to the right of Susan Collins.

HOLDER: Along the same lines, sir: there's a Boy Scout jamboree at an isolated compound in West Texas this fall. I'll stage a variant of the Waco siege to incite Cruz, Jindal and Rand Paul to make inflammatory statements about both of us.

WILLIAMS: *MSNBC* will run 24/7 to frame the hotheads as a threat to civil order and lump them in with the GOP to delegitimize the party.

'PINCH' SULZBERGER: The *Times* can prep the ground. Jason Blair's back on board. Before the raid, we'll run his piece on an Evangelical sect using the jamboree as cover to plot an armed revolution.

OBAMA: One more major distraction. Anyone?

PFEIFFER: You never followed through on your threat of a purge, sir, of people who have given you bad advice.

OBAMA: You, Valerie, Jay . . .

PFEIFFER: Not the inner circle, sir. Scapegoats.

OBAMA: Hmm. Lew's expendable. There's nothing more he can do to undermine faith in our financial system. And Sebelius is getting too big for her britches.

HOLDER: [wagging finger] Careful, sir; such language would be considered sexist coming from anyone not a member of an oppressed minority.

CARNEY: I'm late for my briefing, Mr. President. I should say something to reporters regarding heightened tensions on the Korean Peninsula.

OBAMA: Chuck, what are your sources telling you about Kim Young-un and the Koreas?

HAGEL: We know he suffers from an STD, sir, but I'm not sure it's that one.

OBAMA: Do you have *any* HUMINT for me?

HAGEL: Um, no. May I offer you SPEARMINT, instead? Commerce took over Wrigley's last week because it was too big to fail. Have a stick, sir; it's gummint approved.

I was making a joke, sir.

OBAMA: Chuck, tomorrow I want you to hire an undocumented Guatemalan housekeeper, then resign as soon as you realize what you've done.

OBAMA WAR ROOM: I CAN'T GET NO . . . SADISTRACTIONS

DAN PFEIFFER: You shouldn't have used the phrase "leading from behind" last year when you spoke off the record about Libya, Mr. Vice-President.

BIDEN: Well, I didn't, Danny boy. I said Hillary was leading with her behind. Or maybe I said the whole NATO operation was like the blind leading the blind. I don't remember. The guy misquoted me.

OBAMA: No lasting harm. Research and Destroy knocked that off the front pages fast with the Herman Cain scandal.

JAY CARNEY: Oh, Mr. President, the Smithsonian taxidermist just delivered Gaddafi's head.

OBAMA: Okay. Tell Housekeeping to mount it above the mantel in the Residence, next to bin Laden's. Remind them to leave room for Assad and Boehner.

VALERIE JARRETT: Sir, we're taking a hit in the polls since *Fox News* reported diehard Islamists in Libya and Syria possess Gaddafi's massive stock of surface-to-air missiles.

BIDEN: Damn *Fox*, trying to make people think we shoulda known that could happen.

JOHN KERRY: Mr. President, regarding Syria: the rebel junta has assured me they'll work with us to destroy the country's chemical weapons stock once they use it to overthrow Assad.

OBAMA: Syria's been a useful diversion recently, but attention is swinging back to the economy.

JARRETT: As well as scandals like Gunwalker, Sequestergate, Benghazi, and IRS and NSA abuse of power.

KERRY: Perhaps we need a bank of foreign distractions to draw on through midterms in 2014, sir.

OBAMA: Good thinking. Here's an idea. John, get Supreme Leader Ayatollah Khamenei on the hot line, please.

[pause]

Hello, Ayatollah? It's Barack. Peace be with you, too, sir.

"Death to America"? Ha Ha Haaaa! Funny, you sound just like my former pastor.

No, no, no. I'm doing as little as I can in Syria. And Libya was an aberration. Gaddafi asked for it when he gave up his nuclear program.

Listen, can we meet? Perhaps resolve our countries' differences?

Tehran, September? Absolutely. I'll clear my schedule. Now, my people tell me we shouldn't meet without preconditions. What are your preconditions, sir?

No interference when you make Iraq an Iranian province? Agreed. Out of Kuwait? Okay.

Sure, we'll leave our bases intact for your use should Kuwait become a part of Greater Iran. Waste not, want not. Anything else?

Yes, I'll recall our ambassador to Israel.

Pardon? In fact, I told Netanyahu yesterday I'm implementing a variation of America's "One China" policy *vis-à-vis* the Jewish state and Palestinians. We're calling the initiative our "One Palestine" kowtow.

You'd like a good faith gesture as well? Um, how about our weapons specialists working with Iranian scientists to ensure your nuclear bombs are reasonably clean, limiting damage to the environment when you employ them?

May *I* ask for a good faith gesture in return, sir?

You'll use your influence with al-Qaeda to guarantee captured soldiers will enjoy the option to convert? I don't . . . Ah, conversion entitles them to be beheaded with a sharp knife rather than a dull one. Yes, indeed, Allah is merciful.

See you in September, *inshallah.*

[hangs up]

That went well. Possibly a breakthrough.

BIDEN: Good on ya, Chief.

OBAMA: Okay, Diversion Number Two for, say, next spring? Anybody?

KERRY: North Korea, sir? We're still dead in the water there.

BIDEN: I say we pursue a, whatchamacallit, *quid pro nililum* approach with the Hermit Klingon: unabashed groveling absent expectation of anything in return.

KERRY: Kim Young-un will expect us to offer something concrete in exchange for nothing, sir.

OBAMA: I'll authorize HHS to extend ObamaCare coverage to North Korea's 23 million . . . [Kerry whispers into his ear] Oh? Since yesterday? All right, North Korea's 22 million people.

KATHLEEN SEBELIUS: In fact, the "North Korea Wellness Program" was originally incorporated in the PPACA, sir: page 1889, Title VIII, Section 8004, Article 9, Subset a, 3.

KERRY: Preliminary talks with Kim on this matter took place just after the election, sir. He insisted end-of-life counseling be mandated for all North Korean citizens, regardless of medical condition.

OBAMA: Wily troll. Who says he doesn't care about his people?

[enter First Lady]

MICHELLE: I just talked with Rosalynn Carter. Put "Comparable Worth for First Spouses" at the top of your agenda. You hear me, Barack?

OBAMA APPEALS TO NATION'S LITTLEST CITIZENS—AGAIN

REP. CHARLES RANGEL: Hiya boys and girls. It's me again, your Uncle Chollie in Washington. I help your Uncle Sam take care of you and your mom, and your dad, too, if he hasn't run off yet.

Once more, I'm here to introduce someone special, a person who can calm the raging [Maxine]Waters, sell solar panels below cost and still make a profit, and cause the stock market to plummet, all with a single word.

C'mon, kids, give it up for the president of the United States, Baraaccck Obama.

[fade to]

A Command and Control bunker deep beneath the White House. Wearing a headset, the president is sitting at a console facing three large-screen HD monitors showing complementary views of a tactical assault in progress. He is issuing orders.

At a break in the action, the CIC swivels to face the camera, covers his mic, and whispers:

Hey kids. Good to see you. Hold on a sec. I'm just finishing up a mission.

He turns back to direct the closing moments of the operation:

Zulu 1: secure perimeter. Henderson: white SUV fleeing site. Task Predator to take it out. Bravo 1: Standoff See-Through Infrared shows targets at top of stairwell. Body signatures confirmed. Authorization granted. [pause] Roger that. Well done. Bring me back some ears.

The president removes his headset, turns to the camera, smiles, and speaks:

PRESIDENT OBAMA: You're probably wondering what *that* was about. Unfortunately, your president's sworn enemies are always probing for ways to attack him and, by extension, you.

This morning, under my direction, crack units of our National Civilian Security Force raided RNC headquarters here in Washington looking for some very bad people. They found them. I assure you, I will not rest until all those who threaten the way of life I'm imposing on America are brought to justice.

Before I say more, please stand, place your right hand over your heart, and recite along with me:

I pledge allegiance to the president of the United States of America, and to our decline, for which he's planned, one nation, under him highly risible, with penury and animus for all.

Okay, sit now, kids. Last year I spoke to you about the importance of education. This year I'll explain how you can help me win a third term that will allow me to abandon all pretense of being a uniter and cement my role as Divider-in-Chief.

People say I hate being criticized. That's not true. I don't mind criticism, as long as it's unspoken. The First Amendment to the Constitution doesn't allow people to get on my case. The United States Supreme Court ruled you may not yell "fire" in a crowded theater or shout "You lie!" during a presidential address to a joint session of Congress.

Thanks to Mr. Holder, who's been monitoring Americans since I became president, we know the grown-ups who are publicly *and* privately abusing their free speech rights to pile on me; what I don't know is, which kids hear bad things about me at the dinner table and repeat them at school.

So, I'll ask a favor. In lunchrooms and bathrooms, during gym class and math class, if you witness a classmate dissing me, report it to the political officer at your school. (Just find out who the teachers' union rep is.) And if you're too shy to speak up, e mail the information to me at http://www.AttackWatchJr.com.

I'll bet you sometimes feel powerless at home. Maybe TV time is limited, or you aren't permitted a computer in your bedroom.

I believe in empowering young people. At my request, satellite and cable companies now include a children's blocking option on their menus. Teachers will pass out codes for providers where you live. This means, when your folks tune in to *Fox News*, say, or a rerun of Supernanny, they'll be redirected to *MSNBC*.

Boys and girls, everything I've done to America to make poorer countries less envious of us will be undone if I'm not reelected in 2016. No, you can't vote—yet; but you can use your imagination to support me in other ways.

I'm thinking about Mishaha Glynn, a fourth grader from East Abunni, Utah, who's petitioning Family Court to force her parents to tithe her weekly allowance to my campaign.

And another youngster, Ritva Allembe, a sixth grader from Cheeseburg, Wisconsin, who's been stealing her classmates' bag lunches and tossing them into the dumpster after school. Why? More hungry kids, more federal aid, and more people voting for me to keep the aid coming. Ritva calls her initiative, "LunchWalker."

Well, time to leave. I still have trillions of dollars to squander in a sham attempt to fix our broken economy, and there aren't enough hours in the day.

Now, please watch this taped message from two friends, Mr. Hoffa and Mr. Trumka, who will explain how you kids can organize into dues-paying clubs to give you a say in running your school and help finance my reelection campaign to boot.

Thank you, and may God forgive me. [to someone off camera] What? Oh. I mean, may God bless America.

OBAMA WAR ROOM: ROPE-A-DOPE

KERRY: Russia, China, Iran, North Korea—they're pushing our buttons and watching you for decisiveness, sir. I'll form a "Commission on Foreign Provocations." Recommendations by fall.

OBAMA: No. We act now. Suggestions?

KERRY: Regarding the Russians: I suggest a *quid pro quo*: we won't object to Russian attack subs patrolling Long Island Sound if they don't object to hypothetical musings about missile defense in Eastern Europe.

OBAMA: Ease off, John. They'll never go for that.

VALERIE JARRETT: It's been three weeks since the Chinese sank our destroyer in the South Pacific for operating in their territorial waters, sir. We should respond.

JOE BIDEN: Val's right, Boss. Hit 'em where it hurts, in the pocketbook: order a naval blockade of the Port of Los Angeles. They'll go bonkers with twenty of their container ships offshore, unable to offload cheap goods to our markets.

OBAMA: Okay, Chuck, follow up. But let's remember: Iran's the immediate threat. Sooner or later, they'll nuke Israel, Israel will retaliate, and the mess will distract me from socializing America. What to do?

KERRY: Right now, the Iranians are so focused on Armageddon, they're behaving, sir.

OBAMA: Good. Offer to work with them on "clean bomb" technology; that'll prolong their efforts. Anyone have a brainstorm about the Palestinian problem?

DAN PFEIFFER: If only Israel could kill all the diehards.

JARRETT: The fanatics love death, sir, but a free pass to America trumps 72 virgins. Promise visas to *bona fide* jihadists, Iranian references helpful but not required. They'd find work as *Sharia* enforcers in Detroit and New York Muslim enclaves

BIDEN: I gotta better idea: we convince the Palestinians they'll never beat Israel, but Iran is ripe for the pickin'.

OBAMA: Hmm, turn them on their sponsors. They might buy the notion if we make it worth their while. Jack, can we bury a twenty billion authorization for Abbas in some obscure subsection of Stimulus IV?

JARRETT: Hatred can't be bought off, sir. My advice: we force Israelis to give up their homeland and resettle in Utah.

OBAMA: Tempting. That'd get me points with evangelicals *and* drive the Mormons crazy.

DAN PFEIFFER: Additional benefit, sir: we'd gain a vibrant intranational trading partner, taking some heat off you when you kill NAFTA.

OBAMA: Good point. Chuck, you don't have to raise your hand to say something.

HAGEL: Permission to use the bathroom, sir?

OBAMA: Just hold it for ten minutes . . . I don't mean literally, Chuck.

PFEIFFER: A more drastic alternative, sir: seize the initiative and launch a preemptive nuclear strike on an Israeli city before Iran does. Israelis won't have cause to vaporize Iran, saving millions of lives and denying the ayatollahs and mullahs their martyrdom.

OBAMA: Strangelovian. A nuclear firebreak, risky but forestalling something far worse. And our bomb, unlike the Iranians', would be clean, keeping casualties modest. Val?

JARRETT: The strike would embolden Iranian moderates, sir, and earn us goodwill on the Arab Street.

JAY CARNEY: I can almost see the first line of *WaPo*'s editorial, sir: "President Obama has acted boldly in the Middle East to head off a major conflagration, sending a clear signal to the region that blah blah."

OBAMA: Val, send the launch codes officer in here.

Okay. Chuck, cut the orders. Station relief ships in the Med to assist Israel immediately after the blast. We help our friends. John, tell Iran we'd appreciate help with the relief effort.

KERRY: The target city, sir?

OBAMA: Haifa? Beersheba? Chuck, what do you think? Tel Aviv?

HAGEL: Um, if you say so, sir. Where can I reach Mr. Aviv?

OBAMA: Chuck, head out to Azerbaijan tomorrow to negotiate a status of forces agreement. Stay as long as it takes.

PEACE PRIZE*

OBAMA: [on phone] Sure, Tiger. Stay cool, man. [Hangs up] Finally! An opportunity to show the world I deserve my Nobel. Who else could have persuaded Erin and Tiger to make peace?

JOHN KERRY: Their representatives confirm Sunday's talks at Camp David are on, sir. I bumped the Netanyahu-Abbas summit to next weekend.

OBAMA: Good. As you know, Jesse and Bill here will serve as lead mediators.

JACKSON: Long as they talk and he doesn't stalk, I won't walk.

BILL CLINTON: Nice 'un, Jesse. Lemme try: "If we all pull together, they won't pull apart."

JACKSON: Weak. You feel their pain; leave the wordcraft to me.

OBAMA: John, how do we play this?

KERRY: Stage One: Bill hashes things out with Ms. Nordegren in Rosebud Cabin; Jesse engages Mr. Woods in Dogwood.

JACKSON: Tiger starts jiving', I ain't shrivin'. He's gotta admit, he's gotta submit, he's gotta commit. Or I'm gonna quit.

MICHELLE: Easy, Jesse. Tiger told us he'd do the right thing.

CLINTON: Oh, Hillary refuses to let me participate unless a chaperone is present when I see Elin.

KERRY: Stage Two: multilateral teleconference via secure video uplink in Laurel Lodge's meeting room. Participants: our mediators, the principals, Mr. Woods's mother, Ms. Nordegren's parents, her twin sister, and Dr. Phil.

Ideally, the opposing parties and their sponsors agree to terms and ratify a Memorandum of Understanding. State Department bureaucrats will compose the actual treaty.

OBAMA: Um, this is supposed to be a PR coup for me, John. Where do I come in?

KERRY: Getting to that, sir. Stage Three: a *pro forma* bilateral session. You, Mr. Woods, and Ms. Nordegren in the Presidential Cabin, Aspen Lodge.

Engage in some pleasantries with them, then let the media in. Smile benignly behind the couple as they sign the pact ending the rift. After lunch, you and Tiger head out for nine holes.

OBAMA: Okay, let's all . . .

MICHELLE: Hold on. When Jessie and Bill are done makin' you look like Gandhi, they'll mediate *our* power-sharing dispute. You hear me, Barack?

*A version of this piece originally appeared on americanthinker. com.

OBAMA WAR ROOM: WINNIE THE PUTIN

OBAMA: But *Operation Overreach* has conditioned Americans to my abuse of the presidency.

DAN PFEIFFER: We have to up our game, sir.

OBAMA: I'm already subverting the Constitution and selling out Defense as fast as I can.

PFEIFFER: That's why we suggest hiring David Brock's *Media Matters* to insert, um, an IV disinformation drip into the body politic, relieving the pressure on us to figure out more lines for you to cross here and abroad.

JAY CARNEY: Brock's just arrived through the tunnel connecting his office to the White House. He'll brief you on *Operation Overreach: Reloaded.*

[enter Brock]

CARNEY: David, offer the president examples of poisonous rumors you'd contribute to the nation's discourse.

BROCK: Let's see, we're arming the *Québécois* for their war of independence.

VALERIE JARRETT: *Vive le Québec libre!*

BROCK: Um, Health and Human Services plans to harvest aborted fetuses, paying unmarried urban women $1000 for each donation.

OBAMA: Wish I'd thought of that.

BROCK: Michelle will stage a pageant commemorating the 166th anniversary of the snowbound Mormon party who wound up cannibalizing . . .

JOE BIDEN: You mean the Donner party?

BROCK: Whatever.

OBAMA: You're hired, David. [exit Brock] Hey, where's Holder?

PFEIFFER: On *Ellen Degeneres*, promoting his new book, *A Nation of Clowards*.

JARRETT: Sir, Alan Dershowitz vowed to fight us if we worked with Brock.

OBAMA: I'll invite both to Camp David this weekend for a wine and cheese and bagel and lox summit.

[red phone rings]

Vladimir, old friend. You accept? Wonderful. We'll sign in Moscow next week.

[hangs up]

Breakthrough: Putin's agreed to missile defense platforms on the continent, as long as they're programmed to target near-earth objects. In return, he'll wait until I'm out of office to release a Russian film version of the bin Laden takedown.

OBAMA WAR ROOM: GRAPES OF ROTH

JOE BIDEN: Man, the wingnuts could smoke us in midterms. You nailed it, Boss; if they win, Boehner and McConnell'll be drivin' the bus while we're sittin' in back scratchin' our butts.

OBAMA: Didn't say that, Joe. Said I was "itching for a fight." There's still hope. Dan?

PFEIFFER: The earlier we go on the attack, the better, sir. Soros's PAC already cut an ad. Opens with a Latino woman breastfeeding her baby at home when Sheriff Joe Arpaio's SWAT team storms in, arrests her for exposing herself to a minor, carts her to the Rio Grande, throws her in, and laughs as she paddles to Mexico.

The voiceover: "It's 2015 and Republicans control Congress."

OBAMA: Okay! What happens to the baby?

PFIEFFER: Orphanage. Right out of Dickens.

JAY CARNEY: Here's another, sir: on background, I'll tell the anchors Boehner wants to discourage abortions by requiring women to register their uteri with HHS. That'll get all the scandals off the front pages for a couple days.

JOE BIDEN: I got one, Chief: a House Democrat switches parties then introduces a bill criminalizing the application of makeup while driving.

OBAMA: Good. We go positive, too. Republicans are gaining traction on immigration and austerity. Let's counter. Janet?

HAGEL: Disband the INS and employ drug traffickers to police our southern border, sir; they know the territory and consider people smugglers scum.

VALERIE JARRETT: That would save us a bundle and show you're serious about stopping uncredentialed landscapers infiltrating from *Juárez* and *Tegucigalpa,* Mr. President.

OBAMA: No good. Streisand has her Shangri-La estate in Malibu where half those people wind up. I lose her, I lose Hollywood. Besides, why stop the flow of irregular expatriates who'll vote for me when I amnestitize them? Anyone else?

JACK LEW: Sell China drilling rights off the coasts of Florida and California, sir, then have our enviros tie up the deal in court. If the court rules for the companies, a DNC black ops team will blow a wellhead, setting exploiters back a decade. Your hands would be clean.

OBAMA: No way we can let those rigs produce. Gasoline's four bucks a gallon right now, a far cry from our $10 a gallon goal. Last thing I want is more product and lower prices.

JARRETT: You haven't responded to China's offer to lease California and build mega-manufactories staffed by restive Muslims from Xinxiang.

OBAMA: I dunno. The Chinese say they just want "Made in the USA" tags on their stuff. Sounds harmless enough, but something smells wrong. Stall them. John?

KERRY: French President Hollande called, sir. He'll accept return of Jefferson's 1803 Louisiana Purchase and refund our $15 million payment, minus a 20% restocking fee.

OBAMA: Tempting. Get rid of Texas and a couple other red states. That it?

LEW: McConnell and Boehner laughed when I suggested Treasury assume management of the trillions sitting in IRAs, sir. Too bad. The investments we might have made in America's future!

BIDEN: Wienies. Argentina's government had the guts to take control of the country's private pension funds. Argentina! A tinpot regime shows the world's most progressive declinin' superpower howda do it.

OBAMA: Jack, what about the windfall tax revenue you promised from this year's one time Roth IRA "Pay the IRS now, profit later" conversion deal?

LEW: The public hasn't bought into the promotion, sir. Frankly, only an idiot would pay taxes proactively while you're in office.

JARRETT: Mr. President, why not go after the Roth trove itself? Most of that money's owned by the richest 40%, people who don't need the funds but invested in Roths to help their children and grandchildren evade responsibility for the fix we're bequeathing them.

BIDEN: Won't work, Val. The Hill will never legislate a surtax on Roth withdrawals.

OBAMA: Val's not talking some measly 10% surtax, Joe. I want it all, Val. How do we do manage that?

JARRETT: Go Argentina one better: citing fiscal eminent domain, nationalize Roth accounts. Holder can drag out the court fight through 2016.

OBAMA: Brilliant! With more money than God, I'll buy off enough legislatures to repeal the 22nd Amendment.

LEW: Related matter, sir: Barney Frank says the Republicans are undoing all the damage he did with Fannie Mae and Freddie Mac during his tenure as Chair of the House Financial Services Committee. He wants a firewall to stop them.

PFEIFFER: Barney's right. Took years of neglect for Fannie and Freddie to become a bureaucratic rat's nest. Republicans are cleaning it out.

OBAMA: I'll appropriate those organizations and place them in trust with Treasury. Jack, recharter the two as "Fannie Mae

I" and "Freddie Mac the Knife," the government's fully owned "tough love" lenders [snort]. I'll ask budget hawks Paul Krugman and John Kenneth Galbraith to serve as CEOs.

PFEIFFER: Galbraith's dead, sir.

OBAMA: True. But when critics say his agency reeks of corruption, we'll have a counter.

LEAKED! FROM THE FILES OF DAVID AXELROD

MEMORANDUM

To: Eric Boehlert, Media Matters
From: David Axelrod
Date: May 27, 2010
Subject: Creaming Breitbart

"James O'Keefe's humiliating guilty plea for trespassing in Senator Landrieu's office"? Is that the best you could do? Perhaps I wasn't clear: I want to destroy Breitbart, not embarrass him. O'Keefe is the means—if we act decisively.

Forget British Petroleum and the Gulf spill. Put Stossel, Beck, and O'Reilly on the back burner. Call in those stringers you've got sitting in toilet stalls around Washington hoping to snag a Republican tapping his foot in the next cubicle. Devote all your resources to morphing O'Keefe's transgression into a McVeigh-level atrocity sponsored by Breitbart.

MSNBC will pound on Breitbart's mania to foster civil chaos in America as long as it takes to make the charge resonate. Expect him to be Olbermann's first "Worst Person of the Millennium."

The *Times* and *Post* assure me they'll give the matter their full Abu Ghraib treatment, starting with above-the-fold articles this weekend. Williams, Couric, and Sawyer confirm they'll jump on the story after a decent interval, citing a "raging controversy."

Time Magazine's cover next week features a caricature of Breitbart setting fire to an SEIU tee shirt in front of the White House, with the headline: "What Are the Limits of Dissent in Obama's America?"

When public indignation peaks, Congressional Democrats (and a few Republican simpletons) will demand Attorney General Holder appoint a Special Counsel to investigate Breitbart's activities. Ramsey Clark is available.

Meanwhile, we'll unleash the IRS to pursue seditionists masquerading as dissenters.

Related matters:

Big Journalism's mascot, Retracto, the Correction Alpaca, has been attacking your credibility with some success. You need a counter. I suggest Rumo, the Calumny Capybara. Appoint him a Senior Fellow. What difference does one more make? Soros is loaded.

Also, we'll offset last week's PR blowback when our stooges laid siege to the house of the Bank of America official and scared the bejesus out of his home-alone kid.

So, be advised, hundreds of SEIU members wearing "Tea Party 2010" tees will descend on the homes of *Media Matters'* Senior Fellows at noon tomorrow (while they're at work) to protest something or other.

Fellows should keep their children home from school, alone and not forewarned: we want the kids to show unfeigned terror at the mock-harassment, including frantic calls to 911 Maddow will replay endlessly.

Questions? Call me. I don't need to tell you the Boss is taking a personal interest in this one. From one "journalist" to another: look how far you can go if you play your cards right.

Now get to work.

CHAPTER 13: DON'T BOTHER ME

OBAMA WAR ROOM: TELL ME SOME LIES

OBAMA: So I said to him, "Whaddaya think, Mitt? Secretary of Business. Economy's beginning to come back, and I need a turnaround guy like you to get it going the other way again so we can push for another stimulus."

[enter Secretaries of State and Defense]

JOHN KERRY: Sir! Sir! We just heard . . .

OBAMA: Stop! Unless it's about which schmo and his family I want taken out with a drone, I don't want to know.

JOE BIDEN: People, do *not* put him in a position where he's forced to delay a decision until the time to act has passed.

CHUCK HAGEL: But Mr. President, China . . .

OBAMA: [covers ears] Na na na na na na na na na . . . [leaves]

BIDEN: Jeez, what's so gawdawful important you couldn't deal with the problem?

HAGEL: A Chinese carrier group is cruising off Santa Monica.

KERRY: The People's Republic declared the Pacific Ocean an extension of China's territorial waters.

BIDEN: So? Get the U.N. involved.

KERRY: Apparently, one of Ming ruler Zhu Di's exploration fleets traversed the Pacific in 1428 and claimed it for the Emperor.

BIDEN: What's the Boss supposed to do?

HAGEL: Stage a benefit for displaced Pacific Islanders?

BIDEN: Betcha Chris Christie would appear.

KERRY: [screaming] I'm not talking about Springsteen!

[Enter president]

OBAMA: Crisis over yet? Yes or no? No particulars.

BIDEN: Sure, Chief. Jay, advise the networks to spike the story. Say, "national security concerns."

CARNEY: I´ll get nailed at my briefing.

BIDEN: Tell them: when the facts are in, the president will meet with the pool and take hard questions off the record. Oughta satisfy 'em.

OBAMA WAR ROOM: NOWHERE MAN

[White House advisors in Washington video conferencing with President Obama in Hawaii]

DAN PFEIFFER: We had to do it, sir. The optics are bad. Even our media lackeys grumbled about your Hawaiian family holiday in the midst of the budget crisis.

OBAMA: I know. If it gets out, though . . . [yelling] C'mon, Michelle. Get your butt back on that board, paddle out, and try again. I'm countin' on you, girl.

VALERIE JARRETT: Excuse me, sir. Air Force One arrives at Dulles around noon. Your double will be whisked to the White House. He'll hole up in the sub-basement until you sneak home next week.

OBAMA: A shame we gotta play these games just so I can kick back for a few more days. Hey Dan, you sure nobody's gonna find out?

PFEIFFER: Reporters returned with your other self, sir. And the Service has created a 25 square mile exclusion zone around the Compound. All locals are being temporarily relocated. We're calling it a precautionary measure to protect the family while you're in D.C.

OBAMA: What about Washington?

PFEIFFER: We'll pass out stills of you pacing the floor in the Oval Office, phone in hand. At his press briefings, Carney will say you're reaching out to the principals in an effort to keep fiscal disaster at bay.

OBAMA: I am?

PFEIFFER: Yes, sir. Your voice impersonator has placed dozens of calls to Boehner, McConnell, Cantor, Reid, Hoyer and others to urge them on. The connection is broken before any substantive discussion ensues.

OBAMA: Is Reid aware I´m not coming back?

PFEIFFER: Yes, sir. He says you might as well be on the moon for all he cares.

JARRETT: We've built a mock-up of the Oval Office in the spare beach house, sir. Later on, you'll deliver that three minute statement I prepared about the need for everybody to get serious as doom approaches.

OBAMA: Awright. Hey Mich, order me up one more Blue Hawaii, easy on the vodka, before I head out for another nine holes. Forget the little umbrella.

JAY CARNEY: [running up, breathless] Sir, sir, agents just caught a *National Enquirer* reporter staked out up a palm tree nearby. He took photos of you and transmitted them by sat phone before we could stop him.

OBAMA: Oh for cripes sake. All right, scratch the double and go to plan B: I stay, and Michelle and the kids head back to Washington until Republicans cave. Jay, call Jill Abramson at the *Times*. I want an editorial about the First Family separated and held hostage by GOP intransigence

IN AN ALTERNATE UNIVERSE: CABINET OF CURIOSITIES 1

January 23, 2013
White House, Cabinet Room
First meeting of President Obama's new team

OBAMA: Okay, folks. Let's begin. After your recess appointments to the Cabinet two weeks ago, I gave you all free rein while I was incommunicado playing golf in Ireland. What's been accomplished? We'll start with Defense.

DENNIS KUCINICH: The fleet's been mothballed and the Air Force grounded, sir. Uniformed services finished mustering out yesterday. Our enemies now understand we mean business when we say we want peace.

OBAMA: Good. How's recruitment going for my Civilian National Security Force?

KUCINICH: The first units are scheduled to graduate from Nation of Islam Training Center on Parris Island this fall, sir. They'll be stationed in hot spots like Lubbock, Texas, Orange

County California, and Oklahoma City. Each recruit will be assigned an aide to carry 5,000 rounds of hollow points drawn from our stockpiles.

OBAMA: Fine. Oh, Dennis, a revenue idea: keep a carrier on duty and retrofit it as a "cruise warship." Incorporate DOD Vacations Unlimited to tap into that niche of travelers who want to tour places like Somalia in comfort and safety. Um, State?

CINDY SHEEHAN: With respect, sir, your order to destroy America's nuclear arsenal was a pathetic, empty gesture. Instead, Secretary Kucinich and I are promoting peace and prosperity through managed proliferation. We've distributed our entire stock of these weapons to every non-nuclear country on earth.

KUCINICH: With everyone except us possessing the bomb, pressure to settle even minor disagreements will be enormous, lest miscalculation lead to mutual annihilation.

SHEEHAN: A side benefit: with nukes, third-world countries won't need expensive militaries that impoverish them. Dictators may spend their peace dividend on their poor.

OBAMA: Impeccable logic. National Security Advisor?

MAXINE WATERS: State notified NATO we're pulling out of the alliance, sir, which means the end of the organization. Its existence was provocative anyway, a finger in the eye of the Russians.

And Secretary Kucinich advised Putin to reconstitute the Warsaw Pact, forcibly, if necessary. The world was a better place when the USSR and her satellite states in Eastern Europe checked American Imperialism.

OBAMA: Excellent. CIA, what's showing up on your radar?

JOSEPH WILSON: Can't talk, sir. My suit against the Agency is pending.

OBAMA: Gotcha. Deputy Director?

MARKOS MOULITSAS: Iran nuked Tel Aviv, North Korea invaded South Korea, and Nicaragua's Ortega seized the remaining Gulf oil rigs. Otherwise, a quiet day, sir.

OBAMA: Jay, issue this statement in my name: "All sides bear some responsibility for these events." Homeland Security?

BARBARA BOXER: We continue to monitor the NSA and CIA to assure neither agency abrogates the rights of al Qaeda sleepers in the U.S.

OBAMA: Good, Madame Secretary.

BOXER: Please don't call me "Madame," Barry. And I'm not a "Secretary," I'm a "Director."

OBAMA: Sorry. Let's move to domestic. Health and Human Services, your country is grateful that you've come back from the grave to serve.

DR. KEVORKIAN: Thank you, sir. It's an honor.

We're into Stage two of ObamaCare, pouring resources into the undocumented citizens' community. Once they're amnestied, we'll shift them into general coverage and begin Stage Three: transforming hospitals and clinics into death traps through staff cuts and underfunding. These measures will reduce the strain on facilities and ease population pressures, too.

OBAMA: Faster, please.

KEVORKIAN: We can attrit physicians further by making them federal employees and capping their salaries.

OBAMA: Smart. They'll quit in droves when they become underpaid government bureaucrats. Replace them with minimum wage, non-English speaking graduates of Internet medical schools based in Honduras and Uzbekistan.

KEVORKIAN: ObamaCare help centers in Pakistan are now open, staffed by Dell tech line rejects. Here's a recording of a recent interaction: [signs to staff to play audio]:

"Yes yes, Mrs. Johnson I *am* trying to help you. You must return the defective kidney before we can approve a new one. My name? It is Achmed. Excuse me? But, but, I *am* a supervisor."

OBAMA: HUD?

ROSIE O'DONNELL: Our "Homeless Eradication Initiative" now includes feral cats, sir. I recommend giving the ASPCA cabinet rank.

OBAMA: Noted. Transportation?

RALPH NADER: Citizens enjoy no constitutional right to a car, Mr. President. Ban individual ownership of vehicles beyond 2015, when traveling by mass transit, whether or not it exists, becomes compulsory. We'll ease the pain with a federal auto buy-back program.

OBAMA: Ralph, tap the Amish for additional public transport ideas. Treasury?

PAUL KRUGMAN: You always do the opposite of what I advise, sir, so I object to a tax on air consumption.

OBAMA: I'll consider it. Justice?

RAMSEY CLARK: Adding to what Director Boxer said, I've taken steps to educate jihadists in our midst to their Miranda rights *before* any are apprehended.

I'm also going after the perpetrators of the war on bugs, sir. The wholesale slaughter—the *insecticide*—waged worldwide by American chemical companies and agribusiness is an offense against common decency.

OBAMA: Agreed. Shut down Monsanto and Du Pont on some trumped-up antitrust suit. Agriculture, put a "Pest Relocation" program in place before the fall harvest. HUD, produce a pamphlet for homeowners: "Living with Your Little Guests." OMB?

JESSE JACKSON: My team of forensic anthropological economists calculated in today's dollars the value of slaves' labor up to Emancipation. We'll move on reparations whenever you say, sir.

OBAMA: Soon. Let's . . .

MICHELLE: I want Reverend Farrakhan's appointment as Vatican Ambassador fast-tracked. Can't wait to see his X men mix it up with the Swiss Guard. You hear me, Barack?

IN AN ALTERNATE UNIVERSE: CABINET OF CURIOSITIES 2

January 23, 2017
White House, Cabinet Room
First Meeting of President Obama's New Team

OBAMA: Listen up, people. I got myself across the finish line but couldn't bring Congress along. That's why you're here. Except for Defense, you represent the first entirely recessed Cabinet in American history. Do me proud.

MICHELLE: I'm the new Chief of Staff. You want to see him, you gotta get past me. Waste my time, I'll cut your budget 10%.

OBAMA: So, propose some fresh ideas. HHS?

MICHAEL MOORE: Now that ObamaCare is the law of the land, amend the program to cover all humanity, sir. Eventually, include lesser beings, as well. Innumerable uninsured creatures are suffering.

OBAMA: Easy, big guy. In stages. After people, we insure the remaining mammalians; then, things with legs; finally, air breathers. Treasury?

GEORGE SOROS: I haff run za numbers, zir: Stimulus IV tips worldwide economy into depression within year.

OBAMA: Good. Inching us closer to the one-world government mankind will demand I lead to left the—I mean, right the—ship. I'm getting bored with the presidency, anyway. Joe?

BIDEN: Everybody who wants dough gets some, Chief, and there'll be plenty left over. How 'bout we go transnational and use foreign aid to bail out Africa? Make you more popular in Kenya than Bush. Call it the WASTE Initiative.

OBAMA: WASTE?

BIDEN: "Welfare for African States with Troubled Economies"

OBAMA: OMB?

BERNIE MADOFF: [videoconferencing from Butner Federal Correctional Complex] George is overly optimistic about how long before we foment a global crash, Mr. President. Economies can be annoyingly resilient. We need a backup plan.

OBAMA: Agreed. Eric, task DOJ lawyers to discover extra-constitutional justification for footing a European bailout. We'll call our proposal the, uh, "Bosom Allies Relief Fund." BARF will overwhelm their monetary system with worthless dollars, bollixing up the euro and paralyzing trade.

RAMSEY CLARK: Sir, *I'm* your new AG; Holder's been in jail since last month, after he was convicted of directing a Gunwalker conspiracy that was adjudged vast and injurious.

OBAMA: Oh, right. I'd pardon him, or at least pull him out of solitary, except, well, word is he's writing a book. Hmm. Ramsey, notify Holder's warden to allow him weekly unsupervised walks in Fort Marcy Park.

KRUGMAN: Sir, Republicans will yell bloody murder when they learn you've BARFed.

OBAMA: Too bad. Alert Senators Collins and Murkowski I'll grant them private audiences if they agree to be bipartisan about my usurpation of Congressional power. Moving on, CIA, what's your take on the ruble these days?

MATT DAMON: Fine choice, sir; go for quality, color, and cut.

OBAMA: Never mind. How are negotiations going with al-Qaeda?

DAMON: I'm close to a gentleman's agreement with al-Zawaheri, Mr. President. He'll give us nonspecific advance notice of an atrocity if we grant him U.S. citizenship and the right to appeal to the SCOTUS any decision to take him out. Proceed?

OBAMA: Yes. Which reminds me. Suppose I'm in the middle of a personal-best round and he manages to hit us? I can't leave the course just to rally the public with insipid assurances. NSA?

SEAN PENN: Tape a general statement in the Oval Office to have on hand in case you're busy, sir. You know, "Let me be clear . . . Make no mistake . . . They'll be held accountable . . ." So forth. We'll label it "live."

OBAMA: Sounds good. By the way, Chico, congratulations on being adopted by Hugo Chavez before he died. A real honor for a "gringo."

PENN: *Gracias, Excelente.*

OBAMA: Now, Matt, I assume the Zawahiri deal wouldn't preclude apprehending him should the opportunity arise. If you tried to lure him to Washington to sign off on our arrangement, would he bite?

DAMON: Very likely, sir. I recommend we equip the arresting Delta Force team with the Ripp® Restraint Protective Mask system guaranteed to frustrate spitters and biters.

OBAMA: [sigh] Ramsey?

CLARK: I advise against such a provocative action, sir. We should open a dialogue with the man. He attacks us, we talk with him. He continues to kill Americans, we talk some more. He dirty bombs New York, say, we threaten to stop talking. That's how to get his attention.

OBAMA: Noted. Defense?

ADAM BALDWIN: I'd sooner arm ourselves to the teeth to make everyone fear us, Mr. President.

OBAMA: Alec, this doesn't sound like you. We can't . . . Wha? Oh Good Lord, I picked the wrong Baldwin!

MICHELLE: Well, he's here. Deal with it, Dumbo.

OBAMA: All right. But I've got my eye on you, Jayne. State?

YOKO ONO: Give some nukes to al Qaeda, sir. With both sides starting from a position of strength, we can talk about our differences openly, without fear.

OBAMA: Make it so, Sudoko. Homeland Security?

SHEILA JACKSON LEE: [interrupting cell phone conversation] What?

OBAMA: Um, any policy revamp suggestions?

JACKSON LEE: In fact, yes. Given the TSA's current emphasis on body scanning, I'm changing the agency's name to the T&A Administration.

MICHELLE: The gate called. Michael Jordan's here for your one-on-one. Don't let him blow by you on your left. You hear me, Barack?

CHAPTER 14: SKEWS OF THE DAY

BUNKER MODE

Washington (AP)—In his new book, *House Afire: Nancy Pelosi's Battle to Remain Queen of Congress, Washington Post* Associate Editor Bob Woodward offers a stunning account of Pelosi's failed efforts to save her Speakership in 2010.

Following is a partial transcript of audio Woodward claims was recorded on Election Eve at DNC Headquarters in Washington.

[klaxon sounds]

NANCY PELOSI: Red Alert! Damn! Get to your stations, people. Moving to DEFCON 1—imminent loss of the House. Steny, what's happening?

HOYER: [points to computer screen] Look here, Commander: pre-election concession rumors, rising in the blogosphere. We're shooting them down as fast as we can, but some are getting through.

PELOSI: Stay on it. Commence firing at their launchers.

TIM KAINE: A *Fox News* recon team is probing our perimeter, sir.

PELOSI: Probably O'Reilly's unit. Keep them off me.

HOYER: Skelton [MO], Spratt [SC], and Dingell [MI] report taking direct hits from precision-targeted spots. They're requesting additional air support. Uh, Commander, we lack the resources to . . .

PELOSI: I know. Triage Grayson [FL], Driehaus [OH], and Perriello [VA].

HOYER: Eliot Spitzer from CNN's Kathleen Parker/Elliot Spitzer show on hold, sir. Might be worth a minute of your time.

PELOSI: On speaker. Eliot, Kathleen. How can I . . . ?

SPITZER: Kathleen's not around, Nancy. What are you wearing?

PELOSI: [hangs up] Geez! I'm a grandmother.

JAMES CLYBURN: It's looking dire in Western Pennsylvania, sir. We need a miracle to avoid suffering heavy casualties. Lord forgive us for sending those poor souls into battle with our pathetic record on their backs.

PELOSI: Don't give up yet. [dials phone] Eric? Activate "Operation Fat Tuesday," Sector Tango. [hangs up; dials another number] Panther Central, this is Mother Load [sic]. You're on.

CLYBURN: What's happening?

PELOSI: Our Philly allies will deliver squads in civvies to designated polling places in the region just before 8:00 p.m. tomorrow. A sympathetic judge has agreed to extend voting hours in those stations until midnight to avoid disenfranchising anyone.

HOYER: Then, under cover of darkness, SEIU press gangs will sweep the streets and homeless shelters, pick up thousands of vagrants, transport them to the polls, and help them cast ballots. It'll cost us some cigarettes.

CHRIS VAN HOLLEN: Commander Reid is on the line from the Senate bunker, sir.

PELOSI: On Speaker. Harry, what's up?

REID: The election is lost.

PELOSI: [signals Hoyer to break connection] Loser.

CLYBURN: The action's heating up in Wisconsin and Minnesota, Commander.

PELOSI: Dispatch force multiplier teams to hot zones in those states. They'll assist indigenous troops in door-to-door and phone bank offenses.

KAINE: Barney Frank is on line 2. He insists on speaking with you, sir.

PELOSI: [grabs phone] Hey Barney, you . . .

FRANK: Don't interrupt me, Nancy. I . . .

PELOSI: [breaks connection] No more calls, Steny.

HOYER: Sir, Senator Boxer's faxed a request. She's ringing GOP stronghold Orange County polling places with acoustic repulsors, but she's running short. Wants to know if we can spare a few.

PELOSI: Negative. Tell her to call the California Prison Guards' Union. Chris, are all our PSYOPS units deployed?

VAN HOLLEN: Yes, sir. Unmarked vans are cruising tossup districts, blasting out, "VOTE REPUBLICAN" at an eardrum-shattering 150 decibels.

HOYER: Situation reports are beginning to come in from the Midwest, Commander. We've identified three dozen contests trending more heavily to the enemy than expected.

PELOSI: Key in the pre-programmed Code Red mass emergency phone notification system for GOP neighborhoods in those precincts. Word the message this way: "Warning: you're advised to lock your doors and stay home until polls close and the danger of voting Republican has passed."

Chris, alert Blitzer and the network anchors to begin spreading disinformation on poll closing times at 4:00 p.m. eastern. What's the status of our efforts to disrupt Fox's reporting?

HOYER: When Hannity comes on, Chris Matthews will place an anonymous call to *Fox* and warn them the show is a bomb in their lineup. Good chance *Fox*'ll misconstrue and evacuate the building.

PELOSI: Our legal teams report in?

HOYER: Yes, sir. All fifty are in place. They'll challenge any contest we lose by ten percent or less. Democratic Secretaries of State are standing by to assist.

CLYBURN: A lot of our people are in harm's way, Commander. A word from you would raise morale.

PELOSI: I'll text them this: "We shall fight them in the sushi bars, we shall fight them on the campuses, we shall fight them in the Starbucks. I shall remain a big spender. I have nothing to offer but mud, debt, and a shot and a beer."

HOYER: Sir, will you pull the trigger on "Operation Scorched Earth" if you lose the Speakership?

PELOSI: Yes, though he doesn't exist, may God forgive me. I'll signal Globe Magazine to drop the "Boehner and the Sheep" bomb in a special post-election edition.

BILL CLINTON: Nancy, no! The fallout!

PELOSI: Who let Clinton in here?

HILL AND BILL ON *OPRAH*

Chicago (AP)—Appearing on an *Oprah Winfrey Special* yesterday, former Secretary of State Hillary Clinton and former president Bill Clinton spoke publicly for the first time about the 2008 primary campaign, her political ambitions, and their personal relationship.

Representatives insisted the joint appearance had absolutely nothing to do with Mrs. Clinton's rumored plan to challenge President Obama's bid for a 22nd Amendment-busting third term in 2016.

The show began with Hill and Bill air-kissing and catching up since they were last together at daughter Chelsea's wedding several years ago.

Winfrey commenced the interview by asking Mrs. Clinton to assess her run for the 2008 presidential nomination.

HILLARY: I'm not one to second-guess, but I wish we had played the race card early in the game.

WINFREY: What . . .

HILLARY: Not me. Bill. The moment Obama emerged, Bill missed the opportunity to demand our party open a national discussion on who was the more authentic black leader, an inexperienced senator with roots in Indonesia or him, the First Black President.

WINFREY: So, you didn't go for it because you assumed you had the African-American vote locked up?

HILLARY: Of course. Jesse Jackson had agreed to endorse me and become Secretary of Reparations in my Cabinet. You, Oprah, promised your support if I pushed Congress to make Kenya our 51st state.

WINFREY: Oh. I remember now.

HILLARY: In addition, we had a powerful ad campaign ready to run in minority communities: "Hillary will end welfare as we know it and go back to welfare as we knew it. She'll extend it, not amend it. Don't have it your way, have it both ways!" That focus-tested off the charts across all demographics.

Then Obama came from nowhere, and Mr. "First Black President" here became just another old white guy with a heart condition.

WINFREY: Mr. President, pick one campaign decision you regret.

BILL: Well, in the run-up to primaries in the battleground states, we cut a great TV ad showing Hillary ready to assume command on Day One. But she thought she looked too butch, so we canned the spot.

WINFREY: The new PBS documentary on the 2008 primary campaign covers this. Let's play a clip.

[Announcer]

Aired publicly for the first time, the ad opens with Senator Clinton in full field gear patrolling Fallujah with a joint American-Iraqi unit.

Barking at her Secret Service detail to keep up, Mrs. Clinton is shown sprinting house-to-house, her modified M14 with a Leupold LR/T 10 x 40 mm carried lightly on her shoulder.

Pausing behind a wall after the patrol takes sniper fire, Hillary speaks to the camera:

"Bush screwed up in Iraq. You trust me with your vote, I'm gonna be hands-on and make things right. [shots] Gotta go. [spits her chaw] Third floor window, left! Jones, Moorehead, cover us! Rest of you, follow me!" [more shots as Clinton and her unit scale the wall, firing their weapons]

[Announcer]

Hillary Rodham Clinton: a fighter, not a divider.

[fade out]

"She's one tough hombre," President Clinton told Winfrey, revealing that Hillary considered taking a week off from campaigning to hunt bin Laden in Pakistan's tribal no-go areas.

"I remember her saying, 'If I find the bastard, I'll saw his head off and give it to the Smithsonian.'

Eventually, Hillary decided to keep the macho side of herself hidden from the public. So she went with the softer image, and you know how that worked out."

Turning to the personal, Winfrey asked Mrs. Clinton to discuss the pitfalls of politics and marital relationships. To everyone's surprise, Hillary addressed nagging questions about her own marriage:

HILLARY: Did Bill abuse women? Yes. Did he ignore his duties to pursue tawdry affairs? Of course. Was I restrained by the Secret Service from clocking him with a lamp? Often. I'm sure Americans wanted to slap him upside the head after Lewinsky. His behavior was wrong.

I thought about leaving him until I realized I could ride the scandal right into my own presidency, serving as a champion of the world's poor and helpless, especially the little ones who . . .

WINFREY: So, you stayed with this lout, uh, the Big He . . . for the children? You knew what he was like from the beginning. Why didn't you leave him thirty years ago?

HILLARY: Well, I figured he was headed for big things, and I needed him to pull me along. Bill wasn't at fault when I failed to get the nomination; he was always there for me. I could no more divorce him than announce I won't challenge Obama in 2016.

WINFREY: Aren't you concerned your husband's behavior will embarrass you again?

HILLARY: A lot has changed. I've hand-picked his Secret Service detail and they are all over him 24/7 now. He can't be alone with a woman who isn't a blood relative without my say-so. Kind of like the Muslim custom for women, but reversed.

With Bill resigned to living the life of a eunuch, I don't worry about bimbo eruptions. Actually, since I cut off his Viagra, his bimbo eruptions are just a memory [cackle].

WINFREY: What a bind I'd be in if I had to choose between you and Barack.

HILLARY: Oprah, we're sisters under the skin. We have our reproductive organs in common, for God's sake. Please give some thought to supporting me. Anywhere in particular you've always wanted to be an ambassador?

PIERS MORGAN TONIGHT: GORE REVERSES, CLAIMS GLOBAL COOLING

Washington (AP)—Appearing on *Piers Morgan Tonight* last evening, former vice president Al Gore spoke publicly for the first time about the *National Enquirer*'s 2010 report he was investigated for soliciting sex from a masseuse in a Portland, Oregon hotel.

> It was all a misunderstanding, Piers. I was indeed staying at the Hotel Lucia that night. Checking my e mail on the lobby computer, I found an anonymous message, with attachments, claiming prominent climatologists I'd been working with had been fudging numbers.

> Visibly disturbed, I printed the material and started for upstairs to study it in private when the night manager noticed I was distressed and asked if he could help. In jest, I replied, 'Yes, find a person skilled in massaging climate data and send that person to my room.'

> Later, someone knocked on my door. It was the masseuse. She told me she had never massaged data before, but she thought shiatsu and a light touch on the keyboard would do the trick. When I explained the mix-up, she laughed. We talked a bit and she left. End of story.

Also appearing on the show with Mr. Gore was the new head of the U.N.'s climate panel, Sucrose Boutros-Ghali, sister of former U.N. General Secretary Boutros Boutros-Ghali. Both she and Gore acknowledged global warming has been exposed as a sophisticated hoax perpetrated by several now-discredited climatologists.

"The scientists responsible were vested in trying to prove something that wasn't so in order to secure grants and garner honors and fame," Boutros-Ghali said. "They assumed they'd never be found out. Shows what they know."

In a startling reversal, Gore claimed global cooling, not global warming, is the greatest threat mankind faces. "The most recent data suggest earth is actually heading into a Little Ice Age caused mainly by human activity. We now believe nuclear weapons testing in the latter half of the 20th century by the United States shifted the planet on its axis, exposing less of the surface to the sun's rays."

Other reasons for the cooling earth, Gore explained:

> Refrigerators, freezers, and air conditioners have become ubiquitous over the last fifty years, even in remote areas, Piers. Every time someone peeks in the fridge to see what's inside, every time someone cranks up the AC, cold air escapes and temperatures decline worldwide. The result: falling sea levels as more and more water becomes locked up in polar caps and glaciers. That means less rain and, eventually, drought, famine, pestilence and a host of Biblical plagues.

What to do? For a start, Boutros-Ghali suggested everyone watch Gore's new feature documentary, *An Inconvenient Truth II: This Time I'm Right.* In the film, Gore offers common-sense solutions to slow planetary cooling, e.g., burning more coal; revoking the ban on CFC compounds [found in aerosol spray propellants and AC units] to open holes in the ozone layer, allowing intense solar radiation to reach the earth; and firing the Amazon rain forest, creating particulate barriers in the stratosphere to keep heat from escaping into space.

The former vice president recently founded Cooler Heads International, LLC, Ontario, (CHILLCO), a Canadian-based firm which invests institutional funds in global warming technologies and concepts designed to combat global cooling.

Gore wants individuals to play a role in saving the planet from another ice age:

> Fling open your doors and windows; turn up your thermostats; de-insulate your homes; instigate heated arguments about politics with your friends on the other side. Every little bit helps. We've got a planet to save here, people.

> Bovine belching and flatulence produce significant quantities of methane gas, as do termite emissions. Because methane is a critical greenhouse gas in atmospheric warming, we must stop targeting certain creatures for consumption or eradication.

Sucrose-Ghali called cattle and termites "mankind's allies in the climate crisis." She promised the U.N. would lobby the world community to declare these life forms protected species.

"Aren't you two suggesting short-term, Band-Aid measures?" Morgan inquired.

Gore's response:

> I'm afraid so, Piers. Our planet is sick. Mankind is the tapeworm in its gut. I am the doctor. My prescription: we eliminate the tapeworm to save the patient. I'd like birth rates at zero in fifty years, humans extinct a hundred years after that. We can't hide the decline anymore, so let's just get this over with. Maybe in ten thousand millennia, we'll climb up out of the muck again and this time do it right.

251

OBAMA TO BEGIN NEW WORLD APOLOGY TOUR IN CUBA

Washington (AP)—When President Barack Obama arrives in Havana for a state visit next month, he will personally apologize to Cuban Premier Fidel Castro for decades of American interference with Cuba's efforts to destabilize the Southern Hemisphere.

Appearing on *ABC*'s new Sunday talk show, *Last Week*, which precedes *This Week*, which is followed by *Next Week*, White House Advisor Valerie Jarrett told host Jesse Jackson that Cuba was the first stop on the president's new World Apology Tour.

"He'll match words with actions," Jarrett said, revealing Obama will give Guantanamo Bay back to Cuba as soon as the imprisoned man-made disaster suspects are transferred to halfway houses in the U.S.

"It is a strictly humanitarian gesture," Jarrett insisted. "Cuba's prison population is exploding. Premier Castro assured us that the whole of Guantanamo would become a *gulag* to hold political prisoners who would otherwise be shot because Cuban dungeons are full."

In another sign of a thaw in Cuban-American relations, President Obama offered blanket amnesty and U.S. citizenship to Cuban provocateurs, assassins, and double agents who wish to remain in the shadows after operating in America for decades.

"It has been hard for us," offered "Francisco," the Cuban Security Service's top spy in Florida since 1987. "My people arrived here in 1980 posing as refugees—'Marielitos.' We've been living in fear ever since, running from safe house to safe house, one step ahead of the FBI. Now we can do our jobs without looking over our shoulders."

Attorney General Eric Holder said the Justice Department would waive the Oath of Citizenship for Cuban nationals who did not want to attend the ceremony and risk their cover.

CIA TAPE SHOCKER: PELOSI IN BED WITH REID

WASHINGTON (AP)—In an escalation of the conflict between the Central Intelligence Agency and former House Speaker Nancy Pelosi, a CIA source has provided the *New York Times* a tape of a July 2007 meeting attended by Pelosi, Senate Majority Leader Harry Reid, and the late Pennsylvania Congressman, John Murtha.

"Normally, we'd spike this story," said Jill Abramson, Executive Editor of the *Times*, "but we need to sell newspapers or we'll wind up being a Paraguayan billionaire's trophy rag.

"There's no money in our budget for voice analysis, so we begged the *National Enquirer* to vet the tape for free," Abramson said. "They confirm it's legitimate. I've personally listened to the audio, and the transcript we've printed is accurate."

In one exchange, Pelosi, Murtha, and Reid appear to be discussing ways to keep a weakened President Bush on the defensive in Iraq:

> **MURTHA**: al Qaeda's taking a hit in Iraq, and the Sunnis are beginning to turn. Not good. We need to buy bin Laden time to revive the insurgency or we're in trouble.
>
> Nancy, why don't you schedule the Turkish genocide vote next week? That'd tick the Turks off and force Petraeus to divert forces to the northern border, easing pressure on jihadists in Anbar Province.

PELOSI: Good point, John. A resolution here, a resolution there, we poison relations with key allies, and then we claim Bush is going cowboy in his so-called War on Terror. Harry?

REID: Let's bring Pakistan and Saudi Arabia into play. I'll schedule a vote demanding the administration take out Pakistan's nuclear facilities. Then we'll pass a bill requiring Saudi Royals family visiting America to submit to body cavity searches.

PELOSI: Sounds good. I'll reach out to Taliban leader Mullah Omar and invite him to be my guest at January's State of the Union. Karzai will pitch a fit, and the Taliban will be re-energized. Bush's numbers'll continue to go south when everyone sees what a mess he's made of Iraq and Afghanistan.

Folks, we've got plenty of options to keep the president scrambling. We owe it to the American people.

SENATOR BOXER: WHITMAN, FIORINA SPREAD 2010 CALIFORNIA FOREST BLAZES FOR SPORT

Sacramento (AP)—In the current edition of *The Nation* magazine, Senator Barbara Boxer charges former GOP rival Carly Fiorina and Republican gubernatorial candidate Meg Whitman behaved badly during the Tehachapi wildfire emergency in 2010 which destroyed forty homes.

"Whitman and Fiorina had finished lunch after campaigning in nearby Bakersfield when they saw smoke and decided to go sightseeing in Whitman's German-made EC135 Eurocopter," Boxer told Katrina vanden Heuvel, editor of The Nation. "Shortly after lifting off, Whitman radioed the Disaster Operations Center to demand that aerial water and fire retardant flights be grounded while she and Fiorina toured the scene."

An environmentalist who had chained himself to a Bigcone Douglas-fir to protest the fire texted authorities minutes before being engulfed that he saw an EC135 hovering ten yards off the ground, while the pilot deliberately used the craft's rotor blades to spread the flames.

Another witness, California Governor Jerry Brown, told forestry officials he was hiking out of the area to escape the conflagration when he observed a helicopter land ahead of an advancing wall of fire. He claimed Whitman and Fiorina emerged from the aircraft, caught fleeing animals, and threw them into the blaze.

In the most shocking revelation, a Sierra Club executive, surveying the devastation later, said he spotted Whitman, Fiorina, and Karl Rove toasting marshmallows in the dying embers of seniors Clarence and Wilma Jones' house as the couple wept close by. Rove, Whitman, and Fiorina then commiserated with insurance company officials who had arrived on the scene to assess the damage to their bottom line.

The Nation has preemptively rejected any criticism for running the piece. "We stand by our story," said vanden Heuvel, "because it could have happened and there's no proof it didn't."

FOUNDATION TO LAUNCH "CASH FOR CONGRESSIONAL CLUNKERS" PROGRAM

Chicago (AP)—The Foundation to Preserve American Values, a private philanthropic group, announced at a news conference today it will distribute up to one billion dollars in grants to selected members of Congress. Ralph Warren, president of the FPAV, called the initiative, "Cash for Congressional Clunkers."

Politicians who stay too long in Washington pollute the national discourse and guzzle media airtime, a finite resource. Schumer of New York is a prime example. We propose to get him and others like him out of Washington before they do any more harm to the country. This means offering them attractive incentives to junk their political careers and force voters to do more than fill in the circle next to a familiar name.

Pelosi and Waxman would command top dollar for resigning. Yes, their seats are safe, and they have perks and influence. We'll make it worth their while to trade up from great power to great wealth.

Pelosi, for example, might receive $100 million if she applies. She'll never worry about Botox injection fees again. Waxman, $50 million. That's enough for him to get his nose fixed. Schumer is a special case. We've been in touch. In addition to awarding him $50 million, the Foundation agreed to sponsor *Late Night with Chuck Schumer* on the Comedy Channel.

Warren said the board would evaluate the success of the initiative after six months. "If we like what we see," 'Cash for Administration Clunkers' will kick off next spring."

ALTERNATE WORLDS/ SPACETIMES NEWS ROUNDUP

DON'T HURT ME

October 3, 2016

New York Times—Hillary Clinton petitioned a Virginia Superior Court judge today to issue a restraining order against *Fox News* contributor Brit Hume prior to tonight's presidential debate at James Madison University.

Clinton stated in her complaint she fears for her campaign and is concerned Hume may "rough her up" in his role as moderator. She wants Hume enjoined from coming within 500 feet of her with a question which might appear harmless but could be used to bludgeon her.

DROP THE BALLOT; STEP AWAY FROM THE VOTING BOOTH

November 8, 2016

Reuters—In a massive protest today against the almost certain election of Republican Jon Voight to the presidency, Democrats across the country avoided the polls, casting the integrity of the results in doubt.

In Washington, Senate Majority Charles Schumer (D-NY) said it was heroic for forty million Democrats to choose self-disenfranchisement rather than allow their votes to count for nothing. An *AP* survey last weekend had Michelle Obama down by twenty points to Voight, despite gross oversampling of Wisconsin academics.

EISENHOWER PLANNING BOLD STROKE

May 23, 1944

Washington Post—Highly-placed officials confirm General Dwight Eisenhower is preparing a massive invasion of Normandy sometime in early June.

"The idea is to make Hitler believe our forces will be coming ashore at *Pas de Calais*," one officer involved in the planning reports. "We're pushing the deception that nothing happens until July, at the earliest."

Military and civilian leaders expressed reservations. "I'm only speaking with you because it's going to be bloody if Ike goes ahead," one senator privy to the plans said. "When the Germans read about this in the *Post*, they'll look harder at Normandy, and Eisenhower would be foolish to launch. He'll probably do so anyway. What happens will be on his head."

SUMMAT FOR NOTHING

November 4, 2013

Boston Globe—Cambridge Police Officer James Crowley of "beer summit" fame was arrested outside his Natick, Massachusetts home today and charged with disorderly conduct after shouting "Calm down!" to a mob chanting "racist pig."

DRIVE ME TO THE MOON

March 12, 2014

Daily News—At a press briefing this morning, New York Governor Andrew Cuomo rejected calls from Republican legislators to abandon his plan to grant drivers' licenses to undocumented New Yorkers with criminal backgrounds. And he raised the stakes:

"Sadly, uncredentialed thugs from points south commit crimes with unregistered, untraceable firearms purchased on the black market when they arrive here," Cuomo said.

"To correct this problem, I've instructed officials to issue concealed carry permits and free handguns to immigrants who apply for a New York State driver's license. They don't have to say, Madre ¿pudeo?

"In time, law enforcement agencies may access a detailed database of naturalized aliens and their vehicles, along with the make, model, serial numbers, and ballistic specifications of the firearms provided to them. Finding bad hombres with all this information will be a whole lot easier."

Cuomo credited Democratic strategist Smith Wesson for coming up with an ad campaign to sell the promotion. "The simple message on billboards and TV throughout Mexico: 'New York: Conduzca uno, consiga pistola libre.'" [New York: Drive One, Get Gun Free.]

SELMA ON MY MIND

May 2, 2015

Washington Post—In an e mail sent to *Post* Editors today, a Senate Democrat who requested anonymity said Reverend Jesse Jackson is advising House Majority Leader Nancy Pelosi to stage a reprise of 2010's disappointingly peaceful march through the heart of a Tea Party rally outside Washington's Capitol Building.

Reprinted by permission, the text in full:

"Jackson urged Pelosi to employ aggressive-passive behavior this time around to provoke demonstrators. Jesse called it a riff on Selma. Told Nancy to station SEIU operatives with fire hoses and dogs along the route of the procession. On her signal, they'd hose the Tea Partiers, sic the animals on 'em, and fall back. That cues Pelosi's marchers to descend on the protestors, beat them with sticks, retreat, and assemble, then wait meekly for retaliation while singing, 'We Shall Overcome.'

"Jackson advised the group, 'When they come at you, an *NBC* crew starts taping; so nobody fight back! You gotta be like Jackie Robinson and take it.'

"To avoid a repeat of Emmanuel Cleaver II's debunked 'I was spat upon' story from the first march, Jackson told Cleaver, 'I'll plant a coarse Kos Kid in the Tea Party crowd. You start talkin', he'll start hawkin'. And when this guy spits, he hits. We'll get it on tape and hold back until Trump offers $100,000 offer for proof.

"Pelosi was certain demonstrators planned to pervert the truth with cell phone video that recorded the actual events. House Whip Steny Hoyer said his contact in the Pentagon Signals Jamming Division predicted 'solar activity' affecting mobiles in the area the whole day, as well as *Fox News* satellite transmissions.

"Pelosi also expressed concern dogs might be hurt during the melee. Nancy knows PETA would be furious with her if that happened. She told Hoyer to have vets on call in case a dog is injured or needs a shot after biting Palin or Hannity."

HILLARY: GORE THREATENED ME WITH ENDORSEMENT IN 2008

Washington *(Reuters)*—In an interview with *Salon Magazine*, former Secretary of State Hillary Clinton charged that in May of 2008, Al Gore threatened to support her for president over her objections.

"When we learned Al planned to come on board, Bill and I were furious. We met with him in a K Street brothel Bill frequents, just the three of us and our Secret Service details. We pleaded with Al to endorse Senator Obama instead. He flatly refused, saying, 'I helped you both get over the Lewinsky, uh, hump in '98, which cost me the presidency in 2000. Well, here comes payback.'

"It got pretty intense," said Mrs. Clinton. "At one point, Bill's face turned purple, and he jabbed his finger into Gore's chest and growled, 'All those times you swore you wouldn't utter a good word about either of us, you were lying, weren't you? Obama put you up to this? Oprah? Ken Starr?'"

A spokesman for President Clinton confirmed the account, adding Mrs. Clinton obtained a restraining order against Gore, prohibiting him from coming within 100 hours of following through on his endorsement threat.

White House Press Secretary Jay Carney acknowledged Gore's role as a key advisor to the Obama campaign during the primaries, but he insisted Gore never supported Obama. "The team knew Al's real interest was in leaving his big carbon footprint on Hillary's back, and they respected that."

Unavailable for comment, Gore is in transit to Altair IV in the Orion Cluster for an interstellar conference on "Cosmic Warming, or, the Heat Death of the Universe."

CHAPTER 15: CAMPAIGN 2012

OBAMA WAR ROOM: AFTER MATH

BIDEN: Um, Where's the Chief, Ma'am?

MICHELLE: Romney beat him like a rented mule in last night's debate. He's stressed out. I'm running things until his therapists clear him for duty. Jay, at your briefing, say the president's decided to hole up in the White House until Election Day to do the work of the American people.

BIDEN: How 'bout tough love, Ma'am. Haul his bony rear end back to the Oval Office and tell him to start actively deferrin' decisions again.

MICHELLE: Eric, Jim Lehrer needs to pay for his even-handedness as moderator.

HOLDER: In custody, charged with failure to report a verbal assault.

MICHELLE: Valerie, reach out to the Commission on Presidential Debates. Tell them he's too busy juggling crises to attend the last two debates, but he'll be happy to ignore questions submitted in writing.

[enter the president in his bathrobe, muttering]

OBAMA: No way out, no way out, no . . .

MICHELLE: Barack! Snap out of it. We can recover.

JOE BIDEN: Hey, let's take a page outta Dolly Parton's book and think outside the buxom.

JARRETT: Outside the . . . ?

BIDEN: Roil the GOPhers: ask Pelosi and Reid to cut ads sayin', "We support Romney because we can work with him, because in four years Obama never gave us the time of day, because . . ."

MICHELLE: We get it, Joe.

BIDEN: The Boss was wishy-washy on Iran. Let's play hardball: jam their communication satellites so they can't get *Dancing with the Stars*.

AXELROD: Go further: if the U.N. is refused access to their nuclear facilities, we'll assume control of their entire broadcast network and show *Fiddler on the Roof* 24/7 until the mullahs cry Uncle Tevye.

OBAMA: You know, if I'm reelected, I wouldn't have to work hard. Yubby dibby dibby dibby dibby dibby dibby dum. All day long, I'd biddy biddy golf . . .

MICHELLE: Where's the aide with his medications?

HEROIC COUPLET*

Though poor his gifts, he rose to craggy heights
(Which fact will give his chon'clers sleepless nights).
A cunning man whose seasoning was spare,
The cupboard of his history strangely bare.
To question where he came from, whom he'd known,
Marked those who asked such racist to the bone.
Despite his wish to throw us off the scent,
We now know something of his youthful bent:
He tacked near shore; no destination marked;

This way and that, upon no quest embarked,
Till Saul and Wright and Ayers and all their kind
Found shelter in the harbor of his mind.

He won! The guise was dropped, the man revealed,
His loathing for our country, unconcealed.
He told the world how wicked we had been;
Obsessed about the color of his skin;
Spent massive sums to fund enviro dreams;
Bowed in obeyance to the Saudis' schemes;
Made "jobs" the word that dare not speak its name;
Used talk of being civil to inflame;
Ignored the rule of law, his oath betrayed;
And for the Constitution, scorn displayed;
Spread shameful lies about a coming boom;
Denied the rights of those inside the womb.

And won again! So all must bear some blame
For guaranteeing four more years of same.
And unresolved: the toughest nut of all:
How this pretender keeps us in his thrall.

*Inspired by Alexander Pope, an 18th century English satirist famous for his satirical verse using "heroic couplets," two rhyming lines in iambic pentameter.

PROCESS OF ELIMINATION

Washington Times—A source inside the Democratic National Committee revealed today that officials considered asking former vice president Al Gore to mount a primary challenge against President Obama in 2012.

According to the source, Party leaders interviewed Gore in the summer of 2011, when the president's reelection chances appeared dim. Present at the meeting: Debbie Whassupman Schultz, National Chair; Mike Honda, Vice Chair; Linda Chavez-Thompson, Vice Chair; Harry Reid, Senate Majority MisLeader; and Nancy Pelosi, Speaker-in-Waiting. Partial transcript follows:

WHASSUPMAN SCHULTZ: Let's get started. Polls indicate anyone picked at random from a Newark phone book would thrash President Obama next year in all 57 states, despite ACORN's Get-Out-the-Dead-Vote project. The down-ticket effects would be equally catastrophic.

PELOSI: No turning back, then. Okay, pass the cigars and smoke up the room. Today, we honor the sainted Boss Tweed by beginning a search for a challenger to President Obama. Mr. Soros will fund our candidate in exchange for an office in the West Wing if we win in November.

WHASSUPMAN SCHULTZ: Mike, ask our guest to join us.

[enter Gore]

Welcome, Mr. Vice President. Please sit. Now, tell us why you think we should . . .

GORE: I have conditions.

WHASSUPMAN SCHULTZ: Conditions?

GORE: Which must be accepted by all.

WHASSUPMAN SCHULTZ: And they are?

GORE: The new Congress's first act: expropriating Lafayette Park and authorizing construction of the world's largest geodesic habitats for endangered flora and fauna, to be named the Green House and Animal House.

WHASSUPMAN SCHULTZ: Hmm. Research and Destroy assures me the IRS has supplied us with enough dirt on GOP candidates to take both chambers if Obama's not on the ticket, so it could be done. Nancy, Harry?

PELOSI: I'll commit to the project when I'm Speaker again.

REID: Me too, long as certain associates get the slots concession for both structures. Okay, we . . .

GORE: I'm not done. Karenna's VP and succeeds me in 2028. Yes, it'll take me four terms to undo the damage done by my predecessors. You'll have to amend the Constitution.

REID: [sighing] I guess. Now . . .

GORE: There's more. An earth-centric agenda rules: returning America to its pre-industrial base, and offering the public option to all mankind, resulting in lower life spans and thus reduced pressure on the planet's resources.

PELOSI: Short-term fixes, Al.

GORE: I know. Long term? Our planet is hopelessly infested with . . . people; Earth is the Sick Man of the Solar System. But I am the Healer of Worlds. My prognosis: Gaia is doomed unless we gradually breed out the rampant species: us.

WHASSUPMAN SCHULTZ: So, you're talking, what, worldwide sterilization programs and zero reproduction mandates, in tandem, leading to man's extinction? I can live with that.

PELOSI: Visionary. Right now, though, voters are concerned about energy costs. Your thoughts?

GORE: President Kennedy electrified America when he pledged to put a man on the moon in ten years. The Gore Administration will inspire the country with an environmental crash program: storing methane from bovine flatulence, a major cause of global warming.

REID: *Merde*! Why hasn't anyone thought of this before?

GORE: In one swell poop, we harness a dangerous greenhouse bio-gas for use as cheap fuel.

REID: American entrepremanures will be all over it like flies on . . .

GORE: If only it were just ruminants. Termites produce methane, too, big time. Unrecoverable, unfortunately. I'd task Predators to take out the largest termite mounds worldwide.

WHASSUPMAN SCHULTZ: Insect rights groups will go bugnuts.

GORE: We also need to look at ourselves. Billions use Earth as an outhouse. To set an example, I'll require waste recyclers in every home and public facility in America by 2018. My first Executive Order: "Harvesting Ordure: Operation Assimilative Heads."

REID: HOOAH?

ALL: HOOAH!!

WHASSUPMAN SCHULTZ: Well, you certainly have your finger on the pulse of today's Democratic Party

GORE: If this doesn't work out, please get a message to Soros that I'd like to talk with him about financing a revolutionary *Flintstones*-type personal vehicle that . . .

WHASSUPMAN SCHULTZ: Thank you, Mr. Vice President. We'll be in touch.

OBAMA WAR ROOM: IT'S YOU AND ME, BABY

OBAMA: Okay, we got the Muslims; the generation ship welfarers; dead urban Democrats; feminists; the Greens, blacks, browns; the jaundiced; academics; the Mediscared; home-grown communists; Jews; gays; enfranchised illegals; Kos Kids living in their parents' basements; and drug cartel members with dual citizenship.

DAVID PLOUFFE: We need another bloc to put us over the top, sir.

JOE BIDEN: How about "Sucker Moms"?

OBAMA: We've lost that demographic, Joe.

BIDEN: Not "Soccer Moms," Chief, "Sucker Moms." Single women who thought the boyfriend would stay around soon's he found out there was a *bâtard* in the oven.

OBAMA: And you're proposing?

BIDEN: Declare marital law, Boss. Or is it "common-law"? Whatever. Then, issue a directive defining "deserter" as any civilian male AWOL from his family unit.

DAVID PLOUFFE: In addition, sir, order Homeland Security to transfer to Washington personnel who are busy ignoring human trafficking on the border. They'd team with FBI agents and MPs to track down deadbeat dads and return them to their home bases.

OBAMA: Not bad.

BIDEN: We also find language in ObamaCare guaranteeing 24/7 Supernanny coverage, contingent on your reelection.

KATHLEEN SEBELIUS: I'd add no-cost tubal ligation. Insurance companies would be free to reject offering these benefits at their peril.

OBAMA: I haven't heard a new dirtball Romney attack yet.

GLORIA ALLRED: I'll hold a presser tomorrow and charge Romney with being a general in the GOP's War on Women. His raging libido's fair game. Five sons! What that man put his poor wife through, popping out all those babies.

DAVID AXELROD: I've had a dozen PIs following Romney around, sitting in toilet stalls and waiting for him to come into the bathroom and occupy the next cubicle, sir. In two instances, he did. My guys slid a foot over and tapped suggestively, but Romney didn't take the bait.

JAY CARNEY: *Media Matters* will release a photoshopped picture of Romney going into a motel room with a transvestite.

OBAMA: Piddling stuff. I want to destroy Romney, not embarrass him.

DAVID PLOUFFE: On another front, sir: SEIU thugs wearing Tea Party tees will attack our supporters at the rally in Columbus tomorrow. After ordering the Secret Service to stand down, you'll wade into the melee and beat back the ruffians by yourself with a teleprompter leg, an American flag wrapped around your shoulders like Superman's cape.

OBAMA: Up up and away!

BIDEN: Only a couple days till the election. We better keep a lid on Iran sinking the USS Abraham Lincoln in the Strait of Hormel.

JAY CARNEY: You mean the Strait of Hormuz, Mr. Vice President. Hormel is an American company that makes Spam.

BIDEN: Why're they in the Strait? Betcha one of Romney's companies outsourced operations there. We'll say he's still involved. We can sic the FCC on 'em, too, Chief. Everybody's always complainin' about spam. You'd be the only one doin' anything about it.

OBAMA: Joe, you're going to be out of action with the flu until November 7.

SOLILOQUY* FROM *OBAMALET*, A TWO ACT TRAGEDY (SUMMER 2012)

To run honorably, or not to run honorably: those are my options.
Whether 'tis wiser in the main to malign
The life and motives of my foe
Or to square off against a host of critics,
And by defending . . . buoy them? To mock; to taunt?
Perhaps. And by these means to goad the Mitt
To err with thoughtless, scurrilous gibes
That mark him petty—a scenario
Most certainly to my gain. To taint; to smear . . .
To smear, perhaps to rouse? O, there's the risk;
For if I soil his name what harm may come
Should he then probe my shady past
Prompts me to hold: thus the upshot
That makes defamation truly fraught-filled.
Why would he brook our lies on church and cult,
His bullying ways, his past as profiteer,
His bent for corrupt deals, his wife's excess,
His countenance of harems, his outsourced jobs,
His tortured dogs found dead in household pens,
And not at once retort with truth about my specious
prov'nance

271

Which would cut badly? We might slanders sling,
To smirch and slime without a conscience tug,
'Cept that the fear of fire coming back,
An incendiary charge from whose blast
No candidate survives, stays our hand
And has us at a loss for what to sow
Than turn to libels that may come back in tens.
Thus caution keeps us playing not to lose;
And thus our sordid scheme to lie and bait
Is sidelined now for fear of what we'll reap.
And chicanery of such guile and lure,
A tack denied, puts victory at risk,
And boosts the case for cheating.
Shush now, fool; Reverend Wright begins his homily.

*Parody of Shakespeare's "To be or not to be" soliloquy in *Hamlet*

BITTER CLINGER

The White House
November 5, 2012
8:01 p.m. EST

THE PRESIDENT:

Good evening.

When I assumed office in January 2009, I swore an oath to preserve, protect, and defend my presidency.

Unfortunately, Rasmussen has Romney winning 45 states tomorrow, prompting the FBI to raise the Republican Takeover Threat Level to "Vermilion."

Fortunately, our Living Constitution authorizes the president, with Senate approval, to declare a national emergency and cling to office by postponing elections and declaring martial law. That resolution passed the Upper Chamber moments ago by what sounded to Senator Reid like a two-thirds voice vote.

The Posse Comitatus Act prohibits American troops from being deployed on American soil. Instead, Homeland Security's new Civilian National Security Force will assume responsibility for keeping the peace.

Yes, things seem bleak now, but we *will* postpone our fiscal reckoning until most of us are dead and gone. We must resist the siren call of painful choices; we must stop gazing longingly at the shore as riptides pull us out to sea.

Yesterday, after burgers and fries on the Truman Balcony with Michelle, I stood alone at the railing and looked south towards the Washington Monument, an unlit cigarette dangling from my lips [cough cough]. I thought about Churchill's "sunlit uplands" metaphor. For a brief moment, off in the distance and deep into my second term, I could almost discern the overcast lowlands where our country's future really lies.

My fellow Americans, I need your apathy if I'm to get us there.

Inshalla, and God bless America.

SONG OF DEMAGOGIA*

Introduction

From the mansion near the river
Where the Sage of Monticello
And the Great Emancipator
Served the people, saved the nation,

273

Sounds a call for civil discord
In the service of ambition
From a man whose God is power,
And his name is Demagogia.

Gathering Storm

To the banner flock his minions:
Come the Panthers, the Acorners,
Come the NOWsers and the OWSers,
Come the KosKids, IRSsers,
All the factions so enchanted
By the whimsies of the Leader
Who wants naught but boundless warrant,
Constitution notwithstanding.

Marching Orders

Demagogia tells his vassals
That the ones arrayed against him
Are ignoble, quite unworthy,
And must not be given quarter
When the battle is enjoined.
"Lay aside all thoughts of mercy:
Smear their people, smear their children,
Plough and salt the ground they walk on."

Engagement

In the cities, in the hamlets,
Over air waves, on the WorldWide,
Campaigns combat, hot and savage,
Demagogia at the forefront,
So much riding on the outcome,
Which determines if his tenure
Is a dream cut short by waking.
Or a nightmare neverending.

Foreboding

In November, morning after,
Demagogia stands triumphant,
Savoring the prize he conjured,
Casts a baleful eye about him,
Smiles grimly, mutters darkly:
"Now be fearful, those who thwart me;
See the Phoenix, rising, rising
From the flame pit, from the ashes . . ."

*A parody of Longfellow's celebrated "Song of Hiawatha"

CHAPTER 16: HILLARY WAR ROOMS—2008 PRIMARY CAMPAIGN

PREPPING THE BATTLEFIELD

HILLARY: Begala! Tell the agents I want my bacon crisp this morning or someone will find himself on the Carter detail tomorrow. Serpenthead, get the photographer in here.

CARVILLE: Yes'm

HILLARY: Stop Fidgeting, Bill. Smile like you mean it.

All right, take the damn picture. [flash] God, I hate these weekly "We're still married" photo ops.

PAUL BEGALA: Standing by your man started you on the road to the White House, Your Grace.

HILLARY: Yeah, maybe. But my negatives, which are the direct result of *his* negatives, are way too high. People need to be convinced we're reasonable human beings. Bill, I want you to go on *Hannity* and sound like you're praising Obama while you're bashing him.

BILL: Hannity doesn't do anything for me, Honey. I'll arrange an interview with Katrina Vander, uh, Huevos Rancheros, of *The Nation*.

HILLARY: Don't argue. Carville, go along and watch him; I don't want the horndog trying to get into some secretary's pants.

CARVILLE: Yes'm. I'll be tighter on 'im than a tick and her babies on a Cajun hound.

HILLARY: And Bill, don't be too good. I want people to hear you and think me. Play this right and you might get an office in the West Wing. Not, and you'll be lucky to have a cubicle in the EEOB. Word to the wise.

BEGALA: Brock's here, Majesty.

HILLARY: Approach me, David. Now, listen up. *Media Matters* didn't meet its slander quota last month.

BROCK: I apologize, my Queen. We'll take Ingraham, Hewitt, and Cal Thomas down this month.

HILLARY: Good. As well, advise your gumshoes you need actionable stuff on the major right-wing bloggers ASAP. Also, reach out to our friend at *Hustler* and tell him that you know he's making a list and checking it twice, but you want the dirt before Christmas.

BILL: Honey, I think . . .

HILLARY: Shuddup, Bill. I'm not keeping you around to think. And mind that zipper or you will be First Eunuch when I win.

I SEE DEAD PEOPLE

HOWARD WOLFSON: Senator Obama just declared he's running for the nomination, Mistress.

MARK PENN: We'll have to watch him, Your Ladyship.

HILLARY: That nobody? Let's begin planning our campaign against the Republican nominee, whoever he is. Mark, what were you saying earlier about the "Dead Pool"?

PENN: Dead Democrats voting in sufficient numbers could put you over the top, M'Lady. By a simple stretch of the imagination, they qualify as absentee voters.

HILLARY: Bringing the deceased out of the shadows—I like it. But how do we sell the concept to the public?

ANN LEWIS: Majesty, introduce a bill to end disenfranchisement of the disembodied. Title it, "S 101, Civil Rites."

HILLARY: Visionary! Who'd challenge that?

PAUL BEGALA: Empress, ensure the departeds' allegiance by championing the next stage in entitlements: eternal Social Security and Medicare.

HILLARY: Marvelous! Ann, channel Betty Friedan. Ask her to found the League of Dead Women Voters. Begala, order up ten million Johnnie Cochranized bumper stickers: "If you've gone and died, don't be denied." And book me at St. Patrick's Cathedral on All Souls' Day.

BILL: Honey, you can't . . .

HILLARY: Shuddup, Bill. I lose, I'll go out like a lion; you, you better go on the lam.

PLANS AND PROVISIONS

HILLARY: I see McCain winning the nomination. We start targeting him now.

PAUL BEGALA: Excellency, your negatives are high. Let's drive up his negatives. Get their base to stay home election night.

HILLARY: Carville, reach out to our friends in the media. Tell them to run stories implying there isn't a nickel's worth of difference between John and me. Our base knows better; theirs, well, let's plant some seeds of doubt.

CARVILLE: Yes'm.

HILLARY: Paul, instruct our sleepers on the right-wing blogs to push the same message: McCain is Hillary in, uh, pants. Mark?

PENN: Mistress, I'll ask the *Times* to run a poll with this question: "Would John McCain's temperament, egocentricity, and latent Post Traumatic Stress Disorder make it more likely or less likely you'd vote for him if he's the Republican nominee?"

HILLARY: Good. Anybody else?

HOWARD WOLFSON: Fuel prices are at historic highs, Holy One. People are ticked at Bush, and by extension, all the presidential wannabes.

HILLARY: Yes, but how do we keep the *status quo* for another year? George, can you convince the Saudis to limit production until the election?

SOROS: Iss done, my Queen. Zey agreed to pump haff uff normal eff I build Empire State-size "Motor City Mosque" un Detroit.

BILL: Honey, that doesn't look . . .

HILLARY: Shuddup, Bill. You forget why you agreed to have your presidential library face east?

HUMANIZE ME

PAUL BEGALA: Obama's on the move, Excellency. Everyone likes him. We've gotta do something before this thing gets away from us.

HILLARY: You all know I'm warm and lovable in private. I just can't fake it before strangers the way Bill does.

BILL: Dear, you could always . . .

HILLARY: This is your fault. Out of office and you're still a rock star with your "Aw, Shucks" shtick. How am I supposed to compete with that?

HOWARD WOLFSON: We need to make you seem like an ordinary woman, Your Highness, and take the spotlight off . . . him.

HILLARY: Here's a thought: we leak word Bill's having an affair. This time, instead of standing by my man, I toss his things into the snow at Chappaqua in front of the cameras.

BEGALA: Nice, Exalted One. Tears, followed by a statement of resolve to dump the "Big He." Shows you're sensitive but tough.

HILLARY: Garnering sympathy and admiration both. My marital Sister Souljah moment. Oprah, Katie, Greta—the calls for interviews will pour in.

BILL: Honey, I'd rather . . .

HILLARY: I don't care what you want. This is in service to the cause. Cooperate, or instead of Ambassador to the World when I'm president, you'll be *chargé d'affaires* in Sierra Leone.

BILL: Yes'm.

MADELINE ALBRIGHT: Speaking of the international scene, Mistress, we should burnish your foreign policy credentials. I suggest a "Listening Tour" abroad.

HILLARY: Excellent! I'll smile, nod, and say nothing; people will attribute my silence to empathy. Madeline, develop an itinerary. Allies, of course, but include North Korea, Venezuela, and Iran. Bush is having some success pressuring them. A private word here and there, I'll muck things up before he gets credit. Richard?

HOLBROOKE: Eminence, unfortunately, our allies are warming to Bush.

HILLARY: Then I'll advise them that expressions of support for Bush 43 will deeply offend Clinton 44. Insurance: Carville, move to the continent and set up a PR operation to revive anti-Americanism before Election Day.

ALBRIGHT: Before your trip, Empress, I'll reach out to our media familiars and tell them to begin the drumbeat: under Bush, America is alone in the world.

BILL: Honey, can I . . .

HILLARY: No, you can't come. You're doing penance. Stay home, eat rubber chicken at fund raisers, and make my campaign rich. End of story. Oh, Albright. Do I ask Kim Jung Il to dance, or do I wait for him to ask me?

NO WAY TO TREAT A LADY

HILLARY: So much for your advice on handling last week's debate, O Master Strategist. No straight answers, you said. Ignore the other candidates, attack Bush, you said. Well, it cost me ten points in the polls.

BILL CLINTON: Honey, I . . .

HILLARY: Quiet! You screw up, but I wind up taking the heat. Now what?

HOWARD WOLFSON: Mistress, Tim Russert was partly at fault for being fair. Take him down, as an example.

HILLARY: Agreed. George, buy *NBC* and cancel *Meet the Press*.

SOROS: Yess, M'Lady. Und, for good measure, I buy *ABC*, *CNN*, und *CBS*. Mr. Potato Head haff nowhere to go.

HILLARY: Good, though I'd rather have his head on a plate. Howard, you'll run *NBC*. From now on, "*NBC*" stands for "Nothing but Clinton." Broadcast a year-long, 24/7 campaign infomercial. Other ideas?

ANN LEWIS: Excellency, refuse to eat unless the other candidates acknowledge your inevitability and withdraw from the race. Women will think you noble; men will admire your resolve.

HILLARY: Interesting! My well-being dependent on the pretenders. They'll drop like flies by "Day 11, the Clinton Watch."

HOWARD DEAN: But Highness, without challengers, the DNC will cancel the primaries. Looks bad. For appearances' sake, I'll jump in when the field is clear.

HILLARY: You're a scream, Howard. Run out and get me some burgers.

WOLFSON: We need to knock Obama out soon, Madonna.

PAUL BEGALA: Let's play the race card and steal his natural constituency. When blacks turn to you, white-guilt liberals will follow. You become "The Ma'am" and Obama's burnt toast.

HILLARY: You're right. Serpenthead, reach out to Reverend Jackson. Offer him the Treasury if he endorses me.

CARVILLE: The cabinet position or the keys to Fort Knox and the mints?

HILLARY: Either. Both.

ANN LEWIS: Majesty, we need Oprah, too. But how do we . . .

HILLARY: Tell her I'll make Africa our 51st state.

WOLFSON: With Obama out and Oprah on board, we'll petition the NAACP to become the "National Association for the Advancement of Clinton's Presidency."

HILLARY: I thought that's what it was.

YOU HEAR ME, BARACK?

BILL: Honey, maybe we should . . .

HILLARY: Shuddup, Mr. "First Black President." You hit the road tomorrow and start preaching my gospel in black churches across America. Otherwise, you'll be housesitting in Chappaqua for eight years. Take your pick.

THE STAND

HILLARY: Assume Obama takes Iowa. I'll need New Hampshire. Suggestions?

PAUL BEGALA: Goddess, blacks are 1% of the state's population, and therefore irrelevant. Appeal to Caucasians. Become a political analog of The Great White Hope.

HILLARY: I concur. Instruct our media people to run spots with this message: "Is America ready for a REAL black president?" Also, have them begin dishing on Oprah. Take her down, Obama goes down, too. What else?

ANN LEWIS: Highness, pledge to build a summer White House in the White Mountains.

HILLARY: Yes! Tomorrow I'll introduce a bill granting the entire state national monument status. Flatlanders can visit and spend money, but they can't settle. The old Yankees will love that.

HOWARD WOLFSON: Excellency, a deal sealer. Exempt current, registered Granite State Democrats from federal income taxes in perpetuity.

BILL CLINTON: Honey, you can't . . .

HILLARY: Shuddup, Bill. Starting tomorrow, I want you eating at every greasy spoon in New Hampshire so I don't have to. I lose, I'm still a Senator. You, you'll be Jimmy Cauterized. Word of warning.

CLINTONISTAS

HILLARY: Obama's winning the black vote even though Bill was our First Black President. Unacceptable!

ANN LEWIS: Majesty, Obama mostly talks white. Run clips on black radio of you talkin' black last week at Mount Carmel Missionary Baptist Church.

HILLARY: Ah, I remember: Opened with "I doan feel no ways tired; I come too far from where I started from." All right. Make it so.

Let's double down. Begala, hire a genealogist to find me a black ancestor, preferably one with Hispanic blood. I need street cred in the *barrio* as well as the 'hood'.

HOWARD DEAN: Smart, *Excelencia*. Hispanics are ripe for the picking now that *Señor* Richardson's dropped out.

HILLARY: Richardson was Hispanic?

BEGALA: *Si, Majestad.*

HILLARY: Whatever. Howard, I want DNC agents manning voter registration field offices at popular border crossings in the Southwest. We'll issue each transient a utility bill to prove residency wherever they settle. Make them understand: they wanna stay, they vote my way.

DEAN: I'm meeting our community outreach coordinators next week, *Jefe*. Soon, your picture will be on walls in every *barrio* in the country. And spray painted beneath: "*Mi Casa Blanca es su Casa Blanca.*"

HILLARY: *Naturalmente*! Begala, get word to influential hombres in legal difficulties: you wanna beg my pardon, you better promise me the Rose Garden.

BILL: Honey, I wonder if . . .

HILLARY: Shuddup, Bill. I catch you chasing *senoritas*, you'll be eating your *fajitas* through a straw. *Comprende*?

LOW ROAD

HILLARY: I win the Pennsylvania primary but Obama picks up steam. Insane! How do we stop him before it's too late?

PAUL BEGALA: Mistress, announce that on Day One of your Presidency, you'll issue a retroactive pardon to Obama for fraudulent use of campaign funds. You'll look magnanimous while suggesting he's corrupt.

HILLARY: I like it! And I'll waive the standard fee just to show how fair I am.

ANN LEWIS: Excellency, ask Bill's Saudi contacts to arrange an Osama Obama endorsement.

HILLARY: Marvelous! *Quid pro quo*: once I'm in, we'll call off Delta Force and sic the U.N. on him.

PAUL BEGALA: Commend Obama on his ability to attract radicals, my Queen.

HILLARY: Yes! I want ads showing Wright and Farrakhan ranting, followed by Obama cozying up to them. To avoid blowback, I'll appear at the end and say, "This is America. Who we hang around with is our own business."

JAMES CARVILLE: Exalted, accept the VP spot. In January, staff the West Wing with attractive, forward young interns who report to you.

HILLARY: I see where you're going: when an Obimbo eruption occurs, we alert the *Times*. Bill skated; Obama won't. Then I step in after he's impeached. Could work, since I'm not gonna be some little woman standing by the Man.

WOLFSON: The "Big He" survived the aftermath, Majesty.

HILLARY: True. And Obama is so into himself, there's no guarantee he'll take the bait. Scratch that idea.

LEWIS: Guest host Limbaugh, Mistress. Appeal to their base to continue Operation Chaos. Our common goal: a brokered convention.

HILLARY: Perfect! I'll [chuckle] "promise" to exempt Rush from the Fairness Doctrine when I'm in.

WOLFSON: Sensei, persuade Obama to drop out of the race by promising to appoint him U.N. Ambassador, where he'd be ideally positioned to lead the fight against U.S. imperialism.

BILL: Hey, that's my . . .

HILLARY: Shuddup, Bill. If we get to the White House, I'll let you "vet" the interns. Meanwhile, you volunteer for Obama's campaign. With any luck, you'll hurt him as much as you've hurt me.

BLOW IT FORWARD

HILLARY: The nomination and presidency were mine until Obama stole them. I don't care what sop he throws me, I want him to pay. How do we hurt the usurper while appearing to support him? Ann?

LEWIS: Highness, publicly petition Bush to pardon Rezko before he leaves office so Obama won't feel obliged to. The argument is this keeps an Obama administration from being distracted by scandal right out of the gate.

HILLARY: Wonderful! I'll appear prescient and concerned.

LEWIS: Mistress, have Research and Destroy photoshop and distribute images of Obama and Ayers clinking glasses in a bar. Then go on *Meet the Press* to decry gutter politics and remind everyone the election is over.

HILLARY: I'll be shaking with indignation.

WOLFSON: Majesty, I'll start a whisper campaign that Obama is considering Minister Farrakhan to be Attorney General. You hold a press conference slamming this vicious rumor.

HILLARY: Nice. Begala, hire an Obama impersonator to call Reverend Wright and ask him to offer the invocation at the inauguration. Tomorrow, Mr. "First Black President" here will appear on Greta to congratulate Obama and announce he's offered to serve as the new administration's liaison to the black community.

BILL: Oh, Honey, I couldn't . . .

HILLARY: Shuddup, Bill. Do what you're told or you go back to Chappaqua and have teas, bake cookies.

ACKNOWLEDGMENTS

First, I would like to thank President Obama and the Democratic Party for providing me a wealth of material in addition to a wonderful challenge: satirizing an administration and political party that are almost beyond parody.

Special thanks to three people who have had more influence on me than I'm sure they realize: Lucianne Goldberg for creating and maintaining her conservative salon, lucianne.com, where she graciously allowed me free rein to refine my skills as a satirist; Michael Walsh, my editor at bigjournalism.com (2010-2011), for nurturing me and bringing out my best because I knew he wouldn't accept anything less; and Scott Ott, who inspired me to try my hand at satire and remains, along with Iowahawk, in the top tier of political humorists writing today.

I'm indebted to my wife Regina and daughter Kathleen for reviewing the manuscript and providing excellent insights about what worked and what needed to be put to sleep. They also proofed what I thought was pristine text and caught numerous errors. Humbling.

Thanks to posters at lucianne.com and the Big sites for their feedback. Without it, I'd be clueless about whether my work was going over.

Glendon Haddix of Streetlight Graphics has been an invaluable resource in getting this book ready for prime time and making it look good. So many design and formatting services out there: I'm fortunate to have gone with Glendon and Streetlight.

Finally, I wish to thank Tom Cigas, a fellow traveler and my sounding board over the years. The spark for so much in this book came from our countless political discussions. No better friend.

ABOUT THE AUTHOR

Steve Grammatico was born in New Haven, Connecticut, and taught language skills in a New York City alternative school for troubled Utes. When the federal government defunded the program in 1994, the Utes returned to their ancestral homeland outside Salt Lake City, and Steve launched a career as a leg shark and loan-breaker for dyslexic mobsters. He considers Paul Krugman the best humorist writing today. In his spare time, Steve avoids watching *The View* and pursues an interest in Biblical archaeology. During his last trip to the Holy Lands, Steve discovered ancient scrolls suggesting that before God rested on the Seventh Day, He decided to give mankind the gift of laughter, and so He created liberals. You can e mail Steve at stevegrammatico@yahoo.com.